CW01085167

PRACTICAL ARTS LIBRARY

THE
ART POTTERS
OF BARNSTAPLE

Fig. 1 Three puzzle jugs , from left to right – Lauder, Brannam, Bara

THE

ART POTTERS

OF

BARNSTAPLE

Audrey Edgeler

NIMROD PRESS LTD
15 The Maltings
Turk Street
Alton, Hants. GU34 1DL

© AUDREY EDGELER & NIMROD PRESS LTD, 1990

ISBN 1-85259-178-1

FIRST PUBLISHED 1990

This book is copyright and may not be reproduced in whole or in part
(except for a review) without the express permission of the publishers
in writing

Printed by Ptarmigan Printers

Publishers:
NIMROD PRESS LTD.
15 The Maltings
Turk Street
Alton, Hants. GU34 1DL

CONTENTS

PREFACE

In writing this book, my purpose has been twofold. Ten years of research, illuminated with the handling and collecting of the work of the three Art potters soon indicated the necessity for more than just a book of quick reference for Art Pottery dealers and collectors. The North Devon pottery traditions and the renaissance of the town of Barnstaple from a decayed borough at the beginning of the nineteenth century up to the increasingly prosperous late Victorian era when the three Art Potters (1879 to 1914[1]) ensured for themselves a unique place in the Art Pottery movement: all this demanded a much fuller, social document. By the use of local archives, contemporary records and first (or second)-hand reminiscences it is my hope that this book will also appeal to all Barumites[2] as a permanent record of the three remarkable men who lived and worked in Barnstaple for a greater part of their lives, bringing distinction and prosperity to the town at a time when these were sorely needed.

This account is, of course against all the rules of present-day publishing, being neither a local history nor a book which recommends itself to the larger publishers of books on Antiques who have created the fashionable trend of the picture book with just a passing reference to the pieces shown; in the firm belief that this is what the collecting public want. They may be right!.. I greatly appreciate the interest and confidence already shown me — mainly by dealers and collectors — as evinced by advance orders and I hope that the book comes up to their expectations.

The opening of the first major museum of North Devon in the old Athenaeum building in the Square in Barnstaple is timed for the late Spring of 1989 — a happy coincidence as the museum officer, Mr. Peter Boyd has designated the pottery industry in the area to be the major attraction and already has a fine, representative collection of Barnstaple Art pottery. Further interest will be provided for visitors to the town when C.H. Brannam Ltd's new purpose-built pottery is opened just outside the town in the autumn of this year. Mr. Simon Fox plans a Visitor's Centre, not only for buyers of his wide range of traditional earthenware but also a display of the firm's own Art pottery collection and pottery records. (The old pottery buildings in Litchdon Street are to be preserved together with the oldest remaining kiln).

1. **For the purpose of the definition 'art pottery'. the date 1914 has been taken to mark the close of this movement in Barnstaple: it also marks the date of Lauder's retirement. However, the manufacture of good quality decorated ware still continued both at Brannam's and Baron's potteries up until the mid-twenties.**
2. **Barumite: citizen of Barum, the old latin name for Barnstaple.**

ACKNOWLEDGEMENTS

The production of this book would not have been possible without the encouragement of relatives and friends; in particular my son John whose interest and advice have been a constant source of energy; and who, together with dear friends Barry and Jane Stock provided the confident backing to ensure its publication. Nearer to home, the personal involvement and advice of old friends Audrey and Ken Lloyd and my daughter Anne and her husband Dave Watkins, aviation historian; provided continuing support and encouragement, especially in the final stages.

In particular I should like to thank the following:
Audrey Lloyd for help in the production of the chapters on Lauder the architect and the Barumite, which she wrote; as well as for her corrections of the script, proof reading and help with the compilation of the Index.
Jim Pinn for his ready professional skill in the production of the three Dating and Recognition Guides to the Art Potters.
Gerry Lee of the Museum of North Devon for his maps, line drawings and chapter headings.
Ken Lloyd for the use of his two original drawings of Lauder chapels.
Peter Boyd, Museum Officer, Museum of North Devon for sparing most valuable free time to take photographs of a few of the pieces in the Museum collection.
Bob Scarbro for his unstinting time and effort in the production of photographs from local records.
John Bartlett for sparing time to take additional photographs.
Andy Robinson and *Joël* for pictures of Ravelin.

The following for the loan of/permission to use photographs/information.
Keith Baker for photographs from his collection and his early personal and professional advice.
Peter and Debbie Gooday for the picture of the Brannam Clock.
Mick and Elaine Davis for two photos (and all their help and encouragement).
Mrs. Aggett of Barnstaple for the pictures of the Braunton pottery.
Phillips Auctioneers for the photo of a large Brannam vase.
Messrs Sothebys for the illustration of Wilkinson's set of Toby Jugs.
The Royal Albert Memorial Museum, Exeter for the three photos of Fishley pieces.
The Directors of the Athenaeum Trust for photographs from their printed records.
North Devon District Council and *Linda Blanchard* for the use of a map and

illustration of a fire-dog from the records of the Rescue Archaeology Group.
The Mayor and Corporation of Barnstaple for photos of pieces in the Guildhall.
David Coachworth of the *Victoria and Albert Museum* for information on Libertys.
Dr. Alison Grant for permission to use information from her scholarly work on North Devon Pottery in the Seventeenth Century.

and to the following:

The late Mr. Peter and Mrs. Brannam for their encouragement, and permission to use illustrations from 'A Family Business'.

Simon Fox, Director of C.H. Brannam Ltd. for his generous loan of the pottery records and permission to use pictorial material.

Geoff King, Central Services Librarian, North Devon Library and Record Office for his assistance in mounting an exhibition at the Library.

The Curator and Staff of the North Devon Athenaeum for their patient and untiring help over a number of years.

Mike Taylor, Town Clerk of Barnstaple for his interest and ready help.

Mary and Brian Chugg for information on the Braunton pottery and helpful advice on writing.

Mary Cornish for her most valuable help with family information and the use of family photographs, together with the loan of her grandfather's earthenware figures.

Maud Lemon, George Ovey, Ron Clements, Reg Burrington, Harry Chichester, Fred Gannoway, the Vernon family and others for recollections of life at the potteries.

LIST OF MONOCHROME ILLUSTRATIONS

Notes and Corrigenda

Page

3 Fig. 7 – spelliing of Pottington Point.

7 Footnote 4– readers should instead, be referred to pages 40–45.

11 Fourth line – the sentence should read; '.....children of the poor'.

20 Fig. 23a features Nelson figures and b. the masks. Courtesy R.A.M.M. Exeter.

24 Fig. 24b is not the property of the N.D.A.

32 Fig. 28 – the pieces shown are courtesy of the M.N.D.

33 Fig. 29 Three jugs by E.B. Fishley b. two with Trojan themes.

51 Fig. 41– the pieces shown are the property of the N.D.A.

55 Fig. 45 – the pieces shown are the property of the M.N.D. only.

58 Footnote 1(in text) – readers should be referred to page 73 for later records of the pottery.

61 Fig. 49b John Henry Lemon at the 'Big Wheel'.

64 Footnote 4 – unfortunately the author was unable to include the relevant illustrations, but readers should be referred to pages 6–7.

72 Footnote 8 – for details of the student/designers see pages 100–125

77 Fig. 58 – the pieces shown are not the property of the M.N.D., but are examples from the author' s private collection.

81 The following description refers to the vase on plate XXXII; '.......orange and brown colouring....'.

82 Footnote 4 – readers should be referred to page 60 – fig.48a&b.

87 Fig. 66 – the pieces shown were probably the work of Baron, as opposed to Brannam.

100 The following references have been omitted; fig. 43 page 53, for jardiniere see plate XXX and for the lion pieces see fig. 74 page 104.

101 For the Bowden piece described readers should be referred to page 97 fig. 72.

102 Footnote 1 – see fig. 74 page 104, and footnote 3 – see page 66 fig .51.

103 For an example of Dewdney's early pate sur pate work see page 88 fig. 67, fig 133 and plate VIII.

108 Fig. 79 – the vase shown is from the Barry Stock collection.

111 Fig. 83 – the caption should read ; The Victoria Jubilee mug.

120 Fig. 91 ab&c are the property of the M.N.D.

122 Fig. 93 a&b courtesy of the M.N.D.

125 Fig. 95 courtesy of the M.N.D.

144–5 Figs 111 and 113 courtesy Keith Baker.

162 Fig.125 courtesy M.N.D.

171 For jardiniere with fish supports see plate XXX.

173 Footnote 3 – readers should be referred to page 204 figs 147 and 148.

177 The jardiniere described can be seen on plate XXX.

185 For illustrations of the 1898 catalogue readers should be referred to page 188 fig.139.

186–7 The caption should read from top (LtoR) – 1912, 1886,1930 and 1923.

188–9 Figs. 188/9 courtesy of the C.H. Brannam Ltd. collection.

216 Line 14 – should read 1950 not 1850.

245 Fig. 169 The caption should read; William Baron and apprentice Eddie Chichester Ridd.

257 Part of line 3 has been omitted; it should read '.......some with experience, others probably young trainees. According to reports from later serving there was a happy atmosphere...'

258 Fig. 177 – the caption should read shrew–bell.

270 Fig. 182 – the captions for b&c should be transposed.

274 Footnote 1– readers should see page 33 fig. 29b.

275 Footnote 1 – see page 33.

288 Fig 195 – the caption should read; Detail of exterior of Ravelin.

Attention should also be drawn to the incorrect spelling of John Broad (Broad, John) in the index.

CREDITS:– Illustrations courtesy of the following;

1) N.D.A. – most of the illustrations in Part I, including those of the Bath and West Show and the Literary and Scientific Institution. Fig. 41 is also the property of the N.D.A.
2) The following illustrations are pieces from the M.N.D. from the N.D.D.C. collection:– figs 24 a&b, 28, 29a, 45, 53b, 91,93.
3) The following illustrations can be attributed to the C.H. Brannam Ltd. collection:– 51, 54, 68, 69, 70, 99, 114, 115, 119, 121, 139, 141, 145, 146.
4) Mr. J. Newell to whom the Brannam headed notepaper on page 46 and fig.102 belong.

LIST OF ABBREVIATIONS

N.D.J.	North Devon Journal.
N.D.A.	North Devon Athenaeum.
M.N.D.	Museum of North Devon.
N.D.D.C.	North Devon District Council.
R.A.M.M.	Royal Albert Memorial Museum Exeter.

Αρτ Ποττερσ

Coloured Plates

LIST OF COLOURED ILLUSTRATIONS

I. Top Left:

Three Owl wall-pockets. Top right, is the prototype from Brannam probably modelled by Baron (dated 1893) who used a very similar design at his own pottery in 1895, (the larger, unglazed piece in white clay – signed W.L. Baron), and the smaller was made soon after. (Baron ware) in red clay, (Lauder version MND).

II. Top Right:

Three grotesque or 'quaint' models by William Baron. On the left, a small, fairly naive model of Kruger as a Boar, complete with beard. Centre, is a teapot in an impish spirit, modelled and covered with a mottled glaze, the details, features etc., emphasised with the use of contrasting coloured slip. The third model is of a dragon candlestick, rather more finely modelled than the Brannam versions, and using just two colours; leaf-green and cream. Ht.4", lgth. 6".

III. Bottom Left:

Two finely decorated pieces by Edwin Beer Fishley. On the left, a tall vase in pale blue and charcoal grey. The design is achieved in thinly applied slip, displaying a perching bird in a leafy landscape with flowers and a butterfly, with a matt glaze. Ht. 12". The smaller vase on the right, in brown and cream has a similar design. Ht. 8". Both have separate designs at the base and near the rim, and both are signed E.B. Fishley, Potter. Fremington, N.D. The central, small jug is by William Fishley Holland, in a similar style to the brown and cream. Bought from a Holland family collection, it is possibly unique. The mark is signed W.F. Holland, Fremington, N.D. None of these pieces bear a date, but they would probably have been made between 1890 and 1910.

IV. Bottom Right:

Four late figures by William Fishley Holland, Museum of North Devon, Athenaeum Collection.

V. Top Left:

Three Brannam pieces with a similar style of decoration, 1890/91. The hanging vase was introduced in 1890 (Cat.1.No.3.). It was suspended by cord or chain. Ht. 14" no mark. The wall plaque was also first made in 1890, which date this bears. This design by William Baron. Span 11 1/2". The unusual shaped pot with a pierced lid does not appear in either catalogue, but is possibly the 'Indian pierce pot' mentioned in the Christmas report for 1891. J.D.

VI. Top Right:

Two Brannam pieces with contrasting techniques. The striking and unusual shaped covered bowl with lizard handles is by Thomas Liverton and dated 1895. Here the ochres and cream are used as detail on a pale blue background, ht. 5". A graceful version of the bottle vase with tapering neck and scalloped rim. The stylised design is enlivened with unexpected and unusual mottling, probably resulting from uneven firing. W.B.

VII. Bottom Left: BRANNAM.

Three vases with bird themes by William Baron. The central piece, dated 1888 shows a strong Doulton influence, especially in the raised dots and base panel. The central lateral design encircling the vase depicts two perching birds in a floral setting. The colours are muted and harmonious. The bottle vase on the right, dated 1889 uses similar colouring and themes. (The 'pair' is in the Museum of North Devon). The third piece, using a flat, dense background to throw into relief the strongly outlined forms of birds and formalised flowers is not wholly successful, the iridescent glaze being somewhat patchy. Nevertheless, a most striking and unusual piece. 1890.

VIII. Bottom Right: BRANNAM.

A very fine pair of vases made in 1888 with designs by James Dewdney. Probably specially commissioned, the potting is exceptional and the decoration finely conceived and executed. This year was notable for fine work from both major artists. 'Ginger' had become a fashionable base-colour, often contrasted with pale blue and cream. The darkish royal blue chosen here for the detail is both unusual and effective. Ht. 9".

IX. Top Left

Figure of monk or dwarf with inverted umbrella. A finely modelled and decorated piece for the wall. Dated 1901, dect. Beauchamp Whimple. Ht. 11", width 8". C.H. Baum. Uncommon.

X. Top Right

Two satyr-headed dragon candlesticks; the larger (ht. 11 1/2") is the prototype, in emerald green with the detail in black and fawn (cat. 2. no. 298). Decorator Frank Thomas 1899. The smaller is dated 1902 and is a modified version without the breast. 1899. This was made in at least two sizes of which this was the smallest – ht. 8", dect. Beauchamp Whimple. (There is a larger size of this version in the Museum of North Devon). C. H. Brannam Barum.

Plate I

Plate II

Plate III

Plate IV

Plate V

Plate VI

Plate VII

Plate VIII

Plate IX

Plate X

Plate XI

Plate XII

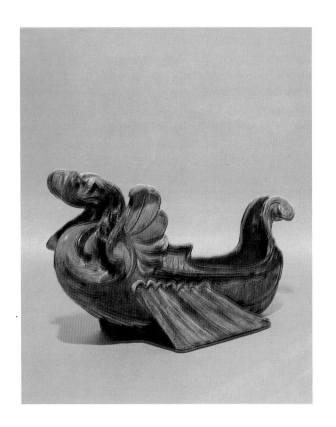

Plate XIII

Plate XIV

Plate XV

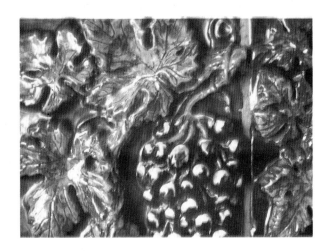

Plate XVI

Plate XVII

Plate XVIII

Plate XIX

Plate XX

Plate XXI

Plate XXII

Plate XXIII

Plate XXIV

Plate XXV

Plate XXVI

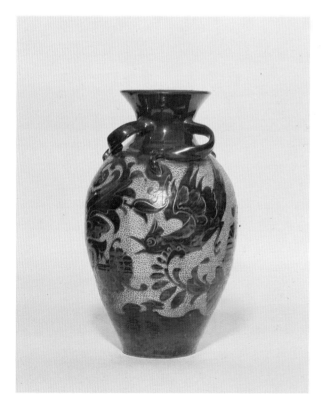

Plate XXVII

Plate XXVIII

Plate XXIX

Plate XXX

Plate XXXI

Plate XXXII

XI. Bottom Left

Three popular 'bird jugs' from drawings by Frank Carruthers Gould who used their main distinguishing features – beaks etc. as points for caricature. Cat. 2. Nos. 281–284 incl., they may be identified and are usually called (L toR) Grebe, Puffin, and Bittern. Made from c. 1898, the Puffin shown is a later, moulded Liberty model, c. 1905 with brilliant blue/green mottled glaze with decoration in greens and brown. Grebe–green with detail in blues and browns. B.W. 1899. On the right, Bittern with fairly lavish decoration by Frank Thomas 1910. Ht. 9 1/2 –10". (Made in four sizes).

XII. Bottom Right

Comparison of the Brannam lion candlestick, c. 1900 and 'modern' copy of old Italian faience design.

XIII. Top Left

Brannam dragon–headed boat (Cat.2.No.2950.A 'gondola for flowers'. Made in three sizes, this was either the smallest or the medium size. c. 1900. Length 13–14". C.H. Brannam Barum.

XIV. Top Right

Detail of Brannam vase 1903. J.D. & assistants. Note heavy layers of slip. Museum of North Devon.

XV. Bottom Left

Detail of tiles from Ravelin fireplaces.

XVI. Bottom Right:

As above.

XVII. Top Left:

A group of three vases by Lauder in mixed clay with a heavy body, dating from 1890–95. All are signed Lauder Barum and rely on pate sur pate for their decoration. On the right is a successful early attempt with an Art Nouveau theme and on the left a charming piece with a rose design in cream, green and pinky browns in a highly glazed dark green body. Centre is a pedestal vase in the classical manner with an all over stylised design using symbols within a linking pattern of diagonals and curves in pastel shades. Ht. 7 1/2–8". Other examples of this period can be found in the Museum of North Devon and the Royal Albert Memorial Museum, Exeter.

XVIII. Top Right

Three very early pieces with the Lauder and Smith mark. The central piece is dated 17/8/89; very heavy, with imperfections in the clay and fairly crude decoration. The other two are probably from the previous year when similar pieces were made with applied designs. These ranged from 6" to 14" or more in height. The body is extremely brittle and it is rare to find a perfect piece. 'Following nature' was the intention and the 'earth colours' of greens, browns and ochres added to this effect. Rose sprays were commonly used but the grape vine was also successfully attempted. Pieces of this type may also be found bearing the oval impressed Devon Art Pottery mark.

XIX. Bottom Left

Two Lauder vases. On left, dated 1893, signed Lauder Barum. Floral sprays on pale blue ground. On the right,

undated, but probably c. 1895–1900 with swirl handles in turquoise unusually contrasted with detail in brown on a cream sgrafitto background. Both pieces are notable for their freely curving lines.

XX. Bottom Right

Three Lauder bird jugs, modelled with worked detail of wings, feathers and features. Bittern, Owl and Kingfisher. Ht. 8 1/2". Lauder Barum, 1890–1900.

XXI. Top Left

Three Lauder pieces relying on sgraffito for decoration, after 1890. Centre is a puzzle jug with the upper part in olive green, and fish design decorated in blue, green, yellow, ochre and cinnamon. Left and right are very individual small vases. Ht. 6 1/2–8 1/2".

XXII. Top Right

A very fine vase by Lauder in his later style, signed Lauder Barum, probably c. 1905. The vase tapers upwards to spread finally to the graceful splayed rim. It falls naturally into two triangular panels, each displaying perching birds on floral sprays, which link naturally below the unusual decorative ring handles. The colour slips are applied in 'stripes' or patches in a random manner to give a pleasing effect of blue, green, and shades of ochre to brown, contrasting with the sgraffito –worked background of cream slip. Ht. 20".

XXIII. Bottom Left

A pair of very fine vases with the mark W.L. Baron, Fremington, Barnstaple 1894; made at the Fishley pottery possibly by E.B. Fishley but decorated by Baron using the Fishley green translucent glaze. The several species of fish are built up very thickly with layers of coloured slip with detail of fins and scales added, while the seaweed is either painted on or laid on in coils. A remarkable and possibly unique pair. Ht. 15".

XIV. Bottom Right

Two early Baron pieces, signed Baron Ware, Barnstaple 1895/6, in white clay. The vase on the left has a typical seascape in translucent green glaze with added slips for detail on cream scratched background. Ht. 12 1/2". The taller vase (14") relies on outline design and linear scratched detail for design in pale colours on a pale lemon base, which presents a strong, bold image on a very stylish body.

XXV. Top Left

Two distinctive Baron vases. On the right, a lightweight piece in white clay, the Art Nouveau style set off to perfection by the carefully defined lines of the clinging vine and pendant bunches of grapes in ochre and pale blue against a finely picked white panel. The piece is unglazed except for the rim and wide panel near the base. An excellent example of this media and style (others may be seen in the Museum of North Devon). Ht. 11". The other vase is most unusual, not being of typical of any other noted. The design of a bramble branch with ripe blackberries appears to have been painted on to the vase very much as if it were a watercolour or an oil on canvas. The result is charming and most natural. Ht.11". Both pieces are signed Baron Barnstaple.

XXVI. Top Right

A Baron bowl using the popular mauve/pink glaze over a trailing, fruitful grape branch. The proportions of the bowl effectively display the design when viewed just below eye level. This colour combination was a favourite of the potters, also used with floral designs, (see Museum of North Devon). This bowl, ht. 52, girth 26".

XXVII. Bottom Left

An early vase marked Baron Barnstaple, with three lateral swirl handles just under the rim. The bold and lively design in a dense green translucent glaze depicts gamecocks in a tropical setting, the whole thrown into relief by the cutaway sgraffito background. Ht. 17".

XXVIII. Bottom Right

Three wall-pockets by William Baron. On the left, one of a pair marked Baron Ware, Barnstaple, in red clay. A modelled piece with scratched and painted detail. The fish wall-pocket in the centre is larger (lgth.12") and intended for use as a flower holder, also one of a pair. Details through linear marking and some build up of slip. Signed Baron, Barnstaple c. 1900. The face on the right is very unusual, its effect reliant on added slip which supplies the beard and moustache, but also suggests a mask or even a dryad. Baron Ware.

XXIX. Top Left

A very fine three-handled vase, full-bodied and featuring three differing ovoid panels, each of a peacock in a floral setting. The finely drawn and detailed designs rely entirely on the artist's incised work for the resulting two-colour harmonious piece. James Dewdney, 1884/85. Ht. 192. span 40".

XXX. Top Right

An early jardiniere of unusual shape; the three incised designs of perching birds in a stylised floral landscape are in a pale blue on a fawn ground, shading to olive brown at the base. The bowl is supported on three ball feet, each being the head of an inverted fish, the tails curving upward to separate the designs. The scales of the fish are finely worked, a feature of the pieces shown at the Devon County Show in 1884. This piece could bear some resemblance to the three jardinieres made for Queen Victoria 1884/85 which featured snake handles. Ht. 10, design by Dewdney.

XXXI. Bottom Left

A very finely worked vase, deeply incised, the 'picked' sgraffito background throwing up the design in strong relief. A typically lively seascape by William Baron displaying a variety of fish basking and feeding among the fronds of luxuriant weed. A wide panel near the base features a continuous stylised pattern of sea-snails. 1889. Ht. 20".

XXXII. Bottom Right

An early Branam vase 1884, Athenaeum Collection, Museum of North Devon.
Plates IV and XXXII courtesy of Beryl Yates.

PART 1

BARNSTAPLE

A

BRIEF HISTORY

Fig. 2 The Barnstaple Great Seal

Fig. 3 The Old Guildhall

Fig. 4   Quay (c. 1837)

Fig. 5 Quay Hall and Ancient Gate (demolished 1852)

Fig. 6 Westacotts Shipbuilding Yard

Fig. 7 Potington Point

Fig. 8   The Raleigh Cabinet Works.   Two views: Past and Present

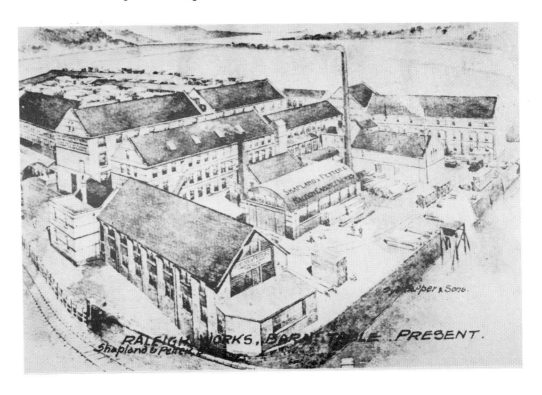

Fig. 9 The Pannier Market. 1885. The earliest known view. Guildhall Collection

Fig. 10 St. Vincent's School. 1903. One of the private schools in Barnstaple

THE TOWN 1800 - 1860

It is truly remarkable that within the seventy years between 1810 and 1880, the ancient borough of Barnstaple, from a depressed and decaying burgh had re-established itself as the chief town and market centre for North Devon. Self-help was perhaps the key to success but mere self-interest on the part of the still-wealthy merchants and traders would not alone have accomplished this 'miracle'. Without the presence in the town of a large number of well-to-do business and professional people with 'reformist' principles it is unlikely that so much would have been achieved in so short a time.[1]

This account is intended to set the scene for the emergence of the Barnstaple Art Potters; flourishing during the last two decades and continuing, though with slackening momentum until the 1920s.

By 1810 the town had fallen on hard times. The recent terminal decline in the once-flourishing major woollen industry; together with the loss of much of the export/ import revenue and a shrinking ship-building industry (both dependent on deep berths and a relatively silt-free estuary and harbour) had brought severe depression and unemployment — a state clearly reflected in the decaying buildings as well as the aspect which greeted visitors arriving from Bristol, Exeter and London: the Square 'an unattractive waste,[2] flanked on the riverside by lime-kilns and the remains of derelict buildings'.

In 1811, in spite of opposition from some members, the Corporation passed an 'Improvement Act' which 'encouraged' property owners to improve their buildings. This, together with a rate of sixpence in the pound allowed for much civic improvement. According to Gribble: 'the conscience of many was stirred — . the inhabitants vied with each other in removing antiquated buildings and replacing them with tasteful and commodious houses ... out of 68 houses running in continuous lines on each side of the street (High Street) 24 have been wholly rebuilt and 25 refronted or had the old fronts modernised.[3]

Within the next twenty years pavements and lighting were provided in the main streets and a new Guildhall built, with a space under for market stalls. By 1863 a full covered market (the Pannier Market) and a row of Butcher's Shops (Butchers' Row) had been built to accommodate the stalls which had previously cluttered the High Street and Cross Street on market days. By mid-century piped water from a reservoir had been provided, while drainage had been greatly improved through work on the embankments. Finally a new riverside road, replacing the old narrow approach through Litchdon Street was built, making access to the town through the Square much easier.

In 1854, the opening of the railway from Exeter brought further prosperity and the growth of a tourist industry, together with its attendant consumer trade. As a measure of the town's new standing in the south west, it was chosen as the venue for the Bath and West of England Agricultural Show in 1859; an event which attracted over thirty thousand visitors during the three public days, and was an outstanding success.[4]

Footnotes *(See footnote numbers in text)*

1. Many of the townspeople were of 'reformist' persuasion. Between 1830 and 1841, one Liberal and one Tory member were returned for Barnstaple, during which period the Liberal party effected the early reforms in the franchise and in education. In 1835, out of a local corporation of eighteen, fourteen were 'reformers'; among them being two bankers, seven merchants and shopkeepers, a surgeon, a solicitor and three of independent means.
2. W.F. Gardiner *Barnstaple: 1837 - 1897* . pub 1897 Ralph Allan, 90 High Street, Barnstaple.
3. John Besly Gribble 'Memorials of Barnstaple 1830'.
4. *See* Page 20.

Fig.11 Barnstaple Congregational Jubilee School. Cross Street
New Alliance House. (Alliance and Leicester Building Society)

Fig. 12 The North Gate (demolished 1852) housing the Old Bluecoat School

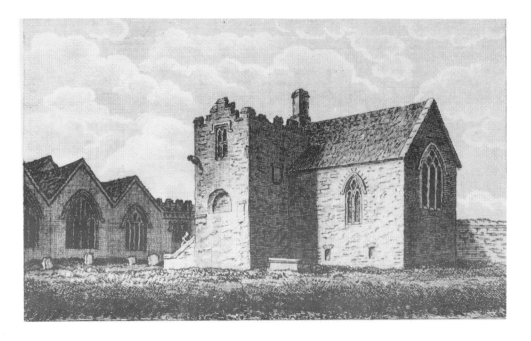

Fig. 13 The Old Grammar School in the Parish Churchyard, now a Museum

Fig. 14 The New Bluecoat School on North Walk

ALICE HORWOOD BLUE COAT GIRLS' SCHOOL.
AD 1659

Fig. 15 The Alice Horwood School for Young Maids

To the Worshipful the Mayor of Barnstaple,

We the undersigned Inhabitants of the Borough of Barnstaple and its vicinity, conceiving that the Establishment of an **INSTITUTION FOR LITERARY AND SCIENTIFIC PURPOSES** would be equally conducive to the welfare of the Town and the improvement and gratification of its Inhabitants; and believing that the present time is peculiarly fitted for the purpose, do request that you will be pleased, at an early day, to convene a **PUBLIC MEETING** to consider the subject; and also to take the necessary steps to carry it into effect.

In compliance with the above Requisition, I do hereby convene a **PUBLIC MEETING** to be holden at the Guildhall in Barnstaple, on Thursday the 7th. of November instant, at 7 o'Clock in the Evening, precisely.

W. F. LATHAM,
Mayor.

Dated November 4th, 1844.

The Petition for an Institution

THE GROWTH OF INDUSTRY

Alongside the promising civic development, new industries were being set up; the first being a Lace Factory, founded in 1821 by John Boden at Raleigh in the rooms of an abandoned mill. Four years later he moved to Stoney Bridge Mill in Vicarage Street (later named the Derby Lace Factory because of the owner's links with that town). The steam-operated machines the owner installed ensured rapid growth in production and by 1828 the factory was taken over by John Miller who, together with three sons and later trustees, guaranteed the continuation of the business until 1927. At one period the three lace-making concerns in the town employed over a thousand people.

Following close on the success of the lace factory, a Mr. Shapland set up a factory at Raleigh in another of the mill buildings, Cabinet making was his trade, and on a trip to America he had seen the great advantage of a machine-made moulding. On his return he was able to produce a similar moulding which he patented and used in his business in partnerhship with Mr. Petter, a retired publisher. When the flourishing factory at Raleigh was burned to the ground, destroying both goods and machinery, the factory moved to new premises on the site of the old shipyard at the end of the Long Bridge. The firm continued to prosper, making quality furniture, and was a major employer for many Years. (In 1897, four hundred hands were employed).

Other small concerns were set up. These included J.D. Young's Iron Works in Silver Street in 1812, and the Carriage Works of Gibbings and Co. At Bradiford Mill, Mr. Hearson made his famous rocking horses; a premises later acquired by Manley and Hayle for the making of brushes (later mechanised and much enlarged by Messrs. Mountjoy and Hancock who supplied much of Devon with a variety of brushes). Mr. Gribble's Iron Foundry on the Newport Road was later continued by the Willshire family, while at Pilton a glove factory was established in 1860 in rambling premises next to the old school. Seven years later, when the old Workhouse was closed, Dornat's mineral water factory was set up there. Lime burning flourished at the beginning of the century: at one time a dozen kilns were being worked in and around the town, but by the end of the century the importing of Guano and the invention of artificial manures had brought the business to a standstill.

THE CHURCHES AND THE GROWTH OF EDUCATION

At the beginning of the nineteenth century there were just two public elementary schools in the town, both charity schools: the Alice Horwood School for thirty 'young maids', established in 1652 and the Bluecoat School, established in 1710. There was, of course the very ancient Grammar School for the education of older boys, with a provision for the admittance of one or two local boys free.

As early as 1805 the first Sunday School had been set up and by 1830 there was provision for over 600 pupils. However, the first denominational day school was the National (Bell's) school in North Walk. Otherwise, children at the poor and less affluent received no schooling until the 1839 Education Act gave grants, mainly to religious bodies towards the foundation of schools. By 1845 three schools had been built and by 1868 seven more had been founded. These included schools of Pilton and Newport as well as those in the parishes of St. Peter's, Holy Trinity and Mary Magdelene. The Wesleyan Schools, in whose development Alexander Lauder was to have so great an interest were started in 1852.

By 1870 the School Board system had been introduced, with grants of £840,000 countrywide. It was hoped to provide universal, free education; though the immediate aims were to encourage regular attendance, to make school compulsory and eventually to raise the school-leaving age. Six years later a Bill forbade the employment of children under ten and stipulated the attendance of those aged between ten and fourteen for at least half time. In 1893 the school-leaving age was raised to eleven and, six years later, to twelve. This placed a heavy financial burden on the sponsors of the Church Schools, but parishioners raised enough money to provide new buildings or to enlarge the schools, and no Board School was set up in the town. In 1895 there were more than 2,700 children attending the local schools. From 1891 the government had paid ten shillings (50p today) per child, per annum, based on the average attendance (calculated from the daily registers). This was in addition to the annual grant. (In 1895 for Barnstaple, Newport and Pilton of £1,325).

CULTURAL AND SOCIAL AMENITIES

From the beginning of the century up to 1891 the town had grown rapidly, the population having trebled — from three and a half thousand to thirteen thousand. However, in spite of the improvements in housing, public amenities and education; before 1845 there were little or no cultural or social amenities. In 1822, a periodical of the time, *The Gossip,* describing Barnstaple as 'an extensive and opulent town' observed that 'it was not to the credit of the inhabitants that the late public library, the only establishment ever formed in it connected with the letters should so speedily have fallen to the ground'. Efforts towards self-help were made, however, but their results were short-lived. The Mechanics Institute, founded in 1830 had at one time a thriving membership of two hundred but foundered and closed nine years later after political dissension.

In 1843 there existed only facilities for the more affluent: two reading rooms and a small circulating library. In the following year a public meeting was convened in

BARNSTAPLE
LITERARY & SCIENTIFIC INSTITUTION.

PROSPECTUS OF LECTURES,

FOR THE FIFTH SESSION.—1849–50.

The Committee have much pleasure in announcing the following series of Lectures, which they anticipate will be delivered during the Session.

THE REV. W. BEAL	Education: in the aspect of Progression as to objective and subjective Knowledge.
MR. SLACK, F.G.S.	Physical Science, (with illustrations.)
MR. PINKETT	The Aborigines of North America.
MR. J. K. MARSH	I. Novels, Novelists and Novels Readers.
MR. J. K. MARSH	II. The same subject concluded.
MR. R. W. COTTON	The North-West Passage—and the Expedition under Sir John Franklin.
MR. CHANTER	I. Astrology, in connection with Astronomy.
MR. CHANTER	II. Astronomy. Both illustrated by illuminated Diagrams and Orreries.
MR. MILLER	Silk: its History, Growth and Manufacture, (illustrated.)
THE REV. S. C. KENT	I. Popular Superstitions.
THE REV. S. C. KENT	II. Mental Improvement; addressed to young Men.
MR. TREGELLES	Rise and Progress of Naval Architecture, (with illustrations.)

A Musical Entertainment will be given in the Christmas Holidays, accompanied by the Exhibition of a new series of Dissolving Views.

It is obviously difficult to assign any fixed time for the delivery of the above Lectures, or even the order in which they will follow each other; but the Committee hope to be able to arrange one for every alternate Tuesday during the session, the usual notice of which will be duly posted at the entrance of the Institution.

The Lectures will commence at Eight o'clock in the Evening.

Members have free admission on presenting their Cards, (which are not transferable.) Non-Members on payment of One Shilling to each Lecture.

JOHN R. CHANTER,
HONORARY SECRETARY.

Dated October 20th, 1849.

BARNSTAPLE
LITERARY AND SCIENTIFIC
INSTITUTION.

W. F. ROCK, Esq., President.

PERSONS DESIROUS OF BECOMING

FREE MEMBERS

On the President's Foundation, must make application on Forms (to be obtained of the Librarian, at the Institution, for that purpose) which are to be filled up according to instructions thereon, and returned before the 25th of March next. The Election of Free Members, by the Council, takes place on the first Thursday in April.

Free Members have the following privileges of the Institution, without any payment whatever :—

Access to the Reading Room (Class II.) supplied with Newspapers and other Periodical Publications.

Use of the Library containing upwards of 5,000 Volumes of Books.

Option of joining Classes to which gratuitous instruction is given in Science, Art, and Languages.

The Free Members are annually elected for the term of one year, which expires on the succeeding 25th of March; but the Council are desirous that they should, nevertheless, attend the General Meeting of Members which takes place in the following week.

R. W. COTTON,
HON. SECRETARY,

February 27th, 1865.

Fig. 16 a. Two posters. Prospectus of Lectures. Notice for Free Members

b The Literary and Scientific Institution Building

response to a petition from 106 inhabitants for the foundation of an Institution for Literary and Scientific purposes. It was hoped to provide a Public and Reference Library, together with public lectures and evening classes for the adult population of the town. Many of the petitioners would no doubt have been anticipating an establishment for a fee-paying membership, with perhaps some social affiliations. Others, with the continued education of the 'working class' in mind may have been hoping for a free library or even free evening classes.

These latter folk must have been greatly encouraged by the early participation of William Frederick Rock, a Barumite and successful London printer. Mr. Rock had been born the eldest son of a High Street cobbler but through hard work and good fortune he had received his education at Christ's Hospital Bluecoat School. Though now moved away, together with his family, he kept in close touch with the affairs of his home town and was kept informed of the townsfolks' efforts to set up an institution.

BARNSTAPLE

LITERARY & SCIENTIFIC

INSTITUTION.

THE COUNCIL ARE DESIROUS OF FORMING

CLASSES

FOR THE STUDY OF

DRAWING

AND THE

FRENCH & LATIN

Languages, for the Winter Season.

Members who purpose to join the respective Classes are requested at once to attach their Signatures to the Requisition in the possession of the Librarian, as the Classes will not be formed until a sufficient number have signified their intention to join them.

☞ The First Meeting of the " Mutual Improvement Class " will take place on Friday, the 22nd inst., at 8 o'clock p.m.

J. G. HAYMAN, Printer, ' North Devon Journal Office,' High-street, Barnstaple.

Fig. 17 Poster. Classes for Drawing, French and Latin

THE LITERARY AND SCIENTIFIC INSTITUTION

At the inaugural meeting the plan was discussed and a committee formed. A letter was read from Mr. Rock, offering to donate £100 annually towards 'the establishment of an instituition calculated to promote general instruction'. A scheme was drawn up, but this proved to have a built-in 'class' structure, with a first and second class membership, separate reading rooms and certain privileges for those who paid most. This in itself was probably acceptable but provision was not made for those unable to afford a fee. Mr. Rock was not amused. He made certain objections and suggestions which stipulated the provision of free membership for those who could not afford to pay. The issue was not immediately resolved, and while the committee went ahead to suggest the issue of proprietory shares for the lease or building of premises; Mr. Rock, on his own initiative took out a lease on premises in High Street where he 'proposed to start a free library ... but was still anxious to merge his plan in any one which might be calculated to diffuse general benefit among all classes'.

The Committee, not wishing to lose his support, fell in with his plans, but the proposed scheme remained, with, however this important proviso:

> ... that in consideration of his annual subscription of £100, he could recommend up to a hundred members as free members (or fifty members plus one hundred subscriptions of six shillings). All members would be free to use the second-class reading room and the library and would have free admissio to the series of lectures to be arranged for the first session. However, the committee insisted that at no time were members to be admitted to classes without the payment of a fee.[1]

The premises at 42 High Street was in many ways ideal for its purpose. The two large rooms facing the High Street became on the ground floor the first-class reading room; with the library above. There was also a second-class reading room and a museum. Initially Mr. Rock presented 600 volumes to form the nucleus of a library, but by 1851 there were over 3,000 volumes and by 1870, 7,000. First-class members paid twenty shillings and second-class members ten shillings per annum.

The course of lectures arranged for the first session proved so popular that late-arriving members sometimes found that the extra fee-paying (one penny) public had filled all the seats, so the fee was later raised to sixpence for non-members! Classes were arranged at various times in the lifetime of the Institution, the first ones in French, Arithmetic and Drawing. There proved to be difficulties almost immediately: teachers who were qualified asked high fees and even then, either through difficulties with discipline or the work proving too difficult for the pupils did not continue their classes. The classes in Drawing, however, originally under the supervision of Mr. Maunder, though lapsing for a brief period proved easily the most popular.

From 1861 onwards, when Mr. Lauder assumed control up until the government

Fig.18 Opening of North Devon Railway 1854

Fig. 19 Mr Rock's House at Blackheath

Mr Rock in the Park

course was introduced and later taken over by the Town Council, the classes continued without a break. The original intention was to provide day classes for those who were free to attend, and evening classes for others, with a special cheap rate for artisans. The latter proved mostly to be Brannam's young designers and the craftsmen at the Raleigh Cabinet Works who learnt design and woodcarving.

The School of Art flourished. New buildings were added and when the library was moved to the new Athenaeum in 1888 the High Street premises were gradually assimilated for Art and Craft teaching. By 1880 the attendance topped one hundred and the success rate was the highest in the country, while in 1894 the School was the most successful in the West of England. Under the headships of J.S. Ireland (three years), and Joseph Kennedy (four years) there was a period of steady progress which came to fruition under the skilled control of Theodore Charbonnier (21 years until 1905). The use of pupil teachers who had qualified through the government examination proved very valuable. Among these were William Baron who later obtained his master's certificate, William Liverton, one of Brannam's most gifted designers and Minnie Croot, probably the most successful of the lady students at the School whose father was a house decorator and oilman with premises in the High Street.

Footnotes *(See footnote numbers in text)*

1. This rule was a bone of contention throughout the lifetime of the Institution. The fee was returned to the student at the end of the course providing that he had attended a prescribed number of lessons and presented himself for examination. This sounds fair, separating the idle from the industrious but, especially in the early years when some of the students may not have been fully literate and numerate and may not have been aware of the standards required; they were probably deserving of more sympathy.

2. Figures from Gardiner (ibid).

Fig. 20 Mr Rock. A Portrait

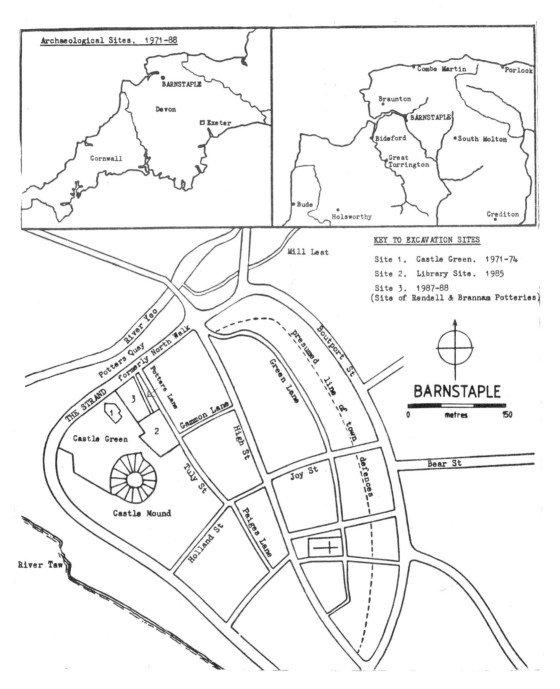

Fig. 21 Map of Barnstaple showing site of early potteries

PART II

THE
POTTERY INDUSTRY
OF
NORTH DEVON

Fig. 22   Detail of Firedog from Mediaeval Pottery NDDC Rescue Archaeology Unit

Fig. 23 a. George Fishley, Fremington. A mantle ornament. On the oval base are four reclining animals. Two masks are applied to the back on either side of a bunch of grapes. All the decoration has been carried out in dark brown and white clays. Ht. 6 3/4"

b. George Fishley, Fremington. A mantle ornament, again the base is oval and supports four reclining animals and 'Nelson' figures to the left and right. Ht. 8 5/8"

THE CLAY

For at least five centuries the potters of Barnstaple, Bideford and Fremington produced common earthenware from the brown clay deposits existing in the vicinity of Fremington, a few miles from Barnstaple. These clay beds lie at the western end of a belt running three and a half miles, parallel to the river Taw, from Lake in the east to the outskirts of Fremington in the west. According to figures supplied in 1890 when a well was dug at Roundswell Farm (towards the eastern end) the thickness of the clay at that point was as much as 78 feet but it lay twelve feet below the surface.[1]

The clay beds at the western end, however were near to the surface; so easily accessible and could be reached with hand tools. The clay was very pure, easy to work and fired to an attractive terra-cotta at the low temperature of 1000 degrees centigrade, which made it ideal for its purpose. The supply, too appeared to be inexhaustible; though early, shallow digging was probably very wasteful as may be seen from the ordnance survey maps of the area which show 'clay coverts' — a large area where the original workings were allowed to become overgrown by scrub and trees. Even later diggers threw the topsoil back or allowed it to fall in, so the remaining clay became adulterated.[2]

Early landowners in the area leased much of their land for clay extraction; leaving themselves enough to keep livestock, grow their own vegetables and build their own house(s). They made sure they were not the losers by asking a low rental for the land but a high annual levy for 'the breaking up of the land in search of clay'.[3] Leases were commonly sold for long periods of up to 99 years, and could be sold to other lessees for the remainder of a term. Typical of these early owners was the Crocker family. Records[4] show that in 1718 Stephen Crocker bought Westlades tenement from Samuel Clark, merchant of London and in the following year purchased the unexpired portion of the 99 year lease from John Sloley for £100. It seems likely that Stephen may have already been potting locally.[5]

By the third generation they had added substantially to their property, a later Stephen's will left land, a house and two pieces of clay-bearing land — Longmoor and Knills Moor. Three sons inherited, but two of these emigrated quite late in life to North America. Either their funds were very considerable or they were good business men; for a direct descendant (George, son of George, who died in 1875, had founded the National Bank of America).[6] The third son, Samuel, the potter and his son, Samuel junior, eventually inherited both clayfields which, of course they not only leased but also exploited both for their own use at their pottery in Bideford and for sale to other potters in the area.[7]/[8]

The transport of clay was not too difficult, except perhaps in bad weather. The Taw and Torridge being tidal rivers, the clay could be taken by boat from the quay at the pottery end of the Pill, seaward to join the river Taw, then down the Torridge to the Strand potteries or those 'East-the-Water' at Bideford. Alternatively they went upriver along the Taw and into the Yeo to unload at Potter's Quay, directly opposite the North Walk potteries in Barnstaple.

Footnotes *(See footnote numbers in text)*

1. Townsend Hall. Lecture to the Devonshire Association 1890. N.D.A.
2. Peter Brannam said that much of the land in the north west corner near to Brannam's pit was no longer workable for this reason. There must remain areas which have never been dug but it has been suggested that it would be uneconomic to excavate further. Before 1880 Brannam's had no lease for digging clay but had it brought in from the pits by a local farmer. 'A Family Business'.
3. Samuel Crocker's son, Stephen paid one shilling per annum rent but £50 an acre for the 'breaking up of the fields'.
4. Documents. N.D.A.
5. An advertisement states 'Crocker pottery, Bideford est. 1688'.
6. Report from the North Devon Journal.
7. It is abundantly clear that the Crockers were very aware of the need for conservation. Under Samuel Crocker's will there were restrictions on the amount of clay taken annually (48 tons from Knills Moor). (Though it should be noted that the Fishleys had a lease on Knills Moor, possibly from as early as 1800). As far as Longmoor was concerned, records show that William Henry Crocker was restricted to taking a maximum of 25 boatloads annually. (A boatload not to exceed twelve tons).
8. The Fishley's first pottery was at Muddlebridge and it seems likely that the potter occupied the original house there. He was obliged to move to Combrew when a member of the Crocker family wanted to occupy the house. The original house was later greatly enlarged and occupied by Eliza Crocker who married Anthony Loveband, a farmer from Yarnscombe. He took the Crocker name and seems to have become the local 'squire'. Stables and outhouses were added and later records describe it as Muddlebridge House. It is a fine house with an extensive walled garden, which is now a guesthouse, with the stables etc. converted to holiday homes. The original part is at the rear.

FUEL

Just as potters preferred to use clay that was readily available and near to hand, so they used fuel that was both cheap and easily obtainable. Thus, Bideford with a natural supply of open-cast coal probably used this in preference to the furze and wood favoured by the Barnstaple potters. In early times this would have been more plentiful but in time the mines were worked out; while wood, besides being used locally for ship building probably became scarcer and more expensive. Furze was reasonably easy to gather and a task for the children.

Brannams are known to have used wood and furze from the first and continued to use it up until the 1880s when they changed to coal. In this Thomas would have been continuing the methods he had learned at the two Rendell potteries where he worked as a young man. Although furze was convenient to gather and cheap to use it was a continual fire hazard, particularly when dry. Potters were prohibited by law from storing it in their yards or building ricks within a certain distance of houses. Nevertheless, accidents did occur. In November 1856 the North Walk pottery was the scene of a fire when furze caught and two sheds were burnt down. Thomas Brannam had neglected to keep up with his insurance premiums and sustained £20 worth of damage. Arson was suspected, and probably proved eighteen years later when, in 1884, a farmer's young son from Tawstock, on leaving the Fortescue Arms at 12.40a.m. was said to have informed the Holland brothers: 'I am going to have a fire tonight'. It was alleged that on the way home to Roundswell he set fire to a large rick of furze at Sticklepath, the property of Charles Brannam, with a loss of several thousand pounds. It is likely that the potter would have been far more prudent than his father!

The Fishleys, at least latterly, preferred the use of coal from the Forest of Dean which was conveniently seaborne, but they also used furze, particularly to raise the temperature of the kiln at the critical point of firing when the glaze began to run.

THE WARE

Early ware for the most part was plain and functional, with a lead-based internal glaze to render it non-porous. However, much evidence has been uncovered to show that over a long period, from early times up to the end of the seventeenth century many potters made fully glazed, twice-fired pieces, decorated with impressed designs, trailing slip or with scratched (sgraffito) decoration. The piece was fired twice, once after decorating and again, at a slightly higher temperature after glazing. The raw lead 'galena' or honey glaze produced two colours — a cream to gold shade over the white slip and a reddy-brown where the terra-cotta base had been revealed or had not been

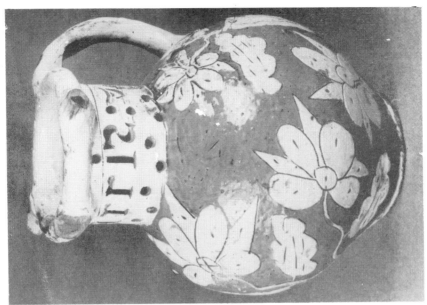

Fig. 24b Early Local Puzzle Jug NDA and MND

Fig. 24a John Phillips Jug 1760

Fig. 25 The Fishley Pottery building at Fremington.
RAMM, Exeter

covered. Most of this decorated slipware was made for special order.

In the main, trade was local, covering North Devon to the south as far as Exeter, and west to Plymouth wherever the roads were adequate; but there was also coastal trade; by boat around the coast to Bristol and Cornwall as well as across to South Wales and Southern Ireland. Additionally, from the middle of the seventeenth century a thriving overseas trade in earthenware grew up between the ports of Bideford and Barnstaple and the new colonies of Maryland and Virginia.

Earlier in the century, the Barnstaple merchant John Delbridge had established trading along the North American eastern seaboard from the fishing fleets of Cape Cod to the Caribbean islands. Carrying emigrants, many probably of Huguenot extraction from North Devon to Virginia, he established and continued to supply settlements. Other local merchants followed suit, some building up small fleets and trading, including earthenware in their cargoes. A good deal of sgraffito ware has been found on sites near Jamestown, Virginia and along the banks of the Potomac in Maryland so it follows that the early settlers, especially those from North Devon used the slip ware and were happy to pay a little more for decorated pieces.[1] Later in the century earthenware was shipped from Bideford to Massachusetts, but there is evidence that supplies were being taken along the coast to New England as early as 1639 when a settlement called Barnstable was founded on Cape Cod.[2]

Towards the end of the seventeenth century the loss of many vessels during wartime trading led to the ruin of many merchants, while the preferred route to the north and the rising port of Liverpool drew trade away from the South-west and gave an opportunity for the Staffordshire potters to enter the American market and to compete for the home trade.[3] Since their ware was finer and more colourful than North Devon slipware, the local potters were now losing their traditional markets. Dr. Grant writes:

'local potteries still produced sgraffito ware harvest jugs and a few other pieces, almost all likely to have been individually commissioned, but archaeologists find little or no decorated ware from North Devon on eighteenth century sites'.

It is not until the middle of the nineteenth century that we are aware of a move locally to reintroduce decorated ware with the work of the Fishley family at Fremington from 1824 (Edmund), and the pieces Thomas Brannam sent to the Great Exhibition of 1851.

Footnotes *(See footnote numbers in text)*.

1. There are dishes in the Colonial National Historical Park in Jamestown.
2. Barnstable is the twin town of Barnstaple.
3. The building of the canals between the potteries and the ports enabled the Staffordshire potters to compete on equal terms.
4. *North Devon Pottery. The Seventeenth Century* Univ. of Exeter. material by courtesy of Doctor Alison Grant.

THE FISHLEY FAMILY TREE

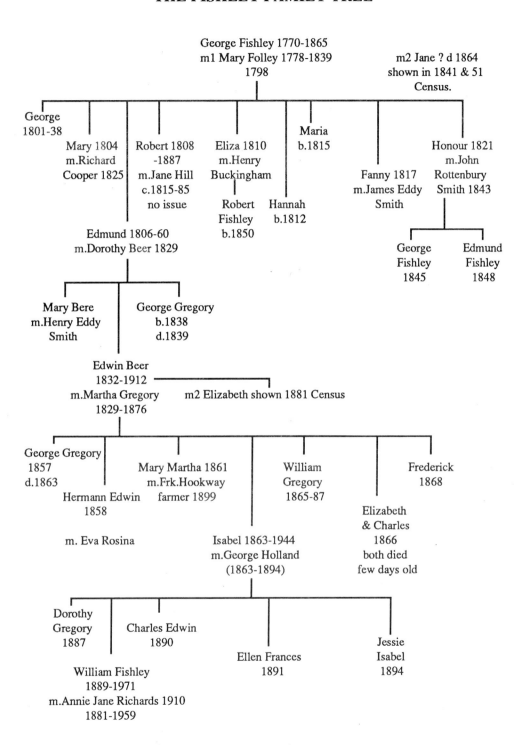

THE FISHLEY FAMILY

It is believed that George Fishley set up his first pottery in 1800 at Muddlebridge, close to Fremington Pill, a small tidal river which flows into the river Taw. At this time it seems very likely that a quay would have already been built for the loading of the clay bound for Bideford and Barnstaple. George may have occupied the nearby house, commonly called Muddlebridge which was considerably enlarged later by the Crocker family.[1] This ties in with the fact that he was obliged to move to another site some fifty yards distant, near to the existing claypits at Combrew. The family occupied the adjacent house there continuously up until 1912, soon after the death of the founder's grandson, Edwin Beer when the pottery was sold.

It seems likely that George would have held a lease on clayfields from early on and records show this to be the case.[1] George established a good reputation for 'sound' pottery which became a 'household word'. (Strong) His two sons, Edmund and Robert worked with him, producing common earthenware of a domestic nature which was sold at the Barnstaple market and in the surrounding area as well as being shipped along the coast to Cornwall and elsewhere. Members of the family also made decorated ware, mostly for special order; in the main harvest jugs for local yeoman farmers and perhaps the landed gentry. Edmund was a skilled decorator who was making specially commissioned pieces from the age of eighteen. He also made a series of posset pots, based on seventeenth century examples made locally.[2] When he died prematurely at the age of 54 as the result of an accident, his son Edwin Beer took over the management of the pottery, at the age of twenty-eight.

George's younger son, Robert certainly worked at the pottery for a number of years but he was a journeyman so probably travelled the country quite extensively, perhaps even as far as Staffordshire (some of his pieces bear a resemblance to the style). He sems to have continued to work at the pottery until his mid-sixties (he was 62 and living at Farm House in the 1871 census). His decorated work which is dated covers a period of twelve years (1836 to 1848). A bowl and cover, dated 1844 shows the use of applied work.[2]

It looks as if the founder, George Fishley waited until near his retirement at the age of seventy before allowing himself the indulgence of making his own decorative ware. This was in marked contrast to the pieces produced by his sons, being modelled in the main rather than thrown. While some pieces employed the 'resist' technique, where leaves were applied to the body before dipping it in white slip, so that after glazing and firing the leaf would be in 'red' with a lighter background, most of his pieces were decorated with applied design of flowers, fruit or leaves. Some pieces featured a recognisable human figure such as Napoleon, Nelson or a Turk.[2] He also used seated or reclining models of cats or dogs, on their own or as part of a group piece.

Often the pieces were intended as mantel ornaments or watch pockets. Colour variations over the white slip were achieved by the use of manganese stains. Peter Brears regards him as 'probably the most important single earthenware potter of the nineteenth century. He was one of the few English coarseware potters able to produce well-executed free-standing figures entirely from his own experience, backed up by his strong North Devon pottery tradition'.[3]

Contemporary studio potters such as Bernard Leach and Michael Cardew were as ready in their praise for the work of Edwin Beer Fishley and later of his grandson's. From 1860 he continued in the traditions of his forbears, producing not only 'sound' but very pleasing and distinctive pottery which attracted visitors to his pottery, not only from the surrounding area; Michael Cardew remembers visiting the pottery often as a boy when the family stayed at nearby Braunton and would make the journey by boat across the Taw. He later visited William Fishley Holland at his pottery in Braunton to watch him at work, and Bernard Leach at one time asked the young grandson to join him at his pottery in St. Ives.

Edwin Beer continued the tradition of making harvest jugs and many are still retained by local families. By the late 1870s, with a competent staff to run the daily work of the pottery, he too became more interested in decoration. Visiting local gentry such as Sir Thomas Dyke Acland and Sir John Walrond encouraged him by sending him designs to copy. But it was J. Phillips, honorary secretary of the Bideford School of Art who claimed credit for introducing the potter to ancient forms and designs by conducting him around 'some of the best collections of pottery in London .. including Schliemanns which he sketched and very cleverly produced'.[4] On his return the potter made a group of three vases which he exhibited at the Plymouth show in 1881 and again at the Newton Abbot show in the following year. One of these, depicting a bearded charioteer driving a team of four horses won the silver trophy at Newton Abbot and was much admired. Many other decorated pieces followed.[6]

In the 1881 census he was employing a staff of eleven men and seven women, among whom was very probably his daughter Mary. She seems to have been of an artistic turn of mind and could have remained working at the pottery until her marriage in 1899 to a local farmer, Frederick Hookway. She is recorded as attending classes at the School of Art in 1890, when examples of her work, 'including several specimens of Fremington pottery which she has decorated', were shown in the annual exhibition. With a natural inherited talent, the training may well have developed in her the gift for design. It would be pleasant to believe her responsible for other fine pieces such as a vase pictured in Plate XXXII. It may seem a trifle odd that neither she nor the other members of the female workforce are mentioned in William Fishley Holland's biography.[5] However, he makes little mention of decoration, nor does he seem to have had much interest in it. (His designer at Clevedon was Bill Janes, and except for very late pieces that he decorated, his concern was primarily with form).

William Fishley Holland was the son of Edwin Beer's eldest daughter, Isabel who had returned to the pottery to look after her ailing mother, and a few years after the premature death of her husband, George who had farmed at Yelland. William learnt all the skills of the pottery but was especially attracted to throwing at which he soon became skilled. At the death of his grandfather in 1912, aged eighty he may have hoped to inherit the pottery but its disposal was left to his two uncles. After continuing and developing the business for a few months, a possible prospective buyer being found, he left to build and manage a new pottery at Braunton. The buyer, Ed Sadler, a potter from Staffordshire had little experience or knowledge of the local techniques and firing, and after a few years sold the pottery to Brannams, who used it for a few years before dismantling the kiln and letting the house.

Footnotes (See footnote numbers in text)

1.   See note 8 page 22.
2.   An exhibition of the work of the Fishley family 'By potters art and skill' was mounted at the Royal Albert Memorial Museum, Exeter in May and June 1984, followed by a showing at Birmingham Museum and Art Gallery from June to August; after which a reduced exhibition was shown in Museums in Devon and Somerset. The catalogue produced is both informative and attractive and has illustrations of some of the pieces shown.
3.   *The Collector's Book of English Country Pottery.*
4.   *The Potter's Art in Devonshire.* Devon Association Transactions. Voluem XII. N.D.A.
5.   *Fifty Years a Potter.* Pottery Quarterly. 1958. now out of print.
6.   See also illustrations of ship jug and beaker with inscriptions on base showing a link with Owen Davis.

Fig. 26 Two Harvest Jugs by E B Fishley

Fig. 27 E B Fishley Jug and base mark showing Owen Davis' interest NDDC and MND

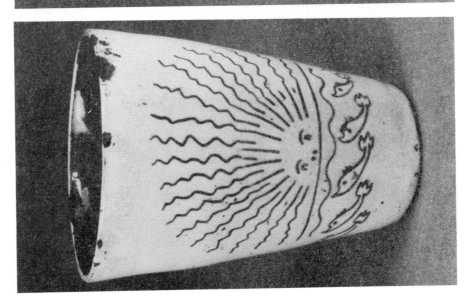

Fig. 28 Three Beakers by E B Fishley

TWO PINE CLASSICAL MODELS.

Three Jugs. E.B. Fishley

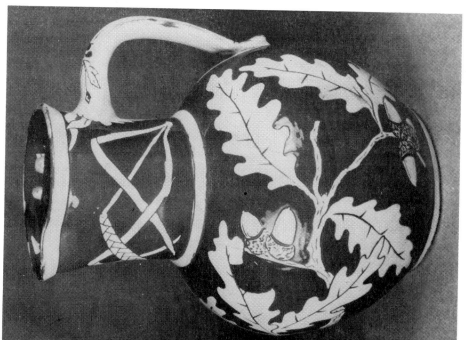

Fig. 29 Jug by E.B. Fishley with oak spray

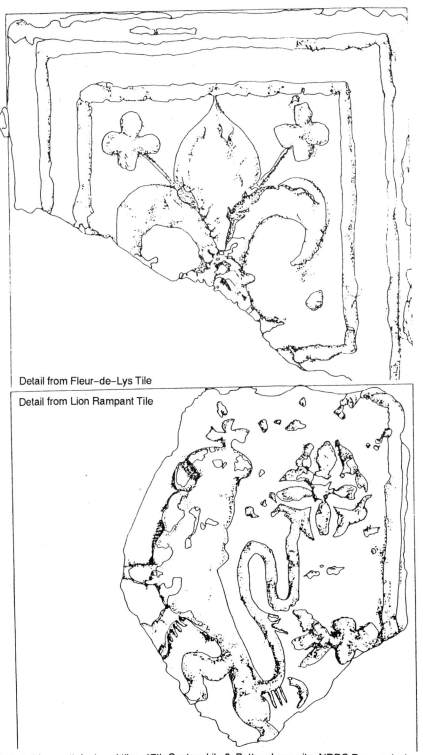

Detail from Fleur-de-Lys Tile

Detail from Lion Rampant Tile

Fig. 30 Detail from relief-glazed tiles, 17th Century kiln 2, Potters Lane site. NDDC Rescue Archaeology Unit

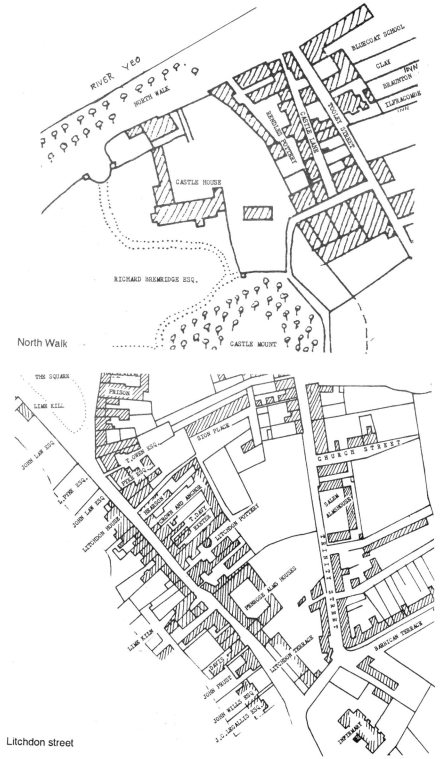

Fig . 30 Map showing the Rendell Potteries, from Pinecombe map

THE RENDELL FAMILY TREE

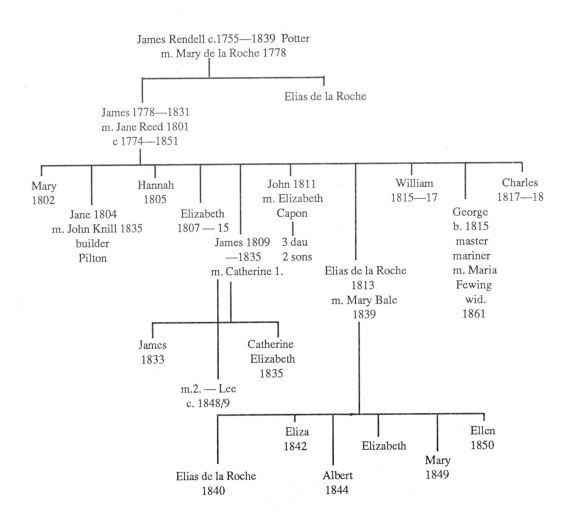

James Rendell c.1755—1839 Potter
m. Mary de la Roche 1778

Elias de la Roche

James 1778—1831
m. Jane Reed 1801
c 1774—1851

Mary
1802

Jane 1804
m. John Knill 1835
builder
Pilton

Hannah
1805

Elizabeth
1807 — 15

James 1809
—1835
m. Catherine 1.

John 1811
m. Elizabeth
Capon

3 dau
2 sons

Elias de la Roche
1813
m. Mary Bale
1839

William
1815—17

George
b. 1815
master
mariner
m. Maria
Fewing
wid.
1861

Charles
1817—18

James
1833

Catherine
Elizabeth
1835

m.2. — Lee
c. 1848/9

Elias de la Roche
1840

Eliza
1842

Albert
1844

Elizabeth

Mary
1849

Ellen
1850

THE BARNSTAPLE POTTERS

There is evidence of potters living and working both in Litchdon Street and in the North Walk area for many centuries. Because the Litchdon Street site has been used continuously as a working pottery from at least 1830, it has not been surveyed by archaeologists;[1] but the North Walk site has been examined recently, in 1973, and last year prior to the building of the new Country Library. The earlier excavations were on the Castle site — the grassed over area below Castle Mound and to the south-west of Potters Lane, where sherds were found of double-fired slipware dating from before 1650 and up to the early years of the eighteenth century. Pieces by William Oliver, John Leachland and others are representative of the sgraffito-decorated ware that was being produced.

Last year's work on the North Walk site uncovered evidence of many potteries from mediaeval times up to the last century. Decorated sherds of mediaeval pottery were found and a mediaeval kiln was lifted for reassembly in the new North Devon Museum, due to open in the Spring of 1989. Pieces from the Castle site include a jug (probably by John Leachland) at the British Museum; a posset pot, probably by William Oliver, at present at the Royal Albert Museum, Exeter; and dishes at the North Devon Maritime Museum, Appledore. There are also pieces in museums in Bristol and Swansea while other examples are retained by the North Devon Rescue Archaeology Group who are engaged in the painstaking work of reassembly!

During the eighteenth century the Litchdon Street pottery was probably used for making bricks, tiles and other coarse earthenware.[2] There was a clay pit on the site worked by a member of the Williams family while another member worked the pottery. At North Walk a Nicholas Thomas had a pottery from around 1715 to 1765, but towards the end of the century a member of the Rendell family[3] was in occupation, and in 1815 James Rendell junior purchased the pottery and house from a member of the Thomas family. The Rendells continued both at North Walk and at Litchdon Street, making bricks and tiles for export to South Wales and probably for local use. They probably also made common domestic earthenware with coloured internal glazes.

In 1847 John Rendell leased the North Walk pottery to Thomas Brannam[4] who had worked at both potteries since coming to the town from Bideford, probably as a young man. In 1853 or thereabouts he bought the Litchdon Street premises, retaining his lease on North Walk. He continued to work both potteries, making common earthenware of a domestic nature as well as tiles and pipes until 1881 when he retired,[5] leaving his son to carry on the business.[6]

Footnotes *(See footnote numbers in text)*

1. In the event of the present Brannam pottery moving to new premises in the near future, there could then be an opportunity to excavate the site.
2. Rate Books.
3. See family tree. James (son) at Litchdon Street until his premature death in 1835 when Elias Rendell assumed control until James' widow sold the property to Thomas Brannam. John at North Walk (Castle Lane) until his mother died and Brannam took out the lease on the property. George, master mariner was responsible for the passage of the wares to South Wales.
4. Thomas Brannam's elder brother, James was also working at the Castle Lane Pottery (1841 census) together with his father in law, James Rice. Though still a potter ten years later he is now living in Paiges Lane, though it is possible he still was working with one of the Rendells.
5. An advertisement of January 1859 lists the type of ware manufactured. This included pipes, tiles, flower and paint pots, salting and bread pans, ovens, pigs' troughs, chimney tops, etc., etc. (Goods sent to any part of the kingdom).
6. The 1841 census shows Thomas Brannam at Litchdon Street with a wife and young daughter, aged under two years.

LITCHDON AND NORTH WALK POTTERIES,
BARNSTAPLE.

T. BRANNAM,

GENERAL EARTHENWARE MANUFACTURER, returns thanks to his Friends and the Public for the liberal support he has received for the past ten years; and begs to inform them that he keeps on Sale an assortment of Draining Pipes, Sewerage Pipes, Closet Pans and Traps, Glazed Rolled Crease, Ridge and Pan-Tile, Stink Traps, Flower and Paint Pots, Farriers' Gills, Salting and Bread Pans, Ovens, Pump and Pigs' Troughs, Chimney Tops, &c., &c.
☞ Goods sent to any part of the Kingdom.

Fig. 31 Two advertisements from the Journal. a. Thomas Brannam

BRANNAM & SON,

MANUFACTURERS OF ALL KINDS OF

EARTHENWARE, OVENS,

CHIMNEY POTS,

FLOWER, SEAKALE, AND RHUBARB POTS,
SEWAGE AND FIELD DRAIN PIPES,
OVEN AND FLOORING TILES, &c., &c.
LITCHDON & NORTH WALK POTTERIES,
BARNSTAPLE   [4382

b. Brannam & Son

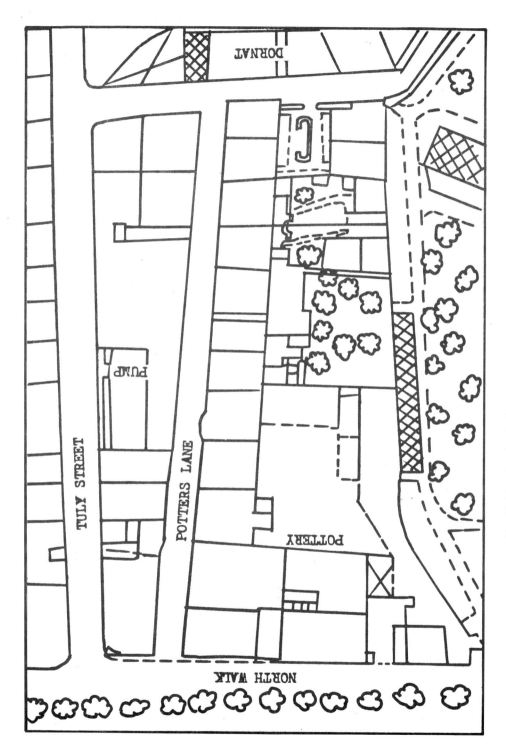

Fig. 32 Map showing the Brannam Potteries on North Walk.1894

BARNSTAPLE IN 1859 — A DIVERSION

It may be truthfully stated that by the second half of the nineteenth century the town of Barnstaple had gained much of its former reputation as the principal town in North Devon. From the decayed and declining borough described by Gribble at the turn of the century there had been an almost complete transformation of the town centre. Much of the High Street had been rebuilt or improved, and, together with the principal streets had been provided with pavements and lighting. The litter of market stalls in the High Street had been removed and a new market built behind the new Guildhall where an area of derelict property had been cleared, while a neat row of shops now housed the butchers of the town.

The entrance to the town from Newport through the Square had been drained and a new road built alongside the river, providing greatly improved access for the coaches and other traffic from Exeter, Bristol and London. A gas supply was available and a satisfactory water supply had been recently installed. The town could now boast ten public elementary schools, a Public Library and Reading Rooms. Businesses were prospering and prospects for employment were encouraging. The very latest wonder, the new railway provided a regular service to Exeter and beyond.

Then, in May 1859 the town was chosen as the venue for the annual Bath and West of England Agricultural Show. A great occasion! Because of the kudos attached to this annual event there was always great competition to be chosen to act as host. It was necessary to provide a convenient site with all amenities and a sufficient sum to finance the undertaking. As well as the provision of a Showground together with fencing, tents and similar undercover accommodation, there were many other expenses such as decorations, civic functions and entertainment of guests and visitors. A subscription list usually provided sufficient funds and in the present case topped the guaranteed amount of £800 by £500.

The area provided for the showground was much larger than usual (18 acres), so there was much more space for exhibitors. The site was on the Pottington Estate and adjacent to Rolle Quay and the Braunton Road. Owned by the Hon. Mark Rolle and farmed by W.B. Fisher it was lent by them for the occasion. The event was reported in full by the *Western Times* (Exeter) as well as in the local press. It lasted five days, from May 30 to June 3 inclusive.

On Monday afternoon the important visitors, who included the Earl of Fortescue and his son were met at the station by the mayor, Richard Bremridge, the principal men of the town and the President of the Society. Contemporary writings recorded:

The bridge across the Taw was spanned by light and elegant arches .. apt and original mottoes overhead expressed the leading thoughts of the Barumites on these occasions ... While guns fired salutes, the

Fig. 33 Views of the Bath and West Show 1859

HE EAST DEVON YEOMANRY CAVALRY BAND will PLAY in the SQUARE PAVILION from 9 to 10 O'CLOCK, A. M.

SHOW YARD ARRANGEMENTS.

Open from 9, a. m. to 6 p. m.   ADMISSION 2s. 6d.

EXHIBITION of Fine Arts and Manufactures.	EXHIBITION of Implements and Machinery.
FLORICULTURAL SHOW.	EXHIBITION of Live Stock of all descriptions.
FRUIT AND VEGETABLE SHOW. (Competition for Prizes.)	THE ROYAL MARINE BAND will play in the Show Yard during the day.
POULTRY SHOW.	PINNEY's BAND will play at intervals during the Show.

THE ANNUAL PAVILION DINNER, at 3 o'Clock,

Open to all Members of the Society, and Visitors.——TICKETS, 4s.——To be obtained on the Grounds, or of Mr. MAY, 71, High Street.

AQUATIC EXCURSIONS ON THE RIVER AT SIX O'CLOCK.

A VOCAL AND INSTRUMENTAL CONCERT at the MUSIC HALL, by the ROYAL MARINE BAND. Conductor, T. WINTERBOTTOM, Esq. Assisted by the principal CHORISTERS OF EXETER CATHEDRAL, under the direction of JAMES INGHAM, Esq. Programme of the Music, Glees, &c., to be obtained in the Room, or of any STATIONER, in the Town. To commence at 8 o'clock.

The E. D. Y. C. BAND will play in the Pavilion at 5, and in the North Walk, from Half past 6, until the commencement of CONCERT in the MUSIC HALL.

THEATRE, AT EIGHT O'CLOCK, Under the Patronage of the PRESIDENT and COUNCIL of the Society.

A GRAND DISPLAY OF FIRE WORKS IN THE NEW ROAD & SQUARE, AT 10.30, P.M.

After the Theatre and Concert have CLOSED.

FRIDAY.

The E. D. Y. C. BAND WILL PLAY IN THE SQUARE FROM 9 TO HALF PAST 10, A. M.

SHOW YARD ARRANGEMENTS.

The Yard will be open at 8 o'Clock, and close at 4. ADMISSION 1s.

All the Exhibitions, as shewn during the previous days, to be open this day.

THE MARINE BAND will play in the Show Yard at Intervals during the day	STEAM PLOUGH at work in a Field near the Show Yard. Admission, One Shilling.
SALE of Prize Fruit and Vegetables, at 2 o'clock.	

A GRAND ILLUMINATED DAY PERFORMANCE AT THE THEATRE, AT TWO O'CLOCK.

E. D. Y. C. BAND will play in the Square Pavilion, North Walk, and Market House during the Afternoon and Evening, commencing at 4 o'clock.

THEATRE OPEN IN THE EVENING AT 8 O CLOCK.

THE MAYOR AND MRS. BREMRIDGE'S BALL, AT THE MUSIC HALL, AT 10 O'CLOCK.

SATURDAY.

THE BAND WILL PLAY ROUND THE TOWN IN THE MORNING, AT NINE O'CLOCK.

Excursions to the surrounding Districts will be formed by Members of the Society, & Visitors.

THE ROYAL NATIONAL LIFE BOAT INSTITUTION WILL EXERCISE THEIR BOATS IN THE RIVER.

Privilege Tickets, admitting to all parts of the Exhibition during the Week. 10s To be obtained only at the Office at the Entrance of the Show Yard.—Children under Twelve Years of Age, 1s.—except Friday, when 6d. only for Children.

THERE WILL BE MORNING SERVICE IN THE OLD CHURCH EACH DAY OF THE WEEK, AT EIGHT O'CLOCK.

BREAKFASTS AND REFRESHMENTS OF EVERY DESCRIPTION MAY BE OBTAINED ON THE GROUND AT ALL TIMES. Purveyor......Mr. MAY. Breakfast and Dinner Ordinaries at the principal Hotels and Inns.   Several Dinner and Refreshment Rooms are also open in different parts of the Town.

GENERAL AMUSEMENTS, &c., during the week.

AN EXHIBITION of Paintings, Articles of Virtu, Curiosities, and Fine Arts, &c., at the ASSEMBLY ROOMS, during the entire Week, Open Daily from 10 a.m. till dark. Admission 1s. One day's proceeds to be appropriated to the North Devon Infirmary. A Refreshment Room attached.

THE PUBLIC READING ROOMS and LIBRARY at the Literary Institution, High Street, are, by the kind permission of the Council of the Institution, Open gratuitously during the Week, from 9 in the Morning, to 9 at Night, to Members of the Society, and Visitors, on presenting their Cards, or entering their Names with the Porter. One of the Rooms is, for the convenience of Strangers, appropriated to the reception of Local Publications, Guide Books, Maps, Local Newspapers, and other matters, relative to Barnstaple, and the North of Devon.

BRITTON'S PHOTOGRAPHIC SALOON, 40, HIGH STREET, OPEN TO ALL VISITORS FREE, DAILY.

THE NEW MARKET will be Decorated and Illuminated as an Evening Promenade, and in the event of the weather proving unpropitious, the Bands will play there instead of the places before appointed.

By permission of the Owner, Strangers may visit and inspect the ancient Danish Mound, and site of the Castle, in the Grounds of Castle House, near the North Walk, by applying to the Gardener.

AGREEABLE WALKS NEAR THE TOWN.—The North Walk.—The Anchor Wood Bank by the River, and Paths extending through the Wood.—The Seven Brethren Bank, above the Bridge.—Pill Grove, by the River, on the Newport side.—Raweigh Lane.— Roborough Hill, and old Roman Encampment, one mile and half,—Tawstock Church, two miles,—and Coddon Hill, three miles from the Town.

Fig. 34 The Bath and West Show. Part of a Programme of Events

Fig. 35 Two vignettes by William Britton. On the Showground

Fig. 36   Two more vignettes.   The Art and Industries Tent

procession crossed the bridge ... The brightest 'belles' of Barnstaple crowded the windows of the houses in High Street and smiled a welcome ... The church bells struck out merrily ... the procession moved on to the Guildhall where the entertainment was provided ... spiced ale was served out of massive silver goblets and small squares of cheese with toast, soaked in spiced liquid. Healths were drunk ... then on to the Parish Church for Divine Service. The venerable Archdeacon of Barnstaple ... in the course of too long a sermon on such an occasion ...later the Exhibition was finally opened.

On Wednesday the mayor gave a banquet for 400 guests and on Thursday evening there was a Vocal and Instrumental concert at the Music Hall. The High Street was decorated with triumphal arches and flags while the Market was brilliantly lit, Mr. Gaydon's illuminated clock proving a great attraction. Printed handbills and posters listed the events and a printed programme gave details of the entries and times of judging, together with a plan of the Showground. As nowadays, there were both trade and competition exhibits. There were three main classes for competition: Implements, Livestock, and Arts and Commerce. The first two days were reserved for the mounting of the show and for private visitors with privilege tickets. On Tuesday the implements were judged, on Wednesday the Livestock and on Thursday the arts and commerce. Local entries were received in all classes. The show was very well attended, with 6,000 visitors on Wednesday, 8,000 on Thursday and nearly 15,000 on Friday, including children . There seems no doubt that this event was a great success and must have contributed substantially to the reputation of Barnstaple as a new centre for Industry and the Arts.

Footnotes (*See footnote numbers in text*)

1.   Quoted from *The Western Times*.

Information, printed matter and illustrations by courtesy of the North Devon Athenaeum.

BRANNAM, THOMAS, Potteries, Barnstaple. Earthenware, Manufacturer. [E.S.]

		£ s d
1.	6 Vases, 5s, 4s, 3s per pair	0 12 0
2.	6 Dozen Flower Pots, 12s, 9s, 6s, 4s, 2s, 1s per doz.	1 14 0
3.	2 Butter Coolers, 2s 6d each	0 5 0
4.	3 Bread Pans, 2s 6d, 2s, 1s 6d	0 6 0
5.	3 Milk Pans, 6d each	0 1 6
6.	3 Milk Pans, as used in Devonshire, 4d each	0 1 0
7.	Oven for baking bread, &c	0 10 6
8.	3 Chimney Tops, 8s, 4s 6d, 1s each	0 1 0
9.	50 Bricks, 8s per 100	0 4 0

BRITTON, WILLIAM & SONS, No. 40, High-street, Barnstaple Opticians, Photographers, Lathe Makers, &c.

[S.P.]

		£ s d
1.	Six-inch Centre Lathe on Planed bed, and Cast-iron frame, Division Plate, and spring centres, brass and other chucks	
2.	Compound Slide Rest. This tool is an improvement on the ordinary slide rest by the addition of an endless wheel and screws, whereby concave and convex surfaces are easily turned, as well as flat surfaces, and parellel bars, &c.	120 0 0
3.	Elliptical Cutter. This tool is used in the turning lathe for producing various cycloidal patterns on ivory, wood, &c.	
4.	Improved Eccentric Drill, and other Tools, &c., belonging to the Lathe	
5.	Machine for Dividing Micrometers on Glass. It is possible with this machine to make upwards of 100,000 lines within the inch	5 0 0
6.	Compound Achromatic Microscope, with 2 in., 1 in., and ¼ in. Object Glasses, Moveable Stage, Polariscope, &c.	30 0 0
7.	Stereoscopes and Stereographs of local scenery, &c.	
8.	Specimens of Photography, both landscape and portraiture, including Photographs on paper, glass, leather, &c.,&c.	

Fig. 37 Two entries for the show from the programme

LETTERS AND TELEGRAMS MUST BE ADDRESSED—BRANNAM, POTTERY, BARNSTAPLE.

THE ONLY·NORTH DEVON POTTERY.

PATRONIZED BY HER LATE MAJESTY QUEEN VICTORIA,1885 & 1892.

BY APPOINTMENT

H.R.H.PRINCESS CHRISTIAN

H.H. PRINCESS VICTORIA OF SCHLESWIG-HOLSTEIN. SEPT 7TH 1905.

H.R.H. DUCHESS OF TECK, 1893.

H.S.H. PRINCESS MAY, 1893.

H.R.H. PRINCESS EDWARD OF SAXE WEIMAR, 1896

H.R.H. PRINCESS CHRISTIAN. SEPT 7TH 1905.

H.R.H. PRINCESS LOUISE, JUNE 1905.

H.R.H. DUKE OF CONNAUGHT. 1892.

H.R.H. PRINCE ALBRECHT OF PRUSSIA, 1895-1899.

LONDON 1851.   PLYMOUTH 1881.   ROYAL CORNWALL POLYTECHNIC 1881.

POTTERIES. BARNSTAPLE, March 3rd. 1903.

L. W. Wallington Esq.

BOUGHT OF C. H. BRANNAM, Manufacturer.

No 2

NOT RESPONSIBLE FOR LOSS OR DAMAGE IN TRANSIT.   STRAW AND PACKAGES CHARGED.   INTEREST CHARGED ON OVERDUE ACCOUNTS

Brannam Headed Notepaper for despatching orders

Fig. 38 Charles Hubert Brannam, a portrait. Courtesy Mrs. Brannam

Number One Union Terrace (present day)
Charles Brannam's school

UNION TERRACE SCHOOL,
BARNSTAPLE,

CONDUCTED by Mr. FEATHERSTONE
and able Assistant Masters.

Young Gentlemen are carefully instructed in History,
Geography, Arithmetic, Book-keeping, and in all sub-
jects connected with a first-class Commercial Education.
Those intended for Agricultural pursuits are taught to
Survey (practically) and to Plan Estates.

The Classical and Mathematical Courses are arranged
with reference to Matriculation at the Universities, and
to the Preliminary Examinations of Apothecaries' Hall,
and the other Medical Licensing Bodies, whilst all
Students are grounded in those preliminary and general
subjects required at the Oxford and Cambridge Local
Examinations.

French and German, which are now, for various
reasons, so essential to men of business, occupy a prominent position in the daily routine.

The Masters devote their whole time to the School,
and no effort is spared to make the establishment equal
in general efficiency to any in North Devon.

The School was established in 1834, and now numbers
about Seventy Pupils, to whose friends references may
be made.

Terms, which are moderate, may be known on application at No. 1, Union Terrace.

☞ School duties will be resumed on MONDAY, January 21st, 1861.

Notice from the Journal advertising Union Terrace
School

Fig. 39 William Britton's shop at High Cross

BARNSTAPLE
LITERARY & SCIENTIFIC
INSTITUTION.

PRESIDENT of the above INSTITUTION,

W. F. ROCK, ESQ.,

WILL DISTRIBUTE THE

PRIZES

To the various Classes connected with

SOUTH KENSINGTON,

On **FRIDAY EVENING NEXT**, 20th August,

At **EIGHT o'clock, P.M.**,

When Members and their Friends are invited to be present.

ADMISSION FREE.

JOS. J. DUNSTONE,
Hon. Secretary.

Dated BARNSTAPLE, August 18th, 1869.

Poster 1869.   William Henry Rock's Prizegiving

BEGINNINGS

When Charles Hubert Brannam, only son of Thomas Backway Brannam was born in January 1855, his parents had not long settled in the premises at Litchdon Street. His elder sister, Mary Jane (Jenny) was already fifteen. His parents separated during his early years, probably when he was ten, Charles remaining with his father. Jenny had already left home a few years earlier, when she married William Britton junior, son of the optician and photographer with a shop at 40 High Street, Barnstaple.

Charles was educated at number one Union Terrace, next door to the North Devon Infirmary and a couple of hundred yards from the pottery. Mr. Featherstone's school for young gentlemen, a private establishment catering for between 50 and 70 boys was highly regarded locally, giving training for commerce and the professions. The year he left, at the age of twelve Charles won the Art Prize.

It was the custom in Victorian times for at least one son to follow his father in the family business and certainly over the last two or three years Charles would have spent much of his time in and around the pottery, becoming acquainted with the life and probably learning many of the skills on Saturday mornings, during the lighter summer evenings and in the holidays. While obviously showing interest, he was, however keen to continue his Art education and, as a preliminary to this he was enrolled as a first-class member of the Literary and Scientific Institution (initially for one quarter) which made him eligible to join the Drawing classes.

He thus made the acquaintance of Alexander Lauder who, having returned some five years earlier from Edinburgh where he had just finished an extensive education which included studies with the architect, Alexander Black as well as considerable art training; was now teaching drawing to the young art students at the afternoon and evening classes. Lauder would have had no formal qualifications but seems to have been a natural teacher, with more patience than many of the trained teachers employed by the Institution during the early years. His job was not without difficulties, as may be glimpsed from the report he submitted to the Art committee in 1865.[1]

'Originally 38 students presented themselves but only 25 proved effective as students ... the majority had not previously held the pencil ... notwithstanding several of the students have made encouraging progress'. A daunting task; but Mr. Lauder proved to be both a popular and successful teacher who provided useful groundwork for the students who were later to tackle the formidable 'National Course of Instruction' when the classes were affiliated with the government scheme, based at South Kensington. Although overall control was then assumed by the Art and Science master, Mr. Maunder who had run the classes for many years, Lauder continued to give his services free up to when the Town Council took over the running of the classes and a full-time Art master (Mr. Ireland) was appointed. (1877)

Fig. 40 Henry Phillip's Pottery at East the Water.

76, HIGH ST., BARNSTAPLE.

JAMES MOON,
FURNISHING AND GENERAL

IRONMONGER,

BELL-HANGER, WHITESMITH, GAS-FITTER,

Brazier, Iron, Copper, and Tin-plate Worker, Oil and Colorman.

A LARGE ASSORTMENT OF

DRAWING & DINING-ROOM STOVES AND FENDERS,
MARBLE CHIMNEY-PIECES;

BODLEY'S, AND OTHER COOKING APPARATUS.

Brass and Iron Bedsteads of every kind kept in Stock, and fixed
ready for inspection.   Table & other Lamps, Gaseliers, Pendants,
Brackets, and Gas-fittings of all kinds.

WARRANTED TABLE AND POCKET CUTLERY; ELECTRO-PLATED,
NICKEL SILVER, AND BRITANNIA METAL GOODS.

MANUFACTURER      AGRICULTURAL

OF   IMPLEMENTS,

every description of

AGRICULTURAL AND OTHER CASTINGS OF EVERY KIND.

FIRE & THIEF PROOF SAFES, BY THE PRINCIPAL MAKERS.

MAKER OF WROUGHT-IRON CONTINUOUS CATTLE FENCES, HURDLES, PALISADING,
TOMB RAILING, VERANDAHS, &c.   CHURCHES, CHAPELS, MANSIONS,
CONSERVATORIES, &c., HEATED ON A MOST APPROVED PRINCIPLE.

GENERAL SMITHS' WORK, IN EVERY BRANCH,
AND EXPERIENCED WORKMEN SENT TO ANY PART OF THE COUNTRY.

SPONGE, HIP, SHOWER, AND EVERY DESCRIPTION OF BATHS.

Bradford's Patent Wringing and Mangling Machines; Kent's
Knife Cleaner; Mincing Machines, &c.

Branch Establishment:—KING STREET, SOUTH MOLTON.

Advertisement. James Moon

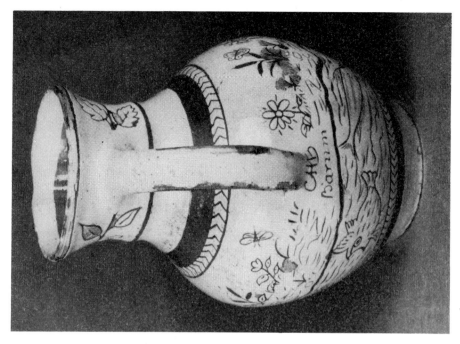

Fig. 41 Very Early Jug by Charles Brannam (two views) NDDC and MND

Fig. 42   Another very early jug by the young Brannam, dated 12.6.79 NDDC and MND

Fig. 43 Alligator on a tile. An early piece by Frederick Bowden NDA and MND

Strap–handled Pitcher, probably by Bowden, (right)and a later copy (left)

Fig. 44 Three early pale blue and chocolate vases with seaweed designs
Left to right no mark, 1888 and 1881 J.D. 8"–10" Barum Ware

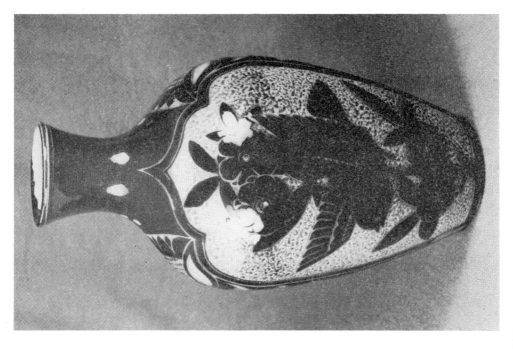

Fig. 45 Two early pieces. a. tankard 9" 1881 b.vase with birds, both MND, NDA

In 1870 Charles Brannam won the prestigious Queen's prize for chalk drawing (aged 15). After this it looks as if he discontinued classes at the school — at least his name does not appear on the records. However it does seem likely that Lauder would have continued to show an interest in the young man's progress and may even have given him private lessons.

There is no reason to suppose that Charles' decision to continue his art training caused a rift in the family; in fact, it seems extremely likely that he combined his studies with work at the pottery. It was probably at about this time that he made the acqaintance of Henry Phillips, the Bideford potter who had been experimenting since the 1860s with designs and glazes on his local earthenware.[5] R.H. Phillips, writing about his ancestor in 'Notes on the Bideford Pottery Industry' says, concerning the glazes:—

'Henry Phillips was a friend of (James) Brannam who was carrying out similar experiments at Litchdon Street pottery, Barnstaple, and it appears likely that they sometimes compared notes, for Henry's will contained a clause that should he die first, his experimental notebooks be handed over to Mr. Brannam. As far as is known this was done on Henry's death'. (Mr. Phillips was presumably referring to *Charles* Brannam, and it seems likely that Brannam's first glaze which produced a pale or midblue originated with Phillips).

Support would also have come from Mr. Rock who is known to have followed the young man's progress with great interest, entertaining Charles at his Blackheath home and taking him on a tour of the London museums where he was made aware of the whole range of ceramic art. It is likely that by now he was relating his artistic ideas to designs for pottery, but Brannam senior had his own problems. For some years he had been struggling to hold the business together; where increasing overheads, falling demand and lower prices had kept his profits marginal. He would not have been prepared to listen to any suggestion which required cash for wasteful experiments requiring special glazes and extra fuel.

Charles[2] decided to join his brother-in-law in his photographer's studio at High Cross, 23, High Street, combining this paid work with keeping his hand in at the pottery. His sister Jenny and her husband, himself an earlier student at the Art school, had always encouraged him in his studies; indeed they may have considered photographic work an outlet for his artistic talent. It is likely that over the next few years he was able to save a certain amount to add to the cash sum of his prize money.

Nearly nine years had passed, during which time business at the pottery became increasingly critical. There is a distinct possibility that Alexander Lauder allowed the young Brannam to work at the pottery *he* had set up at Pottington for he appears to have been working there when his father decided at last to allow the Litchdon Street premises to be used in experiments with Art pottery.[3]

In 1879 Charles Brannam wrote in his Journal:

>...things were going from bad to worse at the pottery, milk pans wholesale 3/- for 12 ... it was difficult to get the wages together. I wanted to get into business on my own account but friends could not prevail upon my father to let me control one of the potteries, but he agreed to my making and decorating pieces of ware by paying the cost of materials and firing.

From small beginnings the experimental pottery became a marketable proposition, attracting attention not only locally but among visitors to the town, including a number of Barumites, keen to help a fellow townsman.[4]

Footnotes *(See footnote numbers in text)*

1. from the Minute books of the Literary and Scientific Institution. (courtesy North Devon Athenaeum).
2. He could have been the 'active intelligent lad, not under 15' advertised for by William Britton in the *North Devon Journal,* June 1875.
3. Information from Mrs. P. Brannam.
4. As noted earlier Barumite — a citizen of Barum: the latin name for Barnstaple.

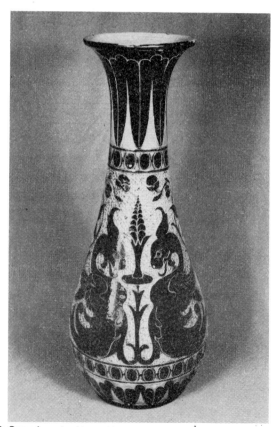

Fig. 46 One of a pair of large blue and chocolate vases with heraldic beasts
20" 1883 J.D. NDA and MND

EARLY DAYS AT THE POTTERY

The initial work force at the pottery was small. It is probable that the making of common earthenware was continued alongside the new work of the finer pottery and since Charles needed skilled staff it seems likely that some of the work force would have been at his disposal. These probably included John Henry Lemon, thrower; Jimmy Stevens, later head-fireman and kiln-setter; and perhaps other experienced older staff, all in their thirties and known to have been potters living in the area at the time:—

Andrew Cox of Silver Street, William Popham living at Belle Meadow, and William Cann living in Trinity Street in 1871. (These names recur in later records of the pottery, probably relatives).[1] (See Page 33).

Frederick Bowden,[2] Charles Brannam 's first modeller who worked at the pottery all his life was probably recruited direct from the Art School. At the age of fourteen he already showed talent; though his early modelling attempts are fairly crude they showed a potential that was to make him an indispensable figure at the pottery. It is likely too that Charles took on new young staff for training in the new processes which required much care and precision.

Not many months after work was started Charles sent a pair of vases to Mr. Rock for his appraisal, and many other eyes were watching his progress. Owen Davis,[3] a successful Barumite who had become a fashionable interior decorator in London sent a design for the potter to copy. Applied to a vase[4] this was well received and led to commissions for more pieces. Then Mr. Davis suggested a contract to supply further pieces of a similar type, exclusively to Messrs Benham and Fround of Chandos Street, London; but the potter did not wish to be tied down in this way and, preferring more freedom to experiment with a variety of styles, signed a contract instead with Messrs. Howell and James & Co.,[5] pottery manufacturers and agents of 5, 7 and 9 Regent Street, London. According to the agreement they were 'to assist him in developing his new ware and to advise him on shape and colour'. (1880).

In January 1881 Brannam was given the best publicity so far when Professor Church,[6] FRS, ceramic scientist and adviser to Henry Doulton at the Lambeth Art pottery used examples of the young potter's work to illustrate the Cantor lecture to the Royal Society of Arts. He referred to some: ...

> fine vases, coloured with glazes of flowing and pulsating hues. The bold foliage work and grotesque animal forms which decorate this 'Barum Ware'[7] remind one at once of the rare 'graffiato' ware and of some of the quaintest and rarest English and Staffordshire productions of the seventeenth century in their picturesqueness and originality.

In May of the same year the *North Devon Journal* reported on the display at Howell

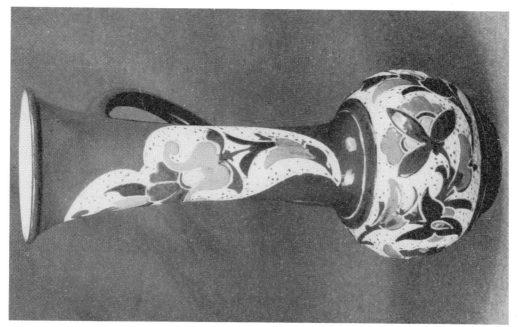

Fig. 47 Two vases, a. with swirled handles, b. with scrolled handles, b. dated 1890, biscuit–fired, WB, both MND

Fig. 48 Two early Brannam Jugs.a. Harvest Jug in the Fishley manner, 8" 1881

b. small marbled jug,1880 signed C.H.B.

Fig. 49 The Potter's Wheel. a. hand–driven.

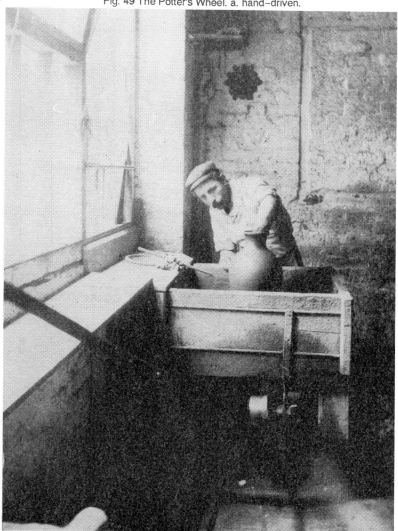

b. John Henry Lemon machine driven

c. 1912

The Staff in theThirties

Fig. 50 Three photos of staff at the Brannam Pottery
courtesy Mrs. Brannam

and James' showroom: ...

> This effective pottery[8] is thoroughly original in method and style, and the quaint designs, executed mainly in dark green and lightish blue are singularly cool and restful to the eye.

(these may have been the first of the designs to achieve a good separation of colour. Some vases presented a streaky appearance over a finely etched design[9]). This fine separation was used in two ways: an etched line was used to separate the two blocks of colour or, the background was pitted to reveal the red clay, so producing the two colours after glazing.[10]

It was clear by now that the pottery had captured the public fancy, both at home and in London. A report in the *Exeter Flying Post* in August, describing Brannam's work at the local exhibition says: ...

> this Barnstaple pottery is all the rage just now ... it is said to have been obtained as a special favour, nearly all that is produced being bought up by a London firm as it is manufactured.

This claim is borne out by Brannam's own note in his Journal that 'the demand was enormous and prices booming'. The pottery was an undoubted success. In November 1881 the following notice was inserted in the 'Journal' ...

North Walk and Litchdon Street Potteries.

> Mr. Thomas Brannam having retired from the above business in favour of his son, Charles Hubert Brannam,[11] notice is hereby given that any persons having claim or debt due from the said Thomas Brannam are requested to send particulars of same to Chanter, Ffinch and Chanter (solicitors).

One may reliably assume that the business had been very near to bankruptcy but that the success of the Art Pottery in under two years had allowed enough profit to be made to pay off outstanding debts and to leave a substantial amount to continue the successful business. For a number of years the making of common earthenware continued. (see Strong's *Industries of North Devon* 1888/9).

On the strength of his success and the taking over of the business, Charles married the girl he had been courting. She was Annie Jeffery Woolacott, third daughter of Jane Lovering Moon Woolacott who kept a pawnbroker's shop at the rear of the family ironmongery business — Moon's at 76 High Street.[12] (Boots the Chemist now occupies the site). The couple went to live in one of the cottages adjacent to the pottery. Within four years they had two sons.

Footnotes *(See footnote numbers in text)*

1. See later chapter on staff at the pottery.

2. The very large model of a lizard on a tile, dated 1880 and with the initials F.B. is in the Athenaeum collection. Bowden was also responsible for an early pitcher with a strap handle and decorated with a lizard. See illustrations.

3. Owen Davis, a convert to the Revival movement was very well known for his designs for furniture, wallpaper, fabrics and stained glass. His designs for the interiors of public buildings were famous: notably the Pompeian designs for the Lyceum, the Bank of England and the Albert Hall. Persian carpet designs for the Empire Theatre and the Willow Plate decor for the Gaiety were also his. (obit notices NDJ and the Cabinet Maker, July 1913).

4. A vase in the C.H. Brannam Ltd collection is in two colours and bears the inscription 'OWD to CHB' as part of the design; there is no mark on the base. Classical in design, it suggests how the potter's style might have developed. Restrained, in impeccable taste and not in the least 'picturesque' or 'quaint' it lacks the exuberance of his later work. Nevertheless, he did use this style for several years (see plates   ) Mr. Len Haskins, who designed a few pieces at the pottery in the early 1980s told me he modelled his work on this vase.

5. information from *A Family Business*.

    In fact, with Howell and James there proved to be little danger that the potter would be tied down; as over the next few years the West Country exhibitions provided him with publicity while from 1886 he had his own new showroom at the pottery.

    Two years later, in 1882 he signed a contract with Messrs Libertys of Regent Street, London; an association which lasted up to the 1930s. At first the firm took certain designs then later had their own exclusive marks (LIBERTY LONDON in a circle). and others. See Dating and Recognition Guide.

6. Professor, later Sir Arthur Herbert Church discovered 'turacin', an animal pigment containing 7% metallic copper and 'churchite', a native cerium phosphate which was used in glazes. (Pottery Gazette article 1931).

7. The earliest mark was 'Barum Ware', incised in a running script, while the potter used the name Barum as part of his registered mark (no. 44561). It has been suggested that he raised objections to Lauder's use of the name (Lauder Barum, Signed) on the pieces during the 1890s.

8. The firing of the pieces greatly affected the colours so that the colouring could be pale blue and chocolate or mid-blue and black, or green and dark brown.

9. Early experiments with blue and yellow glazes were mentioned by Mr. Brannam in an interview he gave to a journalist from the Pottery Gazette in 1931. He recalled that the early streaky glazes resulted from a particular use of wood and furze in the firing which 'broke up the glazes into streaks of various tints instead of yielding one flat colour'.

10. This colour combination together with the use of sgraffito was so popular that Brannam continued to use it right up to the mid 1890s, long after the introduction of coloured slips.

11. Thomas Brannam was then 65 years of age.

12. The unmarried daughters lived with their very deaf mother at number 76 and helped in both shops. The family ironmongery business had once been the largest in the town, with a second shop in South Molton but at about this time the business was sold to Messrs. Noakes and Inns. The pawnbrokers, however continued in the Woolacott family until just after the turn of the century. Annie's sisters never married. Peter Brannam remembered them from duty visits to the house at 61A High Street where they would sit at the upper window. They do not appear to have been very lovable.

THE WORKING POTTERY 1879 — 1903

In this chapter an attempt has been made to trace the progress of the pottery from 1879 to 1903, making use of the Wages Book[1] of 1897 to 1903 and Hugh Strong's contemporary account of 1888.[2] An analysis of deployment of staff and the distribution of wages shows the value placed on certain key workers and the importance of designing and modelling in the Art Pottery. It also indicates the shift of emphasis away from decorating and towards style and new trends in the very early years of the present century, probably to supply the Art-Nouveau requirements of Libertys and changing public taste. Strong's personal visit to the pottery shows work behind the scenes and I am indebted to Maud Lemon, youngest daughter of John Lemon for her early memories.

The first two experimental years were almost certainly run 'on a shoe-string' with just a handful of operators which included John Lemon[3] who had joined the pottery straight from school some five or six years earlier and Frederick Bowden[4] who was already doing modelling work in 1880. Brannam senior's own workforce, numbering at the most a dozen[5] would be continuing with the production of the coarseware on the premises. Though it is possible that their experience was useful it is more likely that Charles probably preferred to train his own young staff in the new and tricky process of glazing and firing the Art Pottery, where there was no room for costly mistakes.

By 1881 and the 'take-over', the successful and rapid progress together with the increasing output suggest that key men were now in charge of slipping, glazing and firing. Jimmy Stevens could have been in charge of the kiln — joining the firm in 1872 he remained in charge for the greater part of his 53 years. By 1887 a second wheel had been installed, leaving Lemon in charge of the original; then ten years later a second kiln was built. The list of 1897 shows the four senior key workers to be Frederick Washer, John Lemon, Bob Smiley; and Charlie Trapnell[6] who came already trained, having completed his apprenticeship at Weston Super-Mare. Tom Lemon had now joined his brother but later moved to Torquay and then to Weston.

By 1881, too the potter had taken on his first designer, and within three or four years needed a second. (James Dewdney and William Baron, both highly trained and talented). Under these two, local youngsters, often straight from school and showing artisitic ability, were trained, and encouraged to attend the evening classes[7] at the School of Art (special rates for artisans). Strong mentions these in his article of 1888. The first of these was probably (John) Arthur Bamkin (first exam success in 1886), followed by Thomas Liverton who became second designer when Baron left in 1893.[8] The next to join was probably Frederick Braddon whose work at the pottery was not, however continuous; though he was the last of the art-designers to be employed,

34

Nov 25th 1891

J. Lemon	14	6
J. Smiley	14	2
Down	16	0
J. Lemon	1	11 7
Passmore	11	0
Driscol	0	0
Williams	4	6
Cox	5	6
Westacott	5	0
S. Pinn	15	0
Crapnell	1	7 4½
Stevens	1	0 0
Bowden	1	12 9
Dobbs	9	0
Copp	19	0
Washer	1	5 7
Thorne	16	0
Paterson	12	0
Chapple	9	11
Popham	8	3
B. Smiley	1	5 0
P.	2	2 0
	1	9 0
	1	6 9
	11	3½
William	12	5½
Bradden	1	6 6
Garland	4	6
Thomas	3	6
Patterson	11	6
Manning	10	
Lemon	1	0 0

282

Aug: 28th 1902

Mr Dewdney		2	2 —
Liverton, T.		1	0 10
Thomas 10/6	Pearse 7/-		17 6
Pinn. S.		1	— 2
Popham. G.			15 6
Lemon Jno		1	13 4
Washer, F.		1	11 6
Stevens Jms		1	4 6
Clarke. W.			17 6
Turner. W.			11 —
Isaac. W.			13 6
Passmore. W.			11 —
Hutchings Jms			12 —
Smiley Jno		1	2 11½
Nutt. W.			16 —
Chapple. W.		1	— 9½
Trapnell. C.		1	10 3
Copp. W.			18 4½
Luscombe N			6 —
Turner A.			6 3
Hemmings			5 6
Sanders			4 6
Gaydon			5 6
Haydon			7 4
Paw			3 6
Cocks Jno			12 6
Cocks Jms			4 2
Pile			3 —
Bowden		1	17 10
Smiley RN		1	2 5½
	£	25	11 9
Pile's Commission 1½	£	2	9 0
		27	18 9

Fig. 51 Two pages from Brannam's wage book C.H. Brannam Ltd.– records

Fig. 52 Three small pieces in blue and chocolate. Left to right: jug 1883, small vase J.D. 1888, pot 1883

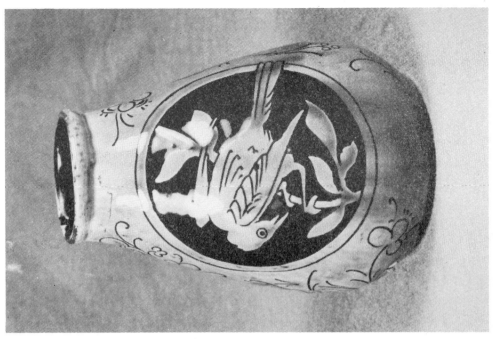

Fig. 53· Two early blue and chocolate pieces from the Museum of North Devon
b. Small vase with perching birds
a. Tankard in pale blue and slate grey, 1881 Brannam Ware NDA

Fig. 54 Jardiniere 1899, presented to the 'Barumites in London' C.H. Brannam Ltd. collection

leaving finally in 1930, when his services wer no longer required. To complete the 1897 list there were two young trainee-designers, Stanley Williams and Beauchamp Whimple and a very new recruit — Frank Thomas, earning the princely sum of three shillings a week! Seven designers in all — probably the largest number engaged at one time. As has already been stated, there was a move away from decorated pieces after the turn of the century, and the 1903 wages list suggests that just four artists were employed full-time — Dewdney, Liverton, Thomas and a recently-recruited Reginald Pearse. (See two photostats from the Brannam Wages Book).

It has been suggested by Peter Brannam that in the early years his grandfather did all the designs himself. In view of the sheer amount of work involved, the excellent, highly individual styles of Dewdney and Baron, as well as Strong's eye-witness account in 1888 —

the design is etched direct upon the pot, there being no previous working out of it on paper';

this claim seems highly unlikely; though there is no doubt that the owner would have done many of the designs for specially commissioned pieces.

The number of men employed in the early years is not known but it would be natural to expect a gradual increase in the workforce as production was stepped up. By 1897 there was a minimum of 28 employed which rose by 1903 to 37. There was little seasonal change except that three men were taken on in the clay-cutting season, one of whom seems to have been kept on for the rest of the year to cart the clay from the pits to the pottery. There is every indication that costing was very carefully controlled — the average weekly bill in the six years covered by the Book varied between twenty-eight and thirty pounds. All the staff, with the exception of Dewdney, who received a salary of two guineas a week basic; were on 'piece work' that is, payment by the hour, so their pay varied from week to week. After Dewdney, the highest paid worker over the period was Frederick Bowden, modeller who averaged from thirty-two to thirty-seven shillings a week. (Baron probably received a similar amount or possibly as much as two pounds). Thomas Liverton earned thirty shillings on average while Arthur Bamkin and Frederick Braddon received around twenty-five.

These latter were on a par with the key workers — Charlie Trapnell from twenty-eight rising to thirty-two shillings, Frederick Washer and Bob Smiley with thirty shillings on average and John Lemon[9] on twenty-eight. The other assistants — throwers, workers in slip and glaze, firemen, packers, down to those involved in preparing the clay and the young lads who made the balls of clay and turned the wheel for the potter earned from three shillings up to twenty-five shillings a week.

The clay-cutters were the exception. Two key men were employed for the season of between 23 and 26 weeks, when the weather was fine, that is between mid-Spring and early Autumn. Cutting was entirely dependent on the weather as the pits flooded after a heavy shower. Thus, in 1902 work was not started until the second week in April and so continued through to mid-October; while in 1900 work was started in mid-March but up to five weeks were lost due to heavy summer showers. Each key man received between seventeen and twenty-two shillings a week plus an end-of-season bonus — in one year a shared ten pounds. This was no doubt 'danger money'. The two reports quoted and Peter Brannam's description of the process, still operating in the late thirties show how hazardous this was for the men involved.[10] It was also very thirsty work, so they received a special cider allowance.

There are no records of other costs but these were obviously considerable, including the following — fuel for the kiln; provision of white clay; material for glazes and colours for slips; stationery; postage; packing and freight charges; advertising; the cost for the upkeep of the horses; cost of repairs especially to the kilns; new tools; wheel and kiln; and many other extras. The early profits were put back into the business in the new building; then, by the turn of the century when the North Walk pottery was closed a row of houses was built in Potters Lane and turning on to the Strand. (Turbit Terrace, now demolished). Land was also purchased in Victoria Road where Clayfield Villas and 'Hayne' were built (later occupied by the potter and his elder son). The potter also built a row of houses at the rear of the pottery, in Trinity Street (Ceramic Terrace) to house those of his workers who wished to rent them. Jimmy Stevens was never an occupier but bought two houses in Belle Alley. John Lemon, however occupied number five for his lifetime and his youngest daughter, Maud lived there until she retired, when she moved across the road to one of the Almshouses.

For a brief look at life in the pottery in the first decade of the present century we have Maud Lemon, youngest daughter of John Lemon with her reminiscences. The family lived at 5, Ceramic Terrace. The rent was 6/6$^{1}/_{4}$, which was deducted from Lemon's pay which he received at the end of the working week soon after midday on Saturday. Maud remembers one occasion when neither boss nor worker had a farthing change. Her father, anxious to be away exclaimed:— 'Forget it then!' 'No Lemon,' was the reply, 'you must look after the farthings and pennies and the shillings and the pounds will take care of themselves'. Miss Lemon was the youngest by twenty years, but most of her brothers and sisters had died in infancy or childhood. She remembers Mr. Brannam as a very careful man; measuring sash cord to the fraction of an inch. The houses were modern, roomy and comfortable and Mr. Brannam paid for the interior decorating but would buy the very cheapest wallpaper at sixpence a piece. If the wife preferred a pattern of her own choice then her husband would have to pay the difference.

Her father worked on the 'big wheel', otherwise the original, needing two assistants to help the thrower. The wheel was situated next to the kiln so that on some days, when the kiln was not in operation it was very cold in winter, while on the firing days it was very hot and smoky, with fumes and dust. This must have affected his chest as after thirty or so years the doctor advised him to change his job which he eventually did, becoming an insurance agent. He returned to work at the pottery during the first World War when they were short of manpower. The family still have a puzzle jug which her father threw for the benefit of an important visitor who was being shown round the pottery. He had to break off from his present task to do this and so 'lost time'. Rather than pay him, he was allowed to keep the jug which was, of course subsequently finely decorated and fired.

Footnotes *(See footnote numbers in text)*

1. Wages book, by courtesy of C.H. Brannam Ltd.
2. Barum Pottery article, first published in the *North Devon Journal* as one of series on Industries of North Devon. Printed in book form 1889 by W. Michael, pub. Barnstaple. Reprinted by David & Charles Ltd., Newton Abbot 1971.
3. John Lemon. Born Barnstaple 1864. Joined Thomas Brannam at North Walk c. 1875 — 6.
4. Bowden's model of lizard, signed F.B. dated 1880 Athenaeum collection.
5. The Census of 1871 showed a staff of 12 men and 2 boys at Litchdon St. Since the pottery had been in decline in the intervening years there were probably far less than this number.
6. Charlie Trapnell. See note of indentures 1882 — 1887. Page 130 'A Family Business' Frederick Washer. 1872 — 1943. Holy Trinity churchyard.
7. In 1881, morning and afternoon classes for one quarter, two sessions a week cost one guinea and fifteen shillings respectively... these no doubt helped to subsidise the evening classes, available for six hours weekly and costing five shillings (3/6 for artisans) Notice in Journal.
8. For details of student/designers see pages 43 — 49.
9. John Lemon's health was not good during his later years at the pottery and he probably worked shorter hours.
10. There are two reports of accidents at the pits. In June 1871 Samuel Emmett, aged 20 was 'a good deal bruised about the head and chest when the soil gave way and he was thrown forward'. Twenty-four years later (November 1895) Samuel Short (55), was 'seriously hurt by falling clay. He survived severe bruising and his collar bone was broken'.
    The method of cutting clay was by 'falling', a process similar to that used by the Fishleys and probably used for many years. This would 'bring down a big chunk of clay which largely broke up when reaching the bottom and could then be loaded away comparatively easily. Chimneys about a foot wide were dug each side of the face and the bottom was undercut similarly so that a massive lump of clay was left suspended. The men then went to the top of the seam and drove down several holes with a long bar ... and filled the holes with water. After a short time ... the whole mass of suspended clay, about fifty tons or more would fall outwards and, with a tremendous thump break itself to pieces on the pit floor'. from *A Family Business.*

SENIOR STAFF AT THE BRANNAM POTTERY, FROM 1872
(and possible forbears)

Name	Dates b. & d.	d of employ	Job	Address(es)
John Henry Lemon	1864-1937	1875- c. 1906	thrower	Zions Place and Ceramic Terrace
Tom Lemon	younger brother of John, later moving to S. Devon ...			
Jimmy Stevens	1860-1940	1872-1925	fireman/kiln setter	Belle Meadow
Billy Chapple	b. 1878	c. 1890-c. 1943	thrower	Zions Place and Ceramic Terrace
Billy and Philly Chapple	possibly sons of above		throwers in charge see p.73 P.B.	
Jimmy Cocks (Cox) John Cocks (Cox) also John Cox	b.1883 poss brother poss relative of above	cont. till retirement shorter period	glazer. potter 1881 census	Silver St.
Charlie Trapnell	b.c. 1870	c. 1887 till retirement Kiln layer previously apprenticed to potter at Weston S.M.		Trinity St.
Frederick Washer	1872-1943	c. 1884 to retirement senior worker, trade? possibly relation of Frk Washer, brickmaker at Fremington, 1881		
Bob Smiley	b. c. 1868	poss c. 1880 to retirement	key worker	Ceramic Terrace
John Smiley	younger brother?	from at least 1897		
Sam Pinn		from at least 1897, later in charge of packing dept. until retirement		
Popham family George and John		from 1890s -	Slipping	
Arthur	b. c. 1880	1890s to 1920s	....	
Henry	b. 1836		in 1851 potter, aged 15	Castle Lane
William	b. 1843		in 1871 potter	Belle Meadow
Cann Family Dick			thrower see P.B.	
William	b. c. 1849		potter 1871	Trinity St.
John		1899-1901	unknown trade	

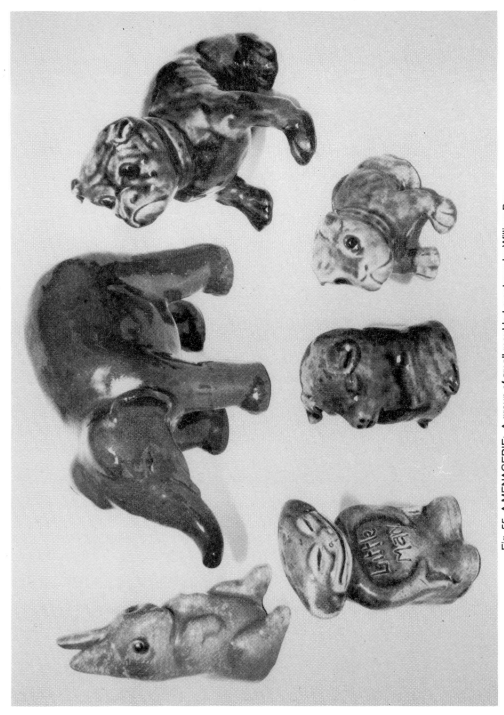

Fig. 55 A MENAGERIE; A group of small moulded creatures by William Baron

Fig. 56 Three late moulded pieces: Brannam dog, bulldog / ashtray, Lauder cat, MND

Fig. 57 A group of Baron cats

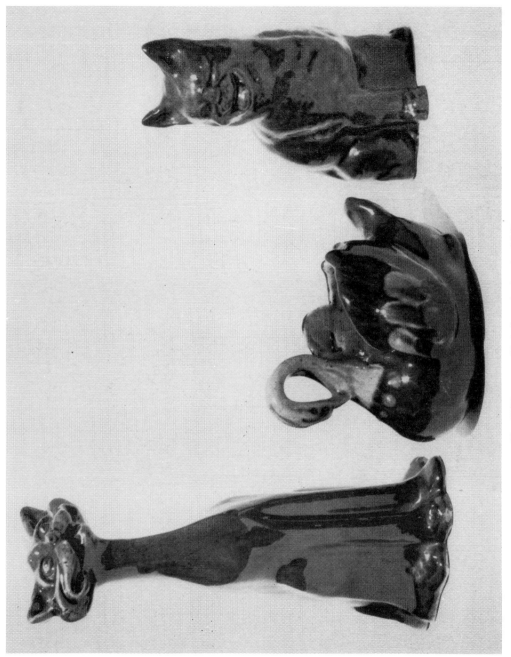

Fig. 58 Three moulded pieces by Lauder MND

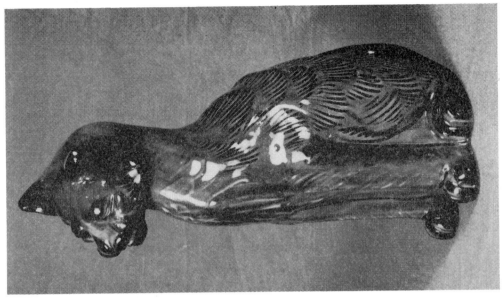

Fig. 59 Two seated Cats. a. by Fishley Holland Braunton 1914 b. by Brannam, MND

Fig. 60 Three Brannam grotesque pieces, collection of Barry Stock, and a moulded Swan by Lauder. MND

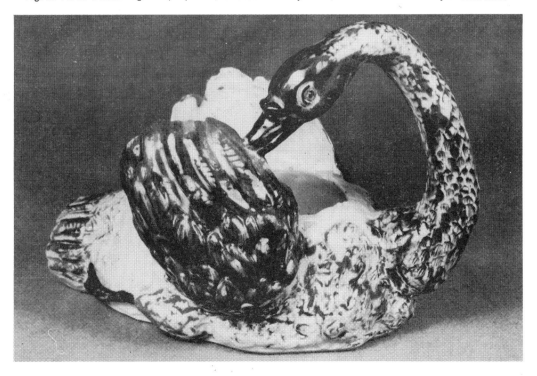

Fig. 61 Two pieces featuring Frogs. a. by E.B. Fishley b. Lauder christening mug

MAINLY PALE BLUE AND CHOCOLATE. 1881 — 84

During the highly successful year of 1881 Brannam engaged his first designer. This was necessary because of the rapid growth of the pottery. It was most important to maintain the high standards as well as to introduce new ideas. More skilled help with designing was urgently needed. The potter's committments of throwing, mixing glazes and the overall supervision of the pottery meant that he could no longer do all the designing work himself. There had not yet been enough time to train local young men (though by the early 1890s he probably had three fairly skilled locally-trained designers[1] — Arthur Bamkin, Thomas Liverton and Frederick Braddon).

By the evidence of his early work James Dewdney was both talented and highly trained. He was also highly valued by his employer. Records of wages are not available before 1897 but in that year and for the next six, he received the top wage of all the workers at the pottery:— two guineas a week, plus two or three odd amounts during the year which could have been for extra work or as a bonus. Dewdney did not live locally but it seems likely that he travelled in daily by train, possibly from Exeter; in which case he probably trained at the School of Art there. His arrival coincided with an increase in the production of the incised ware referred to in the previous chapter. He was now to be responsible for all of the designs (except those made by Brannam himself) until the appointment of William Baron some three or four years later.

In April the popularity of 'the well known blue and black ware'[2] was still high. By the contemporary descriptions it is clear how much the colours varied. In 1888 Hugh Strong wrote:—

> Much of the distinction which causes vases of precisely similar design to differ materially from each other is due to the operation of firing. Two pots going into different kilns or into different parts of one kiln will invariably present great dissimilarity in their finished state, the ware being materially affected by the heat to which it is subjected.[3]

While this led, no doubt to many 'happy accidents' it must have posed serious problems when producing a pair.

Two events during 1882 should be noted, the first Royal order, when the Grand Duke of Hesse (husband of Princess Alice, second daughter of Queen Victoria) chose three pieces from the Howell and James showroom. (Plate IV shows a vase dated 1882 and signed by Dewdney with an orange and brown colouring[4] which could have been similar to one of the royal pieces), and the other two in the new yellow-green tint now so much admired. The second boost came from an article by Cosmo Monkhouse in 'The Magazine of Art', describing the work of the Martin Brothers of Southall together with that of Charles Brannam.[5]

In May 1884, the report of the Devon County Show[6] gives the first mention of the new 'biscuit' firing (once fired) — 'mainly vases of various shapes, some with a bold relief ornament — vine leaves etc., are chaste in design and the modelling is good'. In the 'decorative' class were 'vases with handles in imitation of snakes', goats', and rams' heads ... shapes are ... cylindrical, curved and of every other vase pattern. Around one is a modelled cobra and every one of the scales was worked by hand ... jardinières ... ornamented in the form of panels divided by fern leaves, the decoration being elaborate and the colour excellent ... of that happy character that harmonizes with any surroundings'.

Similar pieces attracted the attention of a certain Mrs. Hanley who 'took an interest in my efforts and was a great help in many ways'.[7] She persuaded a Mrs. Buckmaster to allow four pieces to be sent to the Queen. 'Her Majesty was graciously pleased to order four large jardinières with snake handles. I thought I should never execute the order, the glazes would run dry and I did not know how to correct this; however I stood by the firing and was able to complete it just in time'.

'Just in time' was for delivery in May 1885. Mr. Brannam, with great pride and a sense of occasion immediately adopted the title of 'Royal Barum Ware' for his pottery and inserted a notice in the Journal to the effect that the Art Pottery ordered by the Queen would be on view for two days during the following week.[8] (A duplicate group to be on view at Mr. Britton's, High Cross). It is not known how many similar jardinières were made and sold but the demand both at home and in London must have been tremendous. Unfortunately the pieces are no longer in the Royal Collection nor is there any record of them. Plate II shows a piece made in 1885 and signed J.D. in pale blue and yellow. The ball feet are made from fish heads whose inverted bodies support the piece. The scales are finely worked. The piece could bear some resemblance to the ordered pieces.

Footnotes *(See footnote numbers in text)*

1. See list of designers.
2. North Devon Journal report.
3. From 'Journal article/Industries of North Devon.
4. A reddish glaze had been used from the early days, see example of marbled 1880 jug, signed C H B and 'harvest' jug in the Fishley style, both of which produce brown shades. See Fig 54.
5. See Appendix 2A.
6. Report from North Devon Journal.
7. From the Charles Brannam 'Journal' quoted from 'A Family Business'.
8. At this time Brannam had neither a large window or a showroom at the pottery so the prominent position of his brother in law's shop in High Street was most opportune.

ENTER WILLIAM BARON

It would perhaps be a trifle unfair to link the recruitment of William Baron from the Doulton Lambeth pottery[1] with the appearance of the first coloured slipware produced by Brannam, but in fact the two events did coincide. It is known that William Baron joined Brannam in either the latter part of 1884 or in the early months of 1885. (The pictured Doulton small pot with the initials W B is dated 1884 and Baron exhibited some Brannam pieces at the Exeter Show in September 1885). The earliest example using coloured slips that has been noted is a vase dated 1885 with Dewdney's initials, showing considerable sophistication and control of the medium, suggesting that earlier pieces may have been made. On the other hand, early pieces by Baron have not yet come to light and it seems likely that initially he was kept busy doing modelling work.

The showing of two figures in earthenware at the Exeter Show in September 1885 (which won him a bronze medal) suggests that he may have done similar work for Doultons' — there was after all the excellent example of George Tinworth and John Broad to follow! (they had worked in both the 'stoneware' clay and in earthenware). The first two figures by Baron for Brannam were entitled 'Good for a Yarn' and 'Good for a Gossip'.

They must have been noted by Mr. Rock who, always keen to encourage young talent, gave Brannam a commission to make an earthenware figure to be erected near to the entrance of the new Sports Ground at the end of Rock Park. He wanted a figure that epitomised Sport. No doubt advised by Mr. Charbonnier, headmaster of the School of Art, a model was chosen from the plaster casts. Locally called 'Discobolus, the quoit player' the project was set in motion by the modelling of a trial figure, eleven inches high, standing on a plinth.[2] The completed statue was six feet high on a five foot pedestal and used twelve hundredweight of clay.

It was erected a little back from the path through the Park and close to a pool and fountain. 'The Artist' of December 1887 carried a full report, describing it as the 'chef d'oeuvre of the Barnstaple Art Pottery'. 'At the pottery works of Mr. Brannam has just been produced what is probably the largest statue that exists in terra cotta. It is a slightly enlarged copy of the antique figure known as 'The Fighting Gladiator' which is also one of the most difficult to produce in terra cotta owing to the violent action and want of support for the overhanging parts. The figure was modelled by Mr. W.L. Baron, a designer at the works who is also a student at the School of Art'.

It was, perhaps rather too ambitious. Within a few years Baron was called in to repair a broken arm, and if local reports were correct it was for a long period a prime target for stray stones from passing schoolboys. It was later removed to a new position adjacent to the path, but in the 1930s, after the sportsground site had been filled in with

Fig. 62 The Fighting Gladiator. a. a later small replica in terra-cotta
b. the figure in Rock Park from a postcard

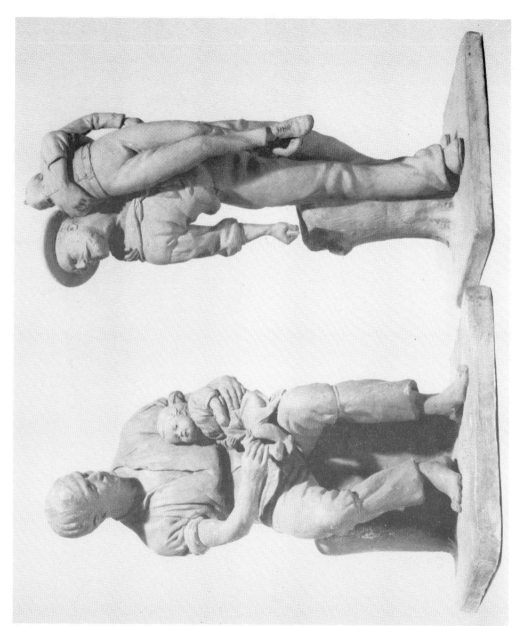

Fig. 63 Two later figures in terra-cotta (family collection) a. The Widower b. The Midshipmite. Height 14"

Fig. 64 Terra–cotta tile, head of Billy in bas–relief MND

Fig. 65 Two small pieces with Baron designs. a. bottle vase, 1885
b. small bulbous vase 6 1/2" 1889, Doulton influence

Fig. 66 Two pieces probably modelled by Brannam. a. double–dolphin bowl, 5" 1891 b. Serpentine teapot, 1891

Fig. 67 Large Vase with early slip design of gamebird by Baron. Height 16", on reverse large chrysanthemum.

Ginger, pale blue and ochres on a cream sgraffito background

refuse and rubble to render it safe from flooding and a new surface laid, the figure had disappeared. An indignant elderly lady visitor to the Athenaeum remembered it being broken down into hardcore for the foundations!

Brannam seems to have had no further plans for terra cotta figures but William Baron made several in later years, probably as part of his work at the School of Art. He was, however almost certainly responsible for designing and modelling various standing modelled pieces for the potter, among them the most popular 'double bowl with dolphin supports', a grotesque teapot and a wall pocket in the shape of an owl's head.[3] There could be many more and he probably shared the modelling work with Bowden. However, these three particular shapes have been singled out for mention as he used all three at his own pottery on Rolle Quay. (He probably considered that he was entitled to use them if they were of his own invention).

However, during the eight or so years he spent at the pottery he did many designs for the bowls, vases and jardinières made there. These were of fine quality and delightful in conception and execution. He preferred natural forms of fish, birds and flowering branches, often showing strong movement and a sense of fun. Two pieces dated 1888 show a strong influence from Doultons. Each uses an Indian bottle shape, which, with its bulbous body is ideal to show off the lateral design of birds in a leafy landscape.

Other designs show his versatility. Much of his spare time was spent as a student and later teacher at the School of Art. He seems to have been an easy-going character who got on well with both his students and fellow workers at the pottery but there may well have been a 'personality clash' between himself and his employer. In 1893 he gave his notice to leave saying 'there was not enough work for him'.[4] Mr. Brannam did not take kindly to the decision, especially when he later became a competitor. The 'reason' for leaving was not taken seriously and he was never forgiven.

Footnotes *(See footnote numbers in text)*

1. More details about Doultons in later account of Baron's early life.
2. This model is still in the possession of the Baron family but has the right arm missing.
3. Pictures show three versions of the owls head, two of the dolphin bowl and two of the grotesque teapot.
4. There were probably other unstated reasons for Baron's decision but there was also some truth in the allegation. The 1897 Wages Book shows seven designers on the pay roll; four years earlier at least four of these would have been senior artists. Baron may have considered he was not getting enough of the 'quality' work.
    A second factor would have been his wish to work out his own ideas without guidance. Also, having qualified as an Art Master he could now teach anywhere (which in fact he did — private lessons from his home and at Chalfoner's School, Braunton). Or simply, it was time to move on.

THE NEW POTTERY 1886 — 87

By 1885, because of the rapid growth in business it had become obvious to Mr. Brannam that his present premises in Litchdon Street would no longer serve. Not only were they inadequate to full production but inappropriate to the quality of the ware he was now offering for sale. They could have even been less than acceptable to his increasingly illustrious clientele. The premises in fact consisted of a row of cottages and several warehouses, one of which displayed the pugmill — a pleasant enough rural sight for a potter of common earthenware but less fitting for an Art Potter with ambition, growing prospects and a certain amount of capital to invest.

A modest showroom on the lines of the Howell and James premises would attract a discerning public; bring business into the town, notably from the rising tourist resorts of Ilfracombe, Lynton and Clovelly; and might perhaps ultimately allow him to dispense with the London agents. A priority, too, was better accommodation for his growing family.

As architect he chose Mr. W. S. Oliver of Cross Street, one of the busiest men in the district. Plans for factories, shops and schools were his special interest and he favoured the use of bricks from the pottery at Petersmarland;[1] bricks whose qualities of strength and durability made them popular with builders and clients alike. There was some delay while the Council debated the possibility of widening Litchdon Street[2] before the new pottery was built, but for various reasons this suggestion was abandoned and the plans were passed.

The project was in two parts;[3] the first for a building to the right of the pottery entrance to house a showroom on the ground floor, the two upper floors to be devoted to family accommodation. The second scheme was for a second building to the left of the entrance and on the side nearest to the Square. This would be of two storeys, the frontage on the ground floor serving simply as a 'shop window', masking the functional rooms of the pottery. An archway surmounting the entrance to the yard would serve to link the two buildings.

During the late Spring of 1886 part of the old property was demolished, and through the summer months work on the Showroom and house went ahead, with the completion in November. The style of the new premises was described by the Journal as 'domestic gothic, freely treated'. Marland brick was used throughout, relieved with bands and arches of red brick. The handsome shop window incorporated the use of stained glass, while an equally handsome porch, featuring pillars and capitals of Barum Ware led into the showroom.

The second building, completed by June of the following year (1887) was built on the site of the old pugmill (though in fact the area behind the new 'showcase' windows continued in use as a clay-processing area up to 1903 when the new large showroom

Fig. 68 The Brannam Pottery, the original showroom

Fig. 69 View of interior of later showroom

Fig. 70 The later Showroom. a. the exterior
                                          b. another view of the interior

was built).[4] A door to the left of the central archway led through this area into the next room where the larger pots were dried, and beyond this was a further room where the potters' wheels and kilns were housed. The original number one kiln had been built at the foundation of the Art pottery; a second block being added in 1895. The first kiln used mainly wood for firing but soon coal was increasingly used, with the addition of faggots; then eventually coal was used exclusively.

The upper rooms of the second building were used for storage and, possibly to accommodate some of the working decorators. The facade of the second building differed in style from the first by its extensive use of wood, both for the two shop and four first-floor windows as well as for the four half-timbered gables. Below the upper windows a wood cornice was supported on curved brackets in which was inserted a band of Barum tiles, modelled in a floral design. Stained leaded glass was used in the upper parts of the first floor windows and continued across the highly decorated archway.

In 1903 further changes were made when a new large showroom was added behind the showcase windows. This was graphically described in the Journal in June. This issue also carried an announcement by Mr. Brannam of the opening, together with his thanks to the public for past support. At the opening over ten thousand pieces were on view. Messrs. Liberty were now sole agents of Royal Barum ware in London. Over the early years altogether three Royal warrants were featured as part of the shop window decoration, while three Royal coats of Arms were secured to the central archway and to two adjoining upstairs windows.

Footnotes *(See footnote numbers in text)*

1.   A brick and clayworks was founded on Claymoor at Petersmarland in 1879 and was capable of producing 100,000 bricks a week, as well as tiles and pipes. They were widely used locally for building. Made from the coloured clays they ranged from cream to pink in colour and are a familiar sight in the town.
2.   This was the last opportunity to widen the road which formed a bottleneck at this point. The plan entailed the purchase of the adjoining Exeter Inn and would have involved the loss of eight feet of frontage for Brannam. The plan fell through but it seems unlikely whether the potter would have readily agreed as the plot was always too small. The bottleneck remains and the street has for some years been subject to one-way traffic.
3.   Information from *North Devon Journal* report and *A Family Business.*
4.   The old showroom was then taken over as a dining room for the family. The window area was retained for a number of years but was later bricked up.

THE GROWING YEARS 1886 — 88

The building programme, with its obvious attendant disruption was not allowed in any way to affect the smooth running of work at the pottery. Decoration involving the use of coloured slips, believed to have been started in 1885 went rapidly ahead. It has been suggested that five or six basic colours were used, probably yellow, red, blue, green and bronze; cream probably occurring naturally from the use of the white slip. According to Strong, in this way 'some forty tints are obtained'. A popular 'colour mix' for 1886, used often by Dewdney in that year and continuing for the next five was the combination of ochres with pale blue and cream. It should be remembered, however that the original two-colour (blue/brown) ware on which the reputation of the pottery had been built was still made (right up to the mid-nineties).

In November of 1887 Sir Francis Cunliffe Owen, the Director of South Kensington Museum visited Barnstaple and presented the prizes to the students of the School of Art whose exhibition featured the work of both Dewdney and Baron. The director had previously visited Brannam's pottery, to which he made a reference in his speech:—

> Mr. Brannam has got in him the certainty of success, because one could see in his quiet modest way, the determination that he had of seeing his native town famous.[1]

The potter, too was taking an increasing interest in the public affairs of the town in connection with the pottery. With the growth of the classes for artisans, he was encouraging his young designers to attend the evening classes, either as Mr. Rock's free students or by profiting from the cheap rates that the school offered. All of his designers attended classes at some time during their working life at the pottery; and both William Baron and Thomas Liverton were allowed time off to attend summer courses at the South Kensington base, probably as part of their training as student teachers; though of course Brannam would not have paid them during their absence.

Further, in November 1887, Brannam gave an hour's instruction on the potter's art in connection with the Radford lectures.[2]

> He gave a practical demonstration, making several pieces from Marland clay — a pretty vase, a jug, then a vase of another pattern. He went on to describe the decorative processes; slipping, glazing, painting, modelling and firing, finally producing a very close imitation of a Greek vase of unique pattern.

(His exhibition at the Devon County Show in Barnstaple the following June was to follow up this public service to his own advantage). Exhibitions at the Royal Cornwall Polytechnic in Falmouth both in 1887 and 88 further advertised his wares. A report in the latter year remarked:—

Later showroom, 1903. The Interior

STAND 34. DEVON COUNTY SHOW.

ROYAL BARUM WARE.

Patronised by H.M. the Queen.
H.R.H. Princess Louise.
H.R.H. Grand Duke of Hesse

9 Silver Medals at Royal Cornwall Polytechnic Exhibition, Falmouth, Exeter, Taunton, London.

A SPLENDID AND ENTIRELY NEW COLLECTION OF THIS

—— CELEBRATED ART WARE, ——

(See Remarks of Sir P. CUNLIFFE OWEN, in *Journal.*)

WILL BE SHOWN.

PATRONISE NORTH DEVON INDUSTRIES, AND SEE POTTERS AT WORK.

Flower Pots, and Devonshire Earthenware.

C. H. BRANNAM Would call Special Attention to the Excellent Quality of these Goods, and trusts Buyers will Inspect the Largest and

BEST ASSORTED STOCK OF

FLOWER POTS, PANS, PITCHERS, STAINS, S ALTING AND BREAD PANS,

DRINKING FOUNTAINS, &c., *Before Purchasing Elsewhere.*

DRAIN PIPES, both Socket and Agricultural, Always in Stock.

TILES OF DIFFERENT SIZES AND PATTERNS.

GLAZED SEWAGE PIPES & SANITARY GOODS.

These Goods are of First-class Quality, being free from cracks of every kind, perfectly smooth, and so do not corrode.

C. H. BRANNAM, Manufacturer,

LITCHDON-ST., BARNSTAPLE.

7603]

ROYAL BARUM WARE.

C. H. BRANNAM

BEGS to thank his numerous Patrons for the Support so liberally bestowed upon him during the past 3½ years, and to inform them the ART POTTERY graciously Ordered by

Her Majesty the Queen,

Will be on View at the POTTERY during TUESDAY and WEDNESDAY, the 5th and 6th of May. Duplicate Group at Mr. W. BRITTON'S, High Cross.

ART POTTERY, LITCHDON-STREET, BARNSTAPLE. 2182

Fig. 71 Two Brannam advertisements for the Journal. a. The Devon County Show 1884
b. The Queen's jardiniere 1885

Fig. 72 The Bowden Wedding Piece. Two views (for description see Bowden MND)

... a splendid collection of Barnstaple pottery (Barumware) ... In its way, nothing excels the beautiful show of Barumware. Mr. Brannam ... is happily never content with resting on his laurels, but each year moves on, in new illustrations of form and ornament.

Earlier that year, in June, he had mounted an important exhibition at the Devon County Show in Barnstaple, on which Hugh Strong reported at length:—

The whole of the art processes are illustrated by the exhibits. Here the article in its 'green' state and then perfected where the ware has been fired... Our notice would be incomplete without mention of the two first class specimens of Art Pottery, designed by Mr. Dewdney, consisting of a mirror frame and a table top in Barum Ware; these are richly painted in pâte sur pâte in colours ranging through blue, green, cream, olive, rich brown etc.

The report gave a full account of the many shapes and patterns now made:—

... The unique dragon pots, three handed pots in numerous pretty designs, glazed pitchers, pots of Venetian design, ornamental nick-nacks in the shape of fishes and a variety of decorated ware; glazed and decorated flower pots, decorated sets of (bedroom)[3] ware, jugs and beakers which by their very appearance would make cooler the refreshing draught; and fantastic tobacco jars in which the smug face of the old smoker invites the lover of the fragrant weed to smoke and be jolly, cheek by jowl with the jovial genii who presides over the jar...

In addition, the potter was on hand to demonstrate the use of a new potter's wheel he had invented which dispensed with the use of both the boy (to turn the wheel) and an assistant to supply the balls of clay to the potter. This was operated by the use of a 'jigger' (a pedal movement) making the potter self-sufficient.

Footnotes *(See footnote numbers in text)*

1. The Director of South Kensington museum had already made a small reference early in his speech to the Mayor's (Alexander Lauder's) rising pottery ... The prizegiving and the 'renaissance' in Barnstaple were reported in *The Studio* for December.
2. The Radford lectures were organised for the benefit of the students as part of the University extension scheme. For the most part they consisted of lectures on the history of Art.
3. It was Sir Philip Cunliffe Owen who had made the suggestion to Brannam to introduce sets of toilet ware into his range of goods. They were probably one of the best-selling 'lines' over the years — until interior plumbing made them redundant. The 1907 catalogue shows four different sets, selling for fifteen shillings for the Art Colour and twenty-five for the decorated. The set comprised jug and basin, small jug and basin, soap dish with lid, tooth mug, shaving bowl and chamber pot. (A jug with set of beakers was sometimes called a lemonade set).

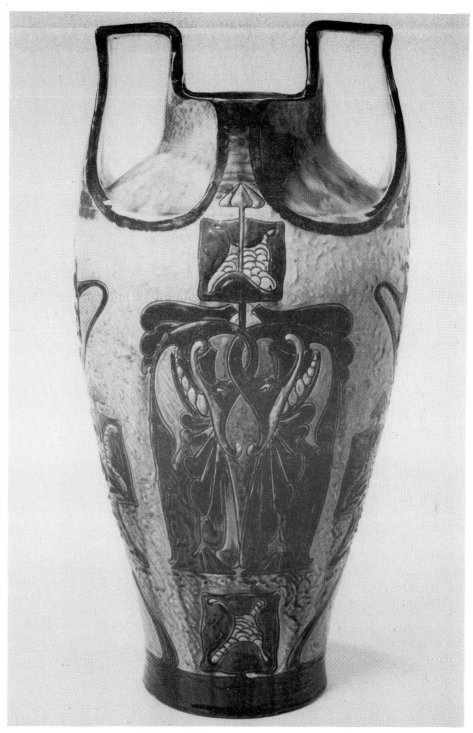

Fig. 73 Art Nouveau Vase with loop handles
courtesy Keith Baker, London

THE DESIGNERS

Frederick Arthur Bowden was arguably the most important member of Brannam's workforce during the life of the pottery. Born in 1865, it is most likely that he joined the pottery straight from school, in 1878 — the year when the potter was conducting experiments prior to taking over the Litchdon Street premises. He was probably already studying at the School of Art where he soon developed an interest in modelling. As early as 1880 Brannam was already allowing him to model and fire large experimental pieces as may be seen from the model of the lizard on a tile (Fig.) now in the Athenaeum collection at the North Devon Museum. The piece is dated 1880 and signed F. B. Though crude, it gives a strong indication of the work that was to follow from this young man of fifteen who was to spend his lifetime at the pottery.

A pitcher, twelve inches in height, with strap handle and a modelled lizard is not signed but it seems likely that it was also his work. The only other early piece that has come to light bearing his initials is a charming seated cat[1] with its paws resting on a bowl (for matches), with the addition of a striker on the side of the base. There must be many more between these dates, both signed and unsigned. He probably did much of the work for the relief ornament on the vases and jardinières shown at the Devon County Show in May 1884 (see Page 34); and would have been responsible for the naturalistic animal shapes for the lion pieces which are probably later copies of an original model. (Fig.   ) (1891 and 1894).

It was in the early 1890s, however that Frank Carruthers Gould[2] sent Brannam drawings for suggested animal and bird grotesques that could be used for useful ornaments, introducing an entirely new and novel series of pieces into the potter's range of goods. Many of these drawings were cleverly adapted and used and proved immensely popular. (By this time, of course William Baron was at the pottery and probably shared the modelling work until he left in 1893). That there was plenty of work for Mr. Bowden is amply demonstrated in the Wages Book[3] (1897 to 1903) where his average wage was second only to James Dewdney, (up to thirty seven shillings). In six years he seems to have had five weeks off work, whether for choice or illness is not known. Since he lived in the Victoria Road area of Barnstaple throughout his life it may probably be assumed that he continued to work at the pottery until his death in 1917 at the age of 53. His private life may be epitomised from the single gravestone in Holy Trinity churchyard,[4] Barnstaple which records his own death and those of his wife and three sons. As may be seen from the family tree, his wife predeceased him by five years at the age of fifty; while all three sons died young, the two elder under the age of twenty two years and the youngest aged sixteen. The last, Hubert could have been a war casualty but it is more likely that all three were victims of that great 'Victorian' killer, tuberculosis. This premise is strengthened by the fact that the daughter, Alma, who married R.H. Davis of Braunton was herself a victim while still young.

This information comes from Mr. William Edward Davis of Braunton whose great-uncle was Frederick Bowden (his mother, Florence Mearles was the modeller's niece). On her marriage to W.L. Davis, Uncle Fred gave her the piece shown in Fig.). This highly individual and decorative ornament[5] he had modelled (and possibly decorated) in 1893. A pair of fish, back to back, hold aloft between their tails a plaque bearing on one side a verse by Edward Capern, the Bideford postman/poet and on the other a formalised design. Uniquely the piece is reversible and has no obvious useful function. The donor chose the popular and striking colour scheme of deep chestnut and cream with decoration in blue and ochre.

It is likely that Bowden attended the School of Art from leaving school until at least the early 1890s. Records show that two pieces by him were exhibited at the school exhibition in 1887 — a lampstand and 'a beautiful Barum Ware vase of splendid proportions, ornamented by a representation of a lobster and a crab'. That same year he presented to the Conservative Association a medallion bearing the profile of the late Lord Iddesleigh. In 1899 a prize-winning model of a squirrel on a bough was shown at the School's exhibition.

A picture emerges of a gifted craftsman, hard-working and versatile, but lacking that good health for his family so desired in Capern's poem.

> 'Good wishes to you my friend
> The best of all wealth
> Love, Comfort & Health
> And a heart that is
> thankful for all'.

BOWDEN FAMILY TREE

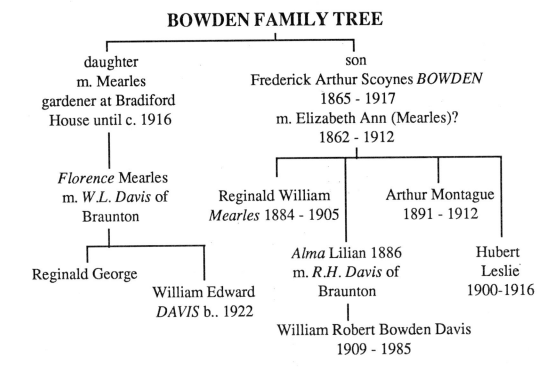

The adoption of the family name of Mearles for the eldest son of the modeller suggests that brother and sister married sister and brother. A further family link was made when the brothers Davis married the cousins Florence and Alma.

Footnotes *(See footnote numbers in text)*

1. See Fig.
2. See Section on grotesques for further information and Appendix B for information on Carruthers Gould
3. See Page
4. The family may have attended Holy Trinity church (where the Brannam family are also buried), though two of the Bowdens were baptised at Thorne's schoolroom (for Methodists) in Barnstaple.
5. This piece will eventually be added to the collection in the North Devon Museum.

Information about *James DEWDNEY* is hard to find. It is likely that he lived in Exeter and had trained at the School of Art there. At any rate, a search through local parish records reveal that he did not live locally. He joined Brannam in 1881, at a critical time, when the potter's early successes demanded fine workmanship in designing work previously performed by Brannam himself and beyond the capabilities of any of his present workforce. The volume of work was increasing and the potter's time would have been fully taken up with his commitments of throwing, mixing glazes and the overall supervision of the pottery without taking on the increasing workload of designing.

From the beginning Dewdney's designs single him out as a first rate ceramic artist who would have graced any pottery. From the peacock designs on the early three-handled pale blue and chocolate vase of 1884/5 to his work on the early pâte sur pâte pieces (see Figs. 48 and 49) he shows his command of the media and his talent for design. His later work is sometimes less effective but perhaps the designs of 1903 shown relied more on a general effect by the heavy impasto decoration, much of it probably finished by the young designers. It is certain that he was highly valued by Brannam, receiving the top wage, at least from 1897 onwards.

Although not living locally, it is certain that he attended the local Art Classes, at least for ten years, between 1887 and 1896. Examples of his work were frequently shown at the school exhibitions, both of Art pottery from Brannams and of designs for cretonne and tapestry. Examples are: in 1888 'a mirror frame and table top richly painted in pâte sur pâte, in colours ranging through blue, green, cream, olive and rich brown' and in 1896 'a set of poultry carvers with ceramic handles and a pair of candelabra'. In the same year he won a prize for a 'richly ornamented pewter dish'.

Members of the Braddon family speak of his friendship with the younger designer. They report that he was known locally as 'the Frenchman' and was called Johnny by his friends. They also believe he too may have died of Tuberculosis. The precedent created by his appointment from outside the pottery was repeated some four years later by the employment of William Baron from the Doulton Lambeth pottery. These two designers contributed very materially to the subsequent success of the Royal Barum pottery.

Thomas Arthur LIVERTON was born in 1875, a younger son of William Liverton, sawyer and later first foreman at Rawle Gammon and Baker's timber yard on Rolle Quay. He probably joined the pottery straight from school, for by 1888 he was already studying at the School of Art where he continued for at leat ten years, taking examinations and later teaching. His principal areas of study were Design, Ornament, Modelling and Model Drawing; all to advanced level. In 1893 he attended the summer course at South Kensington and in the following year passed his examination to qualify as a pupil teacher. The following year he was appointed as pupil teacher at the

Fig. 74 Group of early pieces modelled by Bowden. Left to right: candle–holder 1894, Owl, match–holder 1891, cat match–holder/striker 1886, signed F.B.

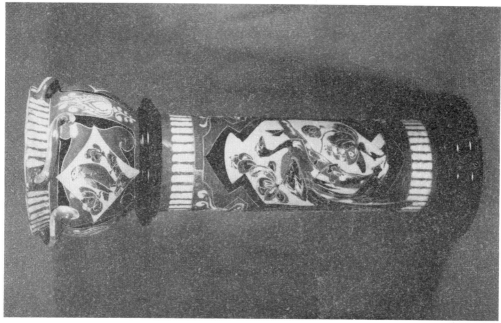

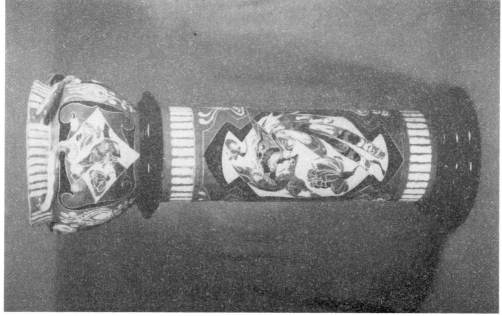

Fig. 75 Jardiniere on a stand. Height: stand 27", bowl 10" J.D. 1898. MND. Both pieces have two panels featuring birds in pale blue, cream, ochres and brown

Fig. 76 Large Vase with birds in a floral landscape. Bold design in ochres and pale blue on sgraffito white slip.
Height 22", J.D. 1890's

Fig. 77 Large Vase with bird handles. Height 20", decoration in leaf green, blue and ochres in several layers of slip.
J.D. 1903

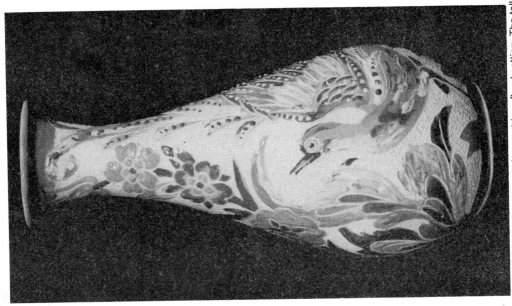

Fig. 79 Vase by Dewdney, pheasant in a floral setting. The tall vase by Brannam dated 1896 with decoration by Dewdney features a pheasant in blues, greens and browns on cream sgraffito ground

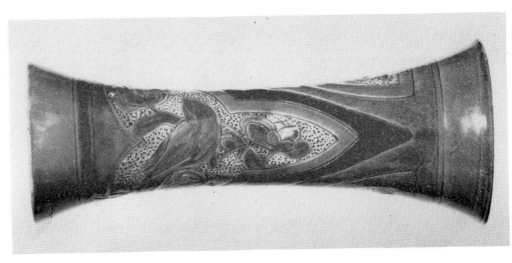

Fig. 78 Cylindrical Vase by Dewdney, 12" with two triangular panels each featuring bird on floral branch. In blue, green and brown. 1898

Fig. 80 Very rare Clock–case by Dewdney. dark green glaze ceramic clock by C.H. Brannam. Approx. length 16", marked 1909 J.D.

Fig. 81 Early design jardiniere with bold bird design by Baron, in chestnut, pale blue, and fawn. Height 10" 1892 MND

Line drawing by Gerry Lee

Fig. 82 Pair of bottle vases with a bird design by Baron in ochres, pale blue and green. 10" 1891

Fig. 83 The Victoria Jubilee jug with motto and design
in pale blue slip and cream. VR. 1837– 1897, height 4 1/2"

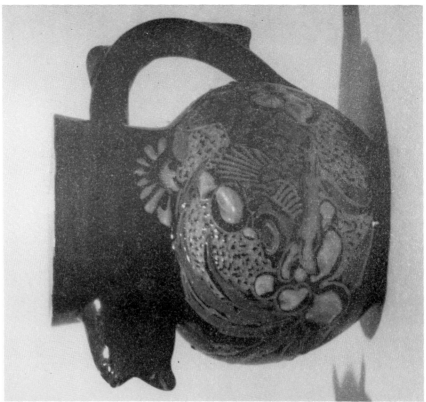

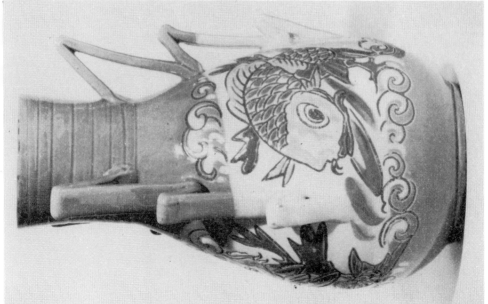

Fig. 84 Two fishy designs by Thomas Liverton.
a. vase with angular handles. 9" 1894. MND
b. fish–mouth jug, brown slip with marine design in cream, pale blue, green and ochres. 6"

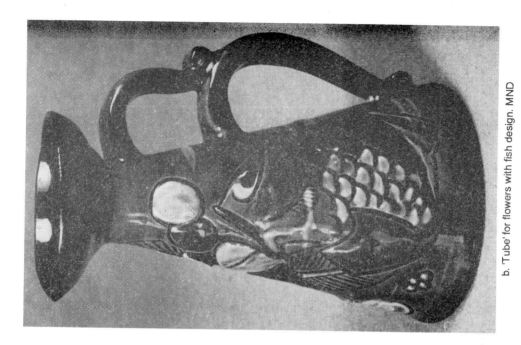

b. 'Tube' for flowers with fish design. MND

Fig. 85 Two more designs by Liverton.
a. double dolphin bowl of less common design, 9" 1894 MND

School of Art at a salary of fifteen pounds a year. (He presumably taught in the evenings as he would not have had time off from the pottery during working hours).

His work at the pottery was extremely individual, often showing art nouveau styles. In the 1897 Wages Book he was second designer, probably having taken over Baron's position. His salary rose to an average of two pounds but by 1902 when the emphasis on design was declining he was one of from four to five designers left on the staff. His designs appear on pieces from the early 1890s up until 1908, when it is likely he left the town, together with his brother William who, since 1891 had owned the China shop, previously owned by Charles Crassweller. Crassweller had owned the premises at 29 High Street since c. 1850. When he died in 1881, William who had been an assistant became the manager, later buying and rebuilding the premises. He was Baron's first agent, in 1893 to possibly as late as 1900, by which time the potter had his own shop.

Frederick John Braddon was born in 1874, son of Thomas Braddon, joiner of Newport. In 1900 he married Edith Harriet Dening, daughter of Samuel Dening, a wine and spirit merchant with a business at 72 High Street, Barnstaple. They had six children, three sons and three daughters. One son died young, of Tuberculosis and another from Meningitis, contracted soon after he joined up in the army in 1917. A granddaughter lives in South Devon.

He attended classes at the School of Art from 1891 to 1895, attaining high marks in his examinations up to advanced standard. His subjects, apart from Drawing were Ornament, Design and Modelling Design. It seems likely that he joined Brannam between 1889 and 1891. However, he probably trained elsewhere during his lifetime and it does not seem likely that his stay with Brannam was continuous. However, it looks as if he worked there continuously from c. 1890 up until at least 1902, and since the following years were early in his marriage and he lived locally, he probably continued up until 1910. During the 1920s and up until 1930 he continued to work at the pottery but the designs were much more simple and sketchy. Many of these were for the vases being supplied to Libertys.

In 1930 he received his notice and a lady designer was employed to do the new styles though it looks as if he may have been recalled to execute special orders. An equal second designer from 1897, his wages rose from thirty shillings to two guineas a week in 1902 and later he probably earnt still more. He later worked for Poole pottery and also at Honiton. In addition he was an accomplished silversmith — among other commissions he made pieces for the monks at Iona. Examples of his work are known to have been on display in the United States and in Germany, possibly in a museum. His style is accomplished and fluent and he was obviously very adaptable, having developed an economic and stylish touch for the Art Nouveau market as well as meeting the demands of the other two potteries for whom he worked.

Fig. 86 Two large Vases made for the Barnstaple Rotary Club, probably decorated by Braddon. Height 12", MND

b. Puzzle Jug with design by Frederick Braddon. Fish/seaweed raised design in blue, ochres and cream on green slip. 6 1/2 1897

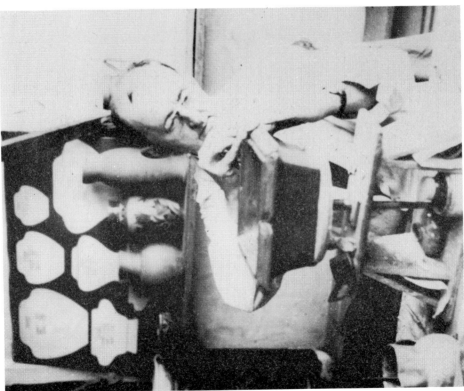

Fig. 87 a. Frederick Braddon in the Pottery c. 1930. Courtesy Mrs. Brannam

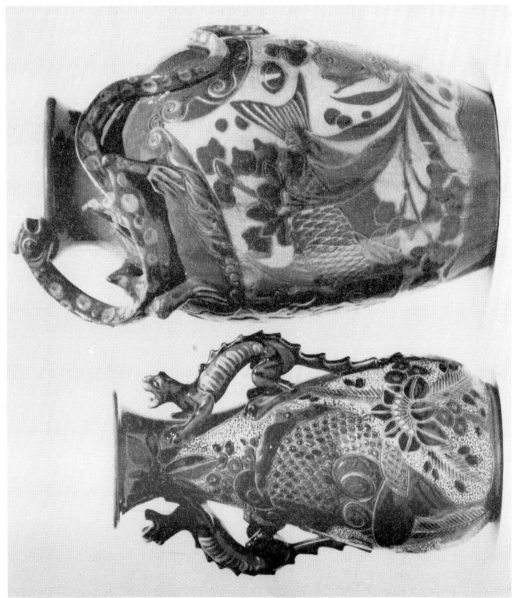

Fig. 88 Dragon–handled vase 1908. Design by Frederick Braddon. Very fine design in blue, green and brown
Lauder Vase with modelled snake decoration

Fig. 89 Four grotesque pieces with designs by Beauchamp Whimple. Barry Stock collection

Another BW design on beaker. MND

Fig. 90 Two pieces decorated by Frank Thomas. a. small teapot, 1908 MND

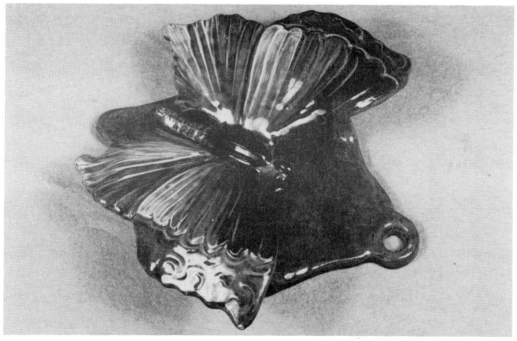

b. butterfly wall–pocket with multi–colour glaze. 1900 MND

Fig. 91 Three late moulded pieces from Brannam.
a. Small jug similar to Baron's owl but with pointed beak b. Marriage Jug. Royal blue/green, detail brown, reversible (scowls/smiles)

c. Fish Jug MND

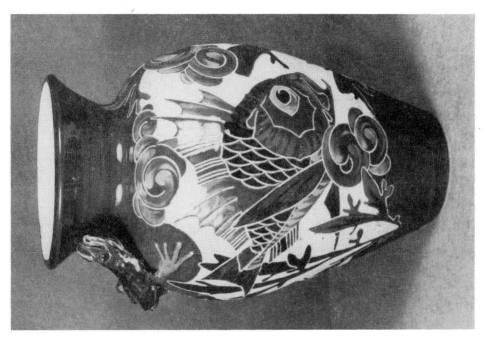

Fig. 92 Two pieces by William Baron a. small vase in white clay. MND b. Vase with decoration of fish and modelled lizard. 12" NDA and MND

Fig. 93 Two late moulded pieces. a. Brannam fish wall-pocket in green glaze

b. Recumbent pig, yellow slip, brown detail 6 1/2" F.B. 1903.

c. group of grotesques from the Brannam records MND

Fig. 94 Two stork/bamboo vases, height 10"
a. the Lauder version, green and blue slip, detail in cream b. the Brannam model (one of a pair), leaf green with cream
and fawn. Impressed LAUDER BARUM   detail. BW 1896

The illustrations show two 'pickle jars, commissioned by the Rotary organisation which were probably made in 1933. One commemorates the presidency of Charles William Brannam in 1928 and the other the secretaryship of C. H. Bradford between 1928 and 1933.

Jno (Arthur) Bamkin signed his pieces A B so it is probably fair to assume that he was known as Arthur. His attendance at the School of Art from 1886 to 1895 suggests that he probably was at the pottery from an early age, though he may not have been allowed to sign his pieces until he was well qualified. He attended the school for at least nine years, studying Drawing, Ornament, Design and Modelling Design to a high standard. In 1897 he was one of the principal designers but examples of his work are not very common. He probably left in the early years of the century.

The work of *Frank Thomas* is very attractive. He probably joined the pottery in 1897 when he was recorded as earning three shillings a week. At the same time he was attending the Art classes and continued to do so until at least 1901, studying drawing and modelling. He obviously made good progress at the pottery for by 1902 he was earning ten shillings and sixpence a week and had been signing his own pieces, (in the main the decoration for grotesque pieces) since 1899.

He may have been a relative of potter/brickmaker Charles Thomas who had a large family and lived at Hardaway Head between 1865 and 1884.

Two pieces are shown — the prototype candlestick dated 1899 and a fantastic bird (the Bittern), 1906 (both in colour).

Little is known of *Stanley Williams* at the present time apart from his name. He attended the School of Art for at least a short period and probably joined the pottery in the early 1890s. The Wages book of 1897 shows him as earning ten shillings and sixpence so by that time he would have probably been responsible for his own pieces for three or four years. He does not have appeared to have stayed longer than 1898 at the latest. Pictured is a Dragon boat, dated 1896 (dust jacket).

Reginald Pearse was probably the last of the nineteenth century designers to be taken on at the pottery. His signature appears on pieces from 1900 up until 1904 though the range of his work could have been much greater. Apart from designs for grotesque pieces-Swan-necked gondola, (1901) and Heron/bamboo candlestick, (1903); he did charming small designs — a jug (1903) and two ashtrays, (1900 and 1904).

Most of the information about *Beauchamp Whimple* comes from his obituary notice in the *North Devon Journal* of June 22, 1905, reporting his untimely death at the age of 25 years. He died in Plymouth of Rheumatic fever. Before going to Plymouth he had resided for a while at Torquay, where 'he had made a wide circle of friends'. The report continues: 'He served his time in the designing department of Mr. C.H. Brannam's famous Barum Ware establishment and was a clever designer. The deceased who had a fine voice was well known in musical circles at Barnstaple: he was for several years a member of Newport choir, afterwards of Holy Trinity choir'.

He probably joined the pottery in 1894 and attended Art classes from 1895 to 98, studying mainly drawing and modelling. The only record of his wage is in 1898 when he was earning fifteen shillings and eightpence in one week. This was a high wage for a young man of eighteen and it looks as if he was very talented and made rapid progress at the pottery. His move to Torquay, probably in 1902/03 was probably to join one of the potteries there, but if examples of his work there exist there would of necessity have been very few.

Pictured are a Heron/Bamboo candlestick (1898), two fantastic birds (Grebe and Bittern) in 1899, a satyr-headed snake candlestick (1902) and the Dwarf/Monk with the inverted umbrella (1901). These show him to be a very fine designer and a great loss to the art world.

Fig. 95
Line drawing of owl design on vase (page 162)

Fig. 96 Two figures from Gould caricatures, Lord Landsdowne and Lloyd George. C.H. Brannam Ltd. collection

The Designers Signatures

Frederick Bowden

Frederick Bowden — *F. B.* / *C.H. Brannam. 1880* *CHB. Barum*

James Dewdney

William Baron

Thomas Liverton

Frederick Braddon

Arthur Bamkin

Frank Thomas

Stanley Williams

Reginald Pearse

Beauchamp Whimple

ROYAL PATRONAGE

In an era notable for the support of Queen Victoria and her consort, Prince Albert of Saxe Coburg to Art and Industry, the Royal seal of approval was greatly prized. That this should be attained within five years of the foundation of his Art Pottery must indeed have been a source of great pride and satisfaction to this modest if ambitious provincial potter; indeed, an honour that no-one, least of all himself would have expected when he was making his first tentative efforts in 1879. In fact, the first known order from a member of the royal family (the Duke of Hesse, husband of Alice, second daughter of the Queen) may well have first brought the attention of her majesty to the rather naive but attractive and novel country pottery. In the event, the potter attracted nearly every member of the royal family as a client, and the firm of C.H. Brannam (Ltd) were eventually to supply its goods to no fewer than five Queens of England, from Victoria to Queen Elizabeth II.

The catalogue of 1907-08 lists no fewer than seven royal clients on its back cover but in fact the number of clients with royal connections could probably easily total a score within the lifetime of the pottery, as the following list would indicate:

The Duke and *Duchess of Hesse (Alice)	1882
H.R.H. Queen Victoria	1885, 1892, 1902
The Princess of Wales, later Queen Alexandra	
H.R.H. the Duke and Duchess of York, later Queen Mary	1894, 1913
(The Duke and Duchess of Teck, parents of Mary, above)	1896
H.R.H. Prince Albrecht of Prussia	1895-99
H.R.H. *Princess Louise, Duchess of Argyll	1891, 1896
H.R.H. *Duke of Connaught (Alfred)	
H.R.H. *the Princess Royal — later wife of Frederick III, German Emperor	
H.R.H. *Beatrice, wife of Prince Henry of Battenburg	1891, 1896
H.R.H. *Helena, Princess Christian of Schleswig Holstein	1905
H.R.H. Victoria, daughter of above, later Princess Louis Battenberg	
(Mountbatten, first Sea Lord, 1912-14)	1905

* indicates children of Queen Victoria.
For other mentions see 'A Peep at the Shops'.

Fig. 97 The North Walk Pottery showing kiln . c. 1900, courtesy P. Newcombe

C. H. BRANNAM'S
ROYAL BARUM WARE

IS MOST SUITABLE FOR

CHRISTMAS, NEW YEAR, AND OTHER PRESENTS,

BEING THE

ONLY North Devon Pottery
Patronised by the QUEEN.

None Genuine without the name, "C. H. Brannam, Barum, N. Devon"

ON EACH PIECE.

WORKS:—LITCHDON-ST., BARNSTAPLE.

Fig. 98 a Brannam advertisement

b. The Royal Coats of Arms, photo Mike Bond

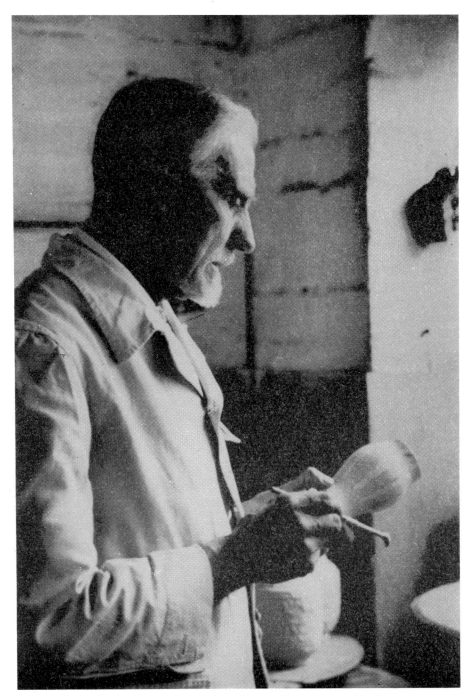

Fig. 99 Charles Brannam at work in the Pottery. 1930s, courtesy Mrs.Brannam

Fig. 100 Group of Commemorative mugs by Brannam. Top row: Four different versions of 1937 Coronation
Bottom row: centre. First commemorative given to all school children. Often unmarked on base

The First Royal Visit — Princess Christian of Schleswig Holstein in 1905.

Though royal patronage came early, the potter had to wait until September 1905 for his first royal visitor, in the person of Princess Christian of Schleswig Holstein (Princess Helena, third daughter of the Queen). The Princess was accompanied by her eldest daughter, Princess Victoria, a lady in waiting and the court Physician, Sir William Taylor. The visit was a private one, a suite of rooms having been reserved for the royal party at the Imperial Hotel, close to the pottery and adjoining the Square. The party arrived in Barnstaple by motor at 6.45 on the evening of Wednesday 6 September, their luggage having been sent on by Great Western Railway. It was only by accident, says the report in the *North Devon Journal*, that the news became public — on the evening of their arrival.

The report continues:

> On Thursday morning Princess Christian and Princess Victoria paid a visit to Mr. C.H. Brannam's Royal Barum ware establishment, situated in Litchdon Street, ... being received by Mr. Brannam and his son Mr. J.W. Brannam who is associated with him in the business. Mr. Brannam conducted the Princesses round the various departments and explained every phase in the process of manufacture, their Royal Highnesses evincing keen interest in the demonstrations. The Princesses were much interested in two specimens which showed the antiquity of Barnstaple pottery, one bearing the date 1686 and the other 1708.
>
> The Princesses were the first persons ever allowed to see the component parts of the glaze for which the firm is famous. Then came a demonstration of 'throwing' and in the firm's system of 'handling'. A process of 'slipping' prepares for decoration and as artists the Princesses were specially interested in a demonstration of the evolution of the superb decoration. The latest style is best represented by a charming chrysanthemum pattern which was much admired. Glazing was the next process and the Princess expressed herself as being highly pleased that the lead poisoning trouble was quite unknown at the Barum works. The final firing which produces the finished article is preceded by a bisque and glaze firing. The Princess warmly complimented Mr. Brannam, saying that they were delighted with what they had seen. On returning from Clovelly in the evening they again visited the showroom where they purchased specimens of all the colours.

Visit to Clovelly

> On leaving Mr. Brannam's establishment about noon on Thursday, the Princesses left Barnstaple in their motor for Clovelly. At the commencement of the Hobby Drive they were met by a carriage and pair, in which they proceeded to Clovelly where they had lunch at the New Inn. It was not known at Clovelly who the illustrious visitors were, and the Princesses had luncheon in the general dining room. Clovelly church was visited and much admired. The Royal party reached Barnstaple in the event shortly after six and dined at eight.

Friday. The Market and Lynton/Lynmouth

> Having seen the market the Princess was surprised to learn that on Fridays the large building was wholly devoted to the sale of country produce. As a trip had been arranged, the visit to the Market had to be made early. They walked from the Imperial to the Market and were not at first recognised but

Fig. 101   Personal headed note paper. Letter to Queen Alexandra, courtesy J. Newell

Fig. 102 Royal Castle Hotel advertisement, from 'Devon Past and Present' NDA

Fig. 103 Woody Bay Station from 'Peacock' postcard

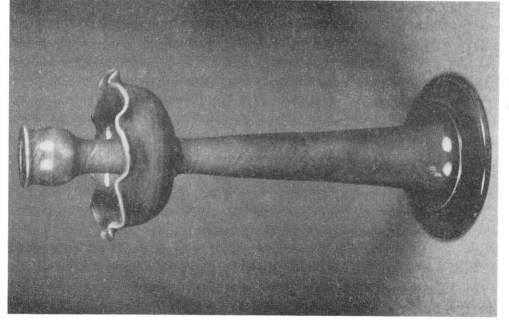

Fig. 104 Two Candlesticks for Libertys. Liberty mark. MND.

a. 13" DuBarry Rose slip   b. 12" Gold

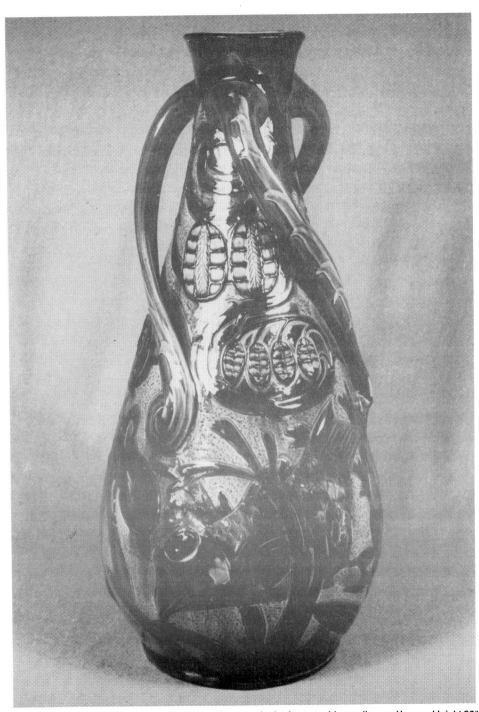

Fig. 105 A large Vase with swirl handles and Art Nouveau design in green, blue, yellow and brown. Height 23"
J.D. 1906 MND

when it became known there was a rush to see them, although the Royal visitors were in no way incommoded. Princess Christian's attention was attracted by the display of blackberries and with the remark that she had not tasted a blackberry for years ordered that a supply should be obtained and prepared for inclusion in the dinner menu in the evening. The Princesses walked from the Market by way of Holland Street to the Town Station and left for Woody Bay by the ordinary train at 10.30. At Woody Bay station they were met by Mr. A. Northcote of the Bear Street Mews, Barnstaple who drove the Royal party round the coast to Lynton by way of Lee Abbey grounds. Luncheon was partaken of at Mr. Tom Jones' Royal Castle Hotel, Lynton, and afterwards the Princesses were conveyed by the Cliff Railway to Lynmouth.

Here a smart carriage and pair (supplied by Mr. Tom Jones) with Mr. H. Saxon as driver was waiting, and the Princesses were driven to Watersmeet and back to Lynton by way of Summerhouse Hill and Barbrook. After tea at the Royal Castle Hotel the Princesses left for Barnstaple, travelling in a special saloon (provided by Mr. C.E. Drewett, the manager of the Lynton and Barnstaple railway) attached to the 4.35 ordinary train. A large crowd assembled at the Town station at Barnstaple and the Princesses graciously acknowledged cheers by bowing.

Mr. Northcote was instructed to call at the Imperial Hotel on Friday evening and he was then complimented by Sir William Taylor on his driving. Permission was given for (him) to make use of the fact that the firm had been patronised by the Princesses. The Princesses concluded their visit to North Devon on Saturday, leaving the Imperial Hotel in their motor for Bath. Their tour will include Scotland and will extend into October. After the Royal party had taken their places in the motor, which stood in front of the Imperial, photographs were (by special permission) taken by Mr. V.G. Vickery of the Bridge-end studio. Princess Christian sat in the car with her lady-in-waiting by her side, the Princess Victoria occupied a seat in front next to the driver. Sir William Taylor reported that the Princesses were charmed with the scenery of North Devon and that they were delighted with Barnstaple. Before leaving the Imperial the Princesses signed the visitors book.

Account from the *North Devon Journal*, slightly abridged.

Fig. 106 Two Lauder pieces

a. tulip pot   b. small milk jug. MND

Fig. 107 Two Brannam Wall Plaques, MND. a. gold slip with central pheasant design by Braddon in browns and green. 9" across. imp. mark. anagram sig. F.B.

b. iridescent green glaze, blue floral boss, 15" across. J.D. C.H. Brannam. Barum ware 1903

BRANNAM AND LIBERTY'S

Throughout the lifetime of the Art Pottery, Charles Brannam retained a firm foothold in Regent Street where Messrs Liberty's were the sole London agent for his pottery.[1] The contract the potter had made in 1881 with Howell and James must have been a short one but it provided ample time for his Barum ware to become well known to the London and visiting public. From the following year (1882) when Liberty's became his sole London agent, the contract was extended, coming to an end in the late thirties. The Barnstaple potter was probably the first of the English country potters to be singled out for inclusion in the firm's new ceramic department (formerly they had dealt only with imported oriental ceramics, particularly blue and white porcelain). Other provincial and country potteries were later patronised, including Aller Vale, Farnham, Della Robbia, Bretby, Burmantofts and Moorcroft; then later, towards the turn of the century and beyond — continental potteries who typified Art Nouveau styles.

It is interesting to speculate to what extent Liberty's interest in Oriental arts and crafts dictated or at least influenced Brannam's choice of oriental themes for his designs. Edmund Capon, in his introductory essay for the catalogue of the Liberty Centenary Exhibition at the Victoria and Albert museum, South Kensington in 1975 notes:

> There was a tremendous fascination for the objects stacked in the original Liberty premises. (218 Regent Street in 1876). The designs ... birds perched at odd angles on flowering branches; sparse bamboo shooting up like an arrow; a solitary crane standing idly in a wistful pool, and of course the occasional but inevitable dragon. Liberty's contribution to the Japanese craze of the late nineteenth and early twentieth centuries and its effect on decorative design, was fundamental. The *Furniture Gazette* of 19 October 1878 carried an announcement of a forthcoming Japanese art exhibition to be arranged at the Burlington Club ... 'present indications would seem to point to the Japanese as the style of the coming season. The most progressive tradesman in Regent Street sells Japanese bric a brac' — no other than A.L. Liberty.

Liberty's interest in the oriental, and in particular the Japanese had begun many years earlier when he was manager of the Great Shawl and Cloak Emporium, also in Regent Street. While there he made important contacts with the pre-Raphaelite artists, Whistler, Oscar Wilde and his group of aesthetes as well as members of fashionable society who were following the current trends of interest in Japanese arts and crafts which had grown rapidly since the International Exhibition of 1862. In 1875, through a loan from his future father-in-law he opened his own shop (East India House) at 118A Regent Street. The business expanded rapidly, from a series of rambling premises to a new property further south (in 1883). Here the basement was devoted to an Eastern Bazaar, a curio department for oriental antiques and an Arab Tea-room,

YULE-TIDE GIFTS

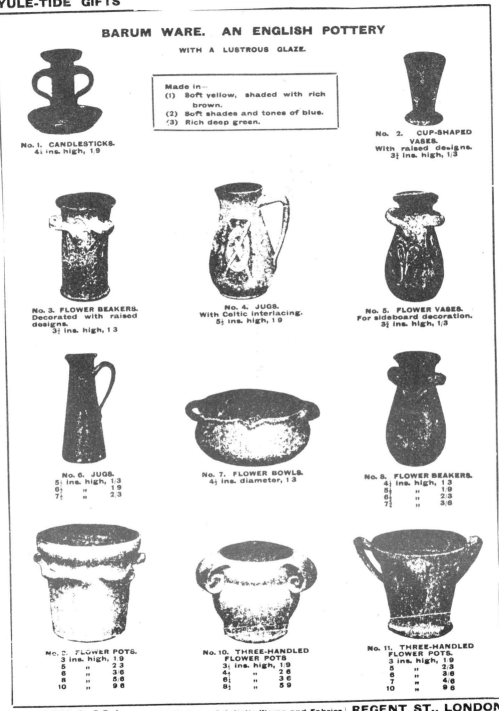

BARUM WARE. AN ENGLISH POTTERY
WITH A LUSTROUS GLAZE.

Made in—
(1) Soft yellow, shaded with rich brown.
(2) Soft shades and tones of blue.
(3) Rich deep green.

No. 1. CANDLESTICKS.
4¼ ins. high, 1/9

No. 2. CUP-SHAPED VASES.
With raised designs.
3½ ins. high, 1/3

No. 3. FLOWER BEAKERS.
Decorated with raised designs.
3¼ ins. high, 1 3

No. 4. JUGS.
With Celtic interlacing.
5½ ins. high, 1 9

No. 5. FLOWER VASES.
For sideboard decoration.
3½ ins. high, 1/3

No. 6. JUGS.
5¼ ins. high, 1/3
6¼   "   1 9
7½   "   2/3

No. 7. FLOWER BOWLS.
4½ ins. diameter, 1 3

No. 8. FLOWER BEAKERS.
4¼ ins. high, 1 3
5¼   "   1/9
6¼   "   2/3
7½   "   3/6

No. 9. FLOWER POTS.
3 ins. high, 1 9
5   "   2 3
6   "   3/6
8   "   5/6
10   "   9 6

No. 10. THREE-HANDLED FLOWER POTS
3¼ ins. high, 1/9
4¼   "   2 6
6¼   "   3 6
8¼   "   5 9

No. 11. THREE-HANDLED FLOWER POTS.
3 ins. high, 1 9
5   "   2/3
6   "   3/6
7   "   4/6
10   "   9 6

LIBERTY & CO [Inventors & Makers of Artistic Wares and Fabrics] **REGENT ST., LONDON**
18

Fig. 108 Liberty & Co. pieces. 1900–1910. Contemporary advertisement

complete with ladies' cloakroom. Following the supply of silk for the productions of 'Patience' and 'The Mikado' at the Savoy Theatre, he embarked on interior decorating, both at the Savoy and other London Theatres. Fashion soon was added to his interests, combined with home dressmaking and soon Liberty's was synonymous with all that was new and fashionable in arts and crafts both in the home and outside it.

Liberty's preferred to use their own mark in connection with art and craft work sold in their store and this was the case with Brannam's pottery from at least 1905. From this date most of the pieces bore a Liberty mark — LIBERTY, LONDON impressed, in a circle; 'Made for Liberty and Co', in a rectangle; or 'Liberty & Co Ltd' impressed. The mark in the rectangle was sometimes preceded by the impressed C.H. Brannam Barum N. Devon. Before the turn of the century there does not appear to have been a Liberty mark and the pieces bore the same mark as those sold elsewhere:— C.H. Brannam Barum, together with a date and usually the designer's initials. Each piece was signed by the potter himself and from 1885 a registered mark was often added:

— Rd. 44561. From 1905 the pottery produced, especially the ware exclusively for Liberty's was far more simple, with sparse decoration, the shape and design reflecting the changing styles of Art Nouveau and later, Art Deco to a limited extent. The illustrations show the type of ware that Liberty preferred, and it may be that Brannam himself, together with his sons were guided by Liberty's own interpretation of future public taste.

Information in this chapter by courtesy of the Victoria and Albert Museum.

Illustrations from Liberty catalogues and others.

Footnotes *(See footnote numbers in text)*

1. **From the twenties.**

Fig. 109 Line drawing by Liverton of geese on a Vase, MND

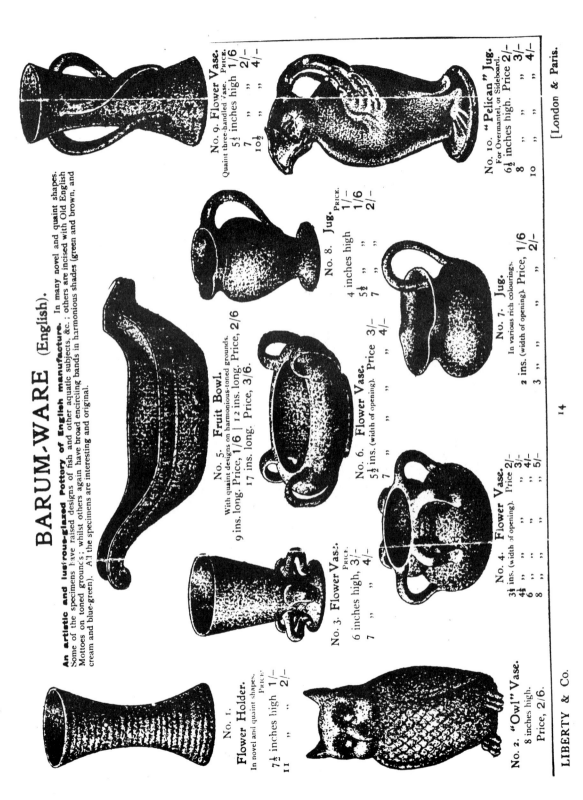

BARUM-WARE (English).

An artistic and lustrous-glazed Pottery of English manufacture. In many novel and quaint shapes. Some of the specimens have raised designs of fish and other aquatic subjects, &c.; others are incised with Old English Mottoes on toned grounds; whilst others again have broad encircling bands in harmonious shades (green and brown, and cream and blue-green). All the specimens are interesting and original.

No. 1.
Flower Holder.
In novel and quaint shapes.
PRICE.
7½ inches high 1/-
11 ,, ,, 2/-

No. 2. "Owl" Vase.
8 inches high.
Price, 2/6.

No. 3. Flower Vase.
PRICE.
6 inches high, 3/-
7 ,, ,, 4/-

No. 4. Flower Vase.
3¼ ins. (width of opening). Price 2/-
4½ ,, ,, ,, 3/-
6 ,, ,, ,, 4/-
8 ,, ,, ,, 5/-

No. 5. Fruit Bowl.
With quaint designs on harmonious-toned grounds.
9 ins. long. Price, 1/6 | 12 ins. long. Price, 2/6
17 ins. long. Price, 3/6.

No. 6. Flower Vase.
5½ ins. (width of opening). Price 3/-
7 ,, ,, ,, 4/-

No. 7. Jug.
In various rich colourings.
2 ins. (width of opening). Price, 1/6
3 ,, ,, ,, 2/-

No. 8. Jug. PRICE.
4 inches high 1/6
5½ ,, ,, 1/6
7 ,, ,, 2/-

No. 9. Flower Vase. PRICE.
Quaint three-handled Vase.
5½ inches high 1/6
7 ,, ,, 2/-
10½ ,, ,, 4/-

No. 10. "Pelican" Jug.
For Overmantel, or Sideboard.
6½ inches high. Price 2/-
8 ,, ,, ,, 3/-
10 ,, ,, ,, 4/-

[London & Paris.

LIBERTY & Co.

14

Fig. 110 More pieces for Libertys from contemporary advertisement

A PEEP AT THE SHOPS

A feature of the *North Devon Journal* from 1887 was a guided tour of the town's shops in the pre-Christmas issues of the newspaper. Starting with a half column it soon became a regular feature, extending to as much as a full-page spread over the two weekly issues preceding Christmas Day. Featured were grocers, butchers, drapers, outfitters, jewellers, china shops, and stores selling fancy goods — in fact any establishment which contributed seasonal offerings in the form of food or presents. Written from information supplied by the traders, the reports were nicely calculated to loosen the purse strings of local shoppers. Barnstaple then, as now served a large rural area and the shops were always well prepared for the Christmas rush.

From the first report up to 1905, Brannam always had a write-up. This, together with a large advertisement well compensated for the fact that the area near the Square no longer was the town centre and that Litchdon Street was perhaps a trifle 'out of it'. From 1906 up until 1912 their name does not appear in the miscellany but for the next three years they advertise again. During the war years the pottery was not advertised at all. For twenty years, however these Christmas reports provide a valuable summary of new trends, in colour, style and decoration as well as information on patrons. These are not always quoted in full, the prefacing remarks almost always being of a fulsome nature, the eulogy being somewhat extreme:— 'Mr. B surpasses former efforts', etc, etc.

In 1886 the firm is introduced, though of course it was in the news often enough during the preceding years. '..showing a grand collection of the famous Brannam ware. Last week a valuable consignment was sent to Messrs Howell and James. To protect the public against imitations, Mr. Brannam places his autograph at the bottom of each piece sent.

In the following year (1887), Mr. C.H. Brannam whose Barum Ware has secured for itself Royal patronage and world-wide celebrity has introduced some novelties this season. These are complete sets of pottery carvers in steel with handsome Barum Ware handles, while there are other knives treated in the same manner. Cheese dishes, milk jugs, cream jugs, vases for table decoration, bouquet vases (painted in plush) and flower bowls are all articles admirably adapted for Christmas presents ... according to a suggestion made by Sir Philip Cunliffe Owen, Mr. Brannam has added toilet ware to his already long list of manufactures.

1888. 'Mr. C.H. Brannam has a splendid show of vases and of ware in forms admirably suited for the purpose of Christmas presents. Amongst the novelties of his show are hanging lamps, Greek hanging pots with brass chains and several other quaintly fashioned pieces of pottery'.

Fig. 111 Group of 'Midget' pieces by Brannam : possibly for dolls' houses

Fig. 112 Buttons and beads by Brannam and Baron

Fig. 113 'A large and amusing Vase',

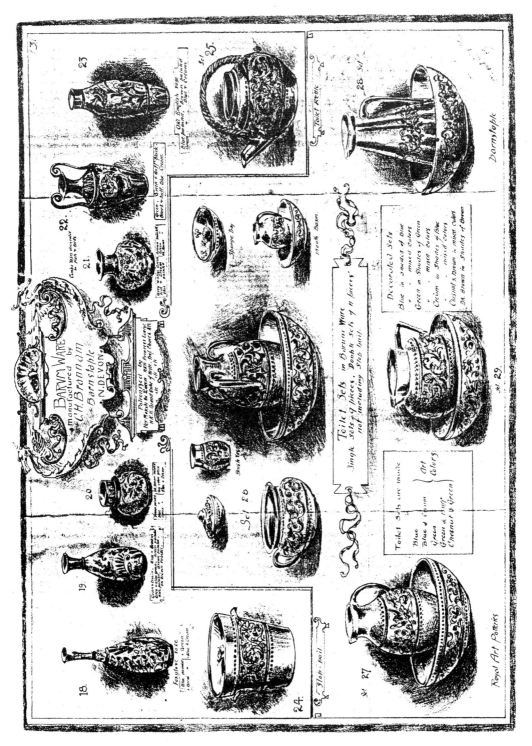

Fig. 114 Early Toilet Ware from pottery records. C.H. Brannam Ltd

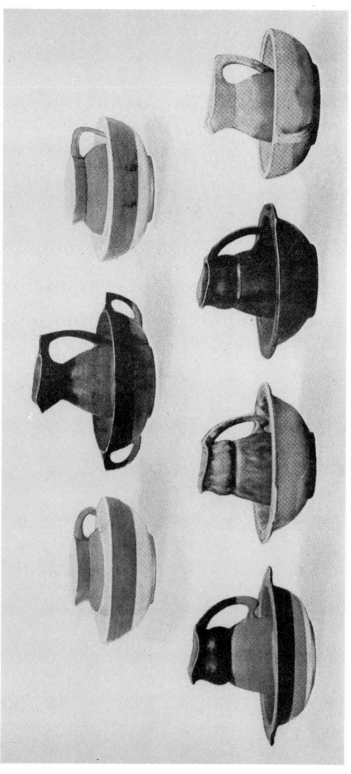

Fig. 115 Later Toilet Ware. From pottery records

Fig. 116 a. Jug from Toilet set 1890 with barley–sugar handle design, by Baron

b. Toilet jug, fish design, green, cream and brown details on leaf green slip. 1917 MND

Fig. 117 Three Ink pots with appropriate mottoes

b. 'Don't forget to write'

c. 'Absent friends are glad of news' MND

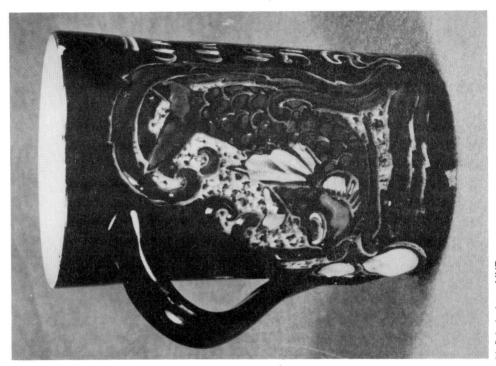

Fig. 118 Two Beakers with fish designs, MND
a. profusion of fish, pale blue/ochres on white slip. 1891
b. with swirl handle, green/yellow/blue fishy design on dark brown. 'Millstone' motto

Fig. 119 Two photographs for second or third catalogue.

Courtesy C.H. Brannam Ltd. pottery records

Fig. 120 Two examples of double dolphin bowl. a. this version of the 'double dolphin bowl' is unmarked. The lively fishy scene is typically Baron, the dolphins very well modelled, and the throwing not typical of Brannam so it is probably an earlyish Baron piece. Colours; blues, ochre and cream on a chocolate ground. The upper bowl bears an unusual scrolling design, ht. 13"

Fig. 121 b. This bowl by Brannam is only 4" high, dated 1890 with a design by Baron in greens and ochre on cream   c. also by Brannam, the cup and saucer, dated 1907 bear the liverton mark with a design in black and cream on green. The mottoes read:– CUP 'Duee mak' yerzel at 'ome' and sauce 'Be aisy / if ye can't be aisy / be as aisy as ye can'.   Collection Barry Stock

1889. '...showing exceedingly pretty ornaments ... quaintly fashioned salt-cellars, drinking cups, flower holders, fish jugs and fish ash trays ... pot pourri vases, persian pots with decorations in chocolate and rich greens ... The new highly successful colour scheme recently introduced add an interest to their display'.

1890. '...Japanese designs figure largely in the excellent Christmas show of Barum Ware ... the decoration and the schemes of colour are alike characterised by their originality and novelty which this Devonshire ceramist strives to perpetuate as characteristic of his choice productions. New uses to which the ware is being put are illustrated with finely fired specimens of plaques, hanging vases and salvers, and there is a varied collection of knick-knacks in ornamental pottery which will form highly acceptable Christmas presents. The larger vases have been skilfully thrown and are very rich in colour'.

1891. '...a delightful display of Royal Barum Ware ... originality of design and of colour conceptions are characteristic of the beautiful productions ... several novelties ... Triplex candelabra and Indian pierce pots are among the newest attractions'.

1892. 'Many novelties are to be seen at the Royal Barum Ware establishment ... in the matter of production (he) is forever moving upwards'.

1893. 'In this display ... Mr. Brannam surpasses former efforts both in regard to grace of design, richness of colour and delicacy of workmanship. Quite recently one of our greatest living Belgian artists has spoken of his ware as being 'incomparable in colour, design and quality' ... in addition to the usual assortment of jardinières, hall stands, vases etc. Mr. Brannam is showing a charming variety of new pieces ... new designs and treatments in quaint motto jugs and cups together with some of the choicest plaques for mural decorations ever turned out of this famous pottery.

1894. '...he is making a speciality of motto goods ... a charming variety of pieces for table decoration ... H.R.H. the Duchess of York bought some Royal Barum Ware last month, this being the second time she has patronised Mr. Brannam's productions'.

1895. '...he has recently made distinct advances ... latest schemes of colour ... there can be little doubt that the visit of Prince Albrecht of Prussia and his suite ... earlier this year ... when many purchases were made by the Royal party ... nerved Mr. Brannam and those in his employ to greater effort both in colour, form and scheme of decoration ... the variety of quaint and beautiful things for table and wall decoration is greatly increased ... some of the best jardinières and pedestals ever produced ... suitable for rooms in any of the prevailing art colours of the day ... stands (just the thing for umbrellas) vases for the hall and drawing room from three feet high to the midget'.

1896. 'Mr. C.H. Brannam has a large share of Royal patronage and quite recently the editor of 'Life' (Mr. Felberman) who is also secretary of the British Committee of the Hungarian Millennial Exhibition (for which Mr. Brannam executed 400 souvenir pieces) has written to say that their Royal Highnesses Princess Louise, Prince Henry of Battenberg and the Duke and Duchess of Teck had been pleased to accept specimens of the new bronze and green produced by Mr. Brannam'.

1897. '...richness of glazes and marvellous purity and range of colour with the perfect harmony to be obtained against backgrounds of gold, terracotta, walnut and cream ... (pay) special attention to vases of various sizes and forms with charming grotesque handles, each separately treated by hand ... jardinières to match, jugs, candlesticks, match holders, ash trays, articles for wall and table decorations in the quaint artistic styles peculiar to this work (over 400 designs stocked)'.

1898. '...because of the concentration of the pottery at Litchdon Street, new kilns were erected in 1898 ... suited to the various colours and glazes ... result in some really marvellous yellowy-green effects, much sought after now to harmonise with delicate tapestries ... each piece now bears the number, 44561 being the registered trade mark'.

1899. '...Mr. Brannam's new colouring effects are in emerald green ... the brilliance of the glaze unequalled ... a feature is made of bird vases from drawings by Mr. Frank Carruthers Gould and of caricature of the day in Mr. Gould's inimitable style. The figures of Mr. Chamberlain and President Kruger as Brer Fox and Mr. Rabbit respectively were recently warmly praised in the *Westminster Gazette*. Most artistic additions to table decorations have been made ... an endless variety of vases for the dining and drawing room. Many beautiful specimens of jardinières and pedestals in studio style. During the summer another visit from H.R.H. Prince Albrecht of Prussia'.

1900. '...Mr. Brannam has recently added many novelties to his stock. Among them are some beautifully modelled swans and dolphin bowls, suitable for junket and salad purposes and as receptacles for flowers for table decoration. Chinese junks have been cleverly treated for table decoration. Pieces executed from designs by F.C. Gould, the distinguished cartoonist are in great demand as are also some 'War' specimens. There are scores of quaint pieces which are sure to attract attention'.

1901. '...some wonderful new shades were recently developed ... one of the most successful of the latest novelties is the Ribbed Devon cyder cup, which is almost identical with an ancient cup found in the Taw. Made in five sizes, the cups have an immense sale for they serve the double purpose of providing a handy drinking vessel and useful flower holder. The graceful daffodil holder (without handles but ribbed) has also proved an exceptionally popular line. Mr. Brannam has been specially successful with his grotesques, all previous records having been surpassed ... with Mother Puss and her kittens — one firm gave an order for 60 dozen for a start'.

1902. '...there is a bewildering variety of productions that are marvels of the ceramic art etc. Mr. Brannam's establishment is working under pressure just now owing to heavy demands for Barum Ware from London houses'.

1903. 'During the past year Mr. Brannam has carried out important alterations and extensions in connection with his establishment in Litchdon Street. There are many novelties ... the production being distinguished by originality of conception, beauty of design, richness of colour, glaze and perfection of workmanship'.

1904. 'Thousands of pieces of the Royal Barum Ware ... there are many delightful novelties. New combinations in colour have recently been introduced with charming results ... several new shapes in flower holders and rose and fruit bowls are to be seen, some treated in a new style of decoration and others being in rich glaze without decoration ... new pedestals in green and brown. A visit to these showrooms is an artistic must.

1905. 'Always attractive, the show at Mr. Brannam's ... is especially interesting this season because of the Royal Warrant just granted by H.R.H. Princess Christian who visited the works and made many purchases last September. Today a window will be devoted to a display of articles in the glorious red tint which gained the special admiration of the Princess and her daughter. Mr. Brannam, whose motto is Exelsior has just produced several new shades of colouring together with a host of new designs. Crushed strawberry and turquoise are the latest tints ... (there are) hundreds of designs of articles of ordinary household utility ... a collection of some 15,000 pieces, offering a bewildering scope of selection ... charming little tea sets bearing Devonshire mottoes are sure to be popular'.

The advertisements of 1907 and 08 both feature the latest novelties in hat pins, buttons and brooches, while the latter year also mentions bulb bowls and tobacco jars.

1912. '...surely ... no more appropriate present ... from a Barumite ... than a piece of Royal Barum Ware which the enterprize of Mr. C.H. Brannam and his sons has made famous in all quarters of the globe ... wonderful range of goods ... something like 20,000 pieces ... latest novelty a series of productions in matt green glaze — a dull glaze that is singularly pleasing ... a recent series ... birds in various shades of green on a blue background ... sold very largely to Libertys ... several new shades and tints include the famous Coronation blue and a du Barrie rose ... a special line of toilet ware and bowls'. (The advertisement features flower vases, bulb bowls, tobacco jars, grotesques, buttons, hat pins and early morning teasets from sixpence to four guineas.

1913. '...a further distinction during the past year, Her Majesty the Queen having honoured the pottery with her patronage ... a special interest is a new line in green matt ... an iridescent green that gives the idea of metal, a great feature of the production being that it is non-porous ... a charming (new) line in the reproduction of Japanese and other noted models ... wide range of pieces ... made by a new process ... specially adapted for the export trade, ... owing to lightness of the pieces ... the Wedgewood blue glaze of the firm is used with exquisite effect. A big demand may safely be predicted for a series executed from designs from Sir Francis Carruthers Gould, the world-famous cartoonist. Lord Halsbury is faithfully depicted in a 'die-hard' Toby jug and a pair of ornaments contain wonderully fine caricatures of Mr. Lloyd George (the Welsh Terrier) and Lord Landsdowne.

'...several notable additions to the range of glazes ... the matt glaze that reproduces the effect of dull gold is a most attractive novelty, and among the other new colours mauve and pink are particularly striking. A new departure that is sure to be popular is the inclusion of tea and coffee sets ... the decorative pieces cover the widest range. There is sure to be a big demand for a patriotic series,[1] which comprises terra cotta busts of H.M. the King, Lord Kitchener, Lord Roberts, Admiral Jellicoe and the King of the Belgians. How the busts can be sold at $6\frac{1}{2}$d is a marvel'. (The advertisement for Christmas also lists General French and General Smith Dorrien).

It is known that Carruthers Gould sent two designs for patriotic Toby Jugs to Brannam but as far as is known these were not used by the potter. The identical drawings were then offered to the Royal Staffordshire pottery and Wilkinsons[2] made a series of eleven. A set fetched almost £1,000 in 1974 but today are worth several times that figure. The set was limited to 350 and the characters are as follows (with captions).

H.M. George V	'Pro Patria'
Field Marshall Haigh	'Push and Go'
Lloyd George	'Shell Out'
Earl Beatty, Admiral of the Fleet	'Dreadnought'
Earl Kitchener	'Bitter for the Kaiser'

Admiral Jellicoe	'Hell Fire Jack'
Woodrow Wyatt	'Welcome Uncle Sam'
President of U.S.A.	
Marshall Joffre	'Ce que j'offre'
Marshall Foch (a bottle)	'Au diable le Kaiser'
General Botha	'Loyalty'

From 1915 until the end of the War there were neither Christmas mentions or advertisements in the Journal.

Footnotes *(See footnote numbers in text)*

1. It is possible that these were based on Carruthers Gould Sketches. They could be produced cheaply because they were made in moulds, biscuit fired and unglazed. They were also very brittle so would have probably had a very short life. Kitchener is only one so far noted.

2. Illustration by permission of Sothebys.

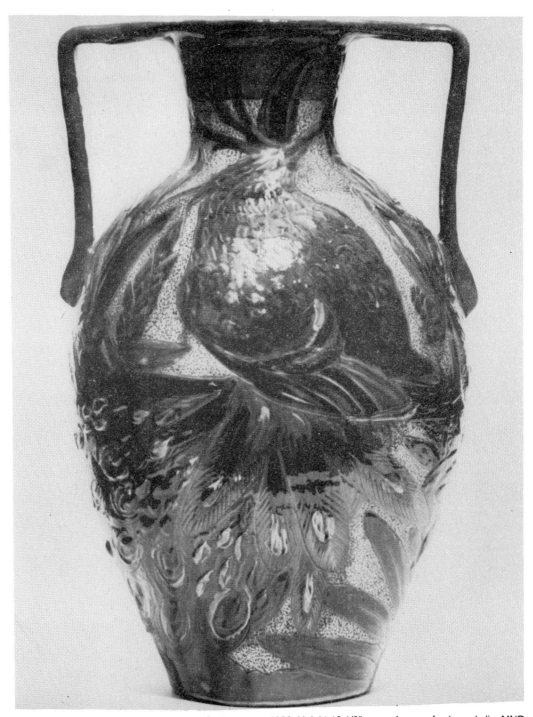

Fig. 122 Large Vase with pheasant design by Dewdney, 1903. Height 19 1/2", many layers of coloured slip. MND

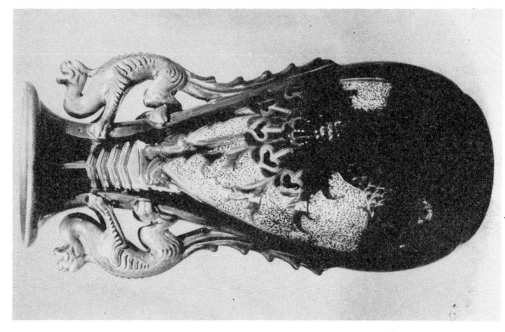

'Fig. 123 Two dragon–handled Vases, Dewdney designs
a. in blue and green with brown detail, two panels. Bird and flower designs,
1910 F.B. MND, height 12"
b. in blue and green glazes, F.B. 1909. Height 15" MND

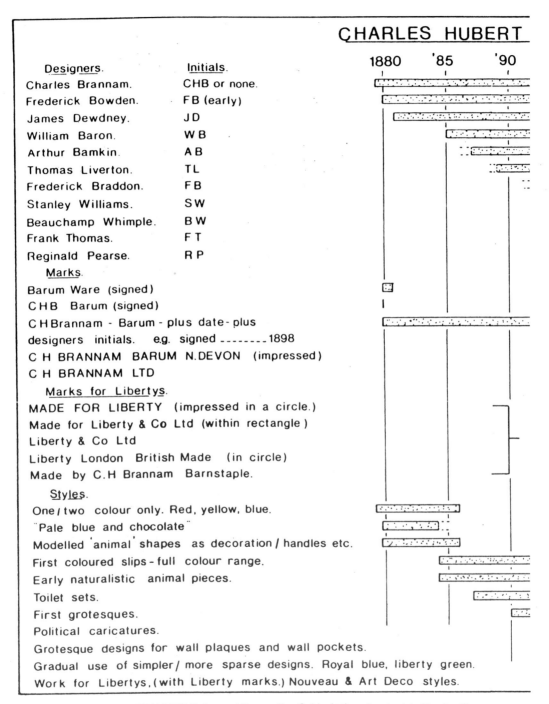

CHARLES HUBERT

Designers.	Initials.	1880	'85	'90
Charles Brannam.	CHB or none.			
Frederick Bowden.	FB (early)			
James Dewdney.	JD			
William Baron.	WB			
Arthur Bamkin.	AB			
Thomas Liverton.	TL			
Frederick Braddon.	FB			
Stanley Williams.	SW			
Beauchamp Whimple.	BW			
Frank Thomas.	FT			
Reginald Pearse.	RP			

Marks.

Barum Ware (signed)

CHB Barum (signed)

CHBrannam - Barum - plus date - plus designers initials. e.g. signed --------1898

C H BRANNAM BARUM N.DEVON (impressed)

C H BRANNAM LTD

Marks for Libertys.

MADE FOR LIBERTY (impressed in a circle.)

Made for Liberty & Co Ltd (within rectangle)

Liberty & Co Ltd

Liberty London British Made (in circle)

Made by C.H Brannam Barnstaple.

Styles.

One / two colour only. Red, yellow, blue.

"Pale blue and chocolate"

Modelled 'animal' shapes as decoration / handles etc.

First coloured slips - full colour range.

Early naturalistic animal pieces.

Toilet sets.

First grotesques.

Political caricatures.

Grotesque designs for wall plaques and wall pockets.

Gradual use of simpler / more sparse designs. Royal blue, liberty green.

Work for Libertys, (with Liberty marks.) Nouveau & Art Deco styles.

Fig. 124 BRANNAM Dating and Recognition Guide designed and printed by Jim Pinn

(Continued on page 161)

BRANNAM   1855 ~ 1937

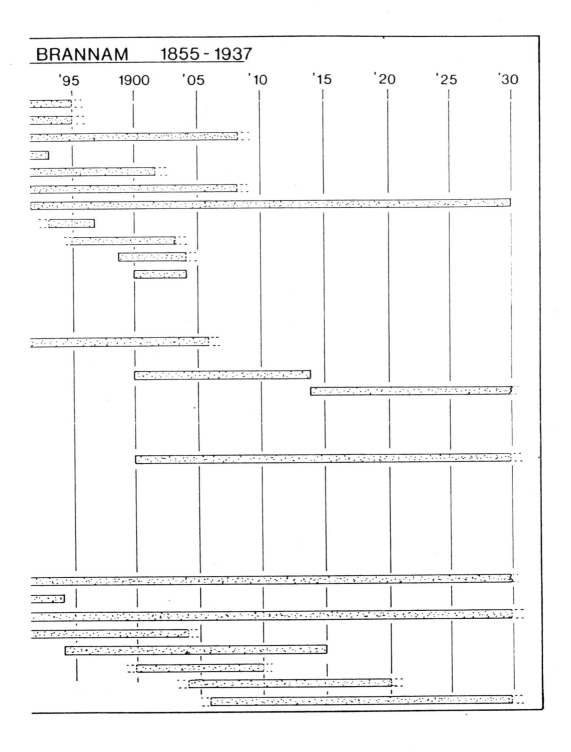

Fig. 125 Large Art Nouveau Vase, one of a pair with Owl design. Height 14" Royal Blue Glaze 1920's

STYLE BRANNAM

Styles and Shapes

Charles Brannam did not base his style on any particular period or movement, but instead allowed it to evolve from its origins in West Country traditional techniques, to an increasingly sophisticated and mature style that was peculiarly his own. He must always have been aware of the importance of good basic shapes that were both functional and pleasing; and from the forms he had used in his father's pottery he now developed a whole new range, but suitable for the drawing and dining rooms rather than the kitchen. Visits to the London museums must have made him aware of a vast range of shapes and styles that were unfamiliar — from early classical forms up to those of the previous century. However, though using shapes and forms from many periods, he was very selective in his choice, rejecting the elaborate and preferring the simple as being more in sympathy both with the medium (earthenware) and his own ideas.

He was looking for shapes that would more readily exploit the designs and decoration that he already had in mind — full-bodied shapes, similar perhaps to the local harvest jugs that had been made over the last hundred years. An early choice was the bulbous jardinière; together with the vase, preferably with a rounded body narrowing towards the neck to finish with an outward curving rim. Both of these shapes were most suitable for either a continuous lateral design or for division into two or three ovoid panels. The vases, especially the larger were often finished with handles, sometimes of a moulded or decorative nature. The very early jardinières were more often purely globular and without handles; while the later, more familiar shape featured an outward curving rim and lateral handles — for practical reasons perhaps. This latter shape was made from small flower vases up to the purely decorative and included the favourite sizes for the aspidistra.

The 'Indian bottle' made an early appearance — with a bulbous lower part and a long tubular neck, straight or curving to a splayed or pinched rim. Then there was the popular waisted cylindrical vase or 'tube', often with two or three vertical swirled handles and sometimes recommended for daffodils. Jugs and pitchers were old friends, and many variations were made. In 1887 the potter produced his first toilet set; eventually extending to four or five different versions, each with a different shaped jug and basin. (There were later versions for the Liberty mark). There were also fish-mouth jugs, puzzle jugs, motto jugs, tankards and three-handled jugs (also called tygs or loving cups).

For the table there were salt cellars, pots and dishes of many different shapes, beakers, mugs, teapots, coffee pots as well as afternoon tea services. There were also ink-pots, candlesticks and spill-holders; and for the smoker match-holders and strikers, ashtrays and lidded jars for tobacco. Among the floor-standing pieces were hall stands or pedestals for the jardinières, umbrella stands and mammoth vases and pots.

With remarkably few exceptions, each and every piece was functional,[1] whether from deliberate intention based on the common sense notion that the practical was the more important aspect or from aesthetic considerations (William Morris) — that utility and beauty were entirely compatible, cannot be determined; but Brannam being a practical man with a strong business sense, the former premise seems more likely. Notable and popular styles were the Stork/Bamboo vase for flowers (or with added socket for candles) made over a period of at least ten years, the double bowl with its linked support of dolphins, and of course the 'chubby dragon' grotesque candle holder.

From the very early days Brannam had used modelling as part of his decoration and from as early 1886 he was producing modelled figures as opposed to thrown pottery. At first these were naturalistic in style such as the cat (1884) and the two lion pieces — a match holder (1891) and a candle holder (1894), but by 1890 he began to make pieces of a grotesque form from drawings by Frank Carruthers Gould.[2] Featuring dragons, fish, insects, birds, frogs and other reptiles they were used for candlesticks, match holders/strikers, flower holders and so on. The creature/boats with dragon heads were supplied with a wire framework to support flowers. From 1900 too there were wall-plaques and, a few years later grotesque wall-pockets or brackets to hold matches, tapers or flowers. The dragon, the lizard and the snake, all used from the early years were popular for applied decoration and especially for handles; indeed the dragon handle has become almost a trade mark of the Barnstaple potters.

There were many free-standing or wall-hanging grotesque pieces which, because of their vulnerability or perhaps because fewer were made of that particular style that are seldom seen today. Many were not shown in the catalogues and others that were pictured are now rare. Some of these are recorded in photographs from the Brannam records, others may exist in museums and private collections. There are also 'one-off' pieces such as those made by James Dewdney for the School of Art's exhibition in 1888 — a ceramic table top, a mirror frame and poultry carvers together with a set of knives with ceramic handles. There were some forms such as the Persian pot, Indian pierce pot, pot-pourri vase, hanging lamp and triplex candelabra which are difficult to identify and may no longer exist, but an example of the hanging flower vase is shown on Plate V.

In 1899 Brannam produced the first political cartoon figures from drawings by Carruthers Gould. These were figures from drawings of Joseph Chamberlain and President Kruger as Brer Fox and Brer Rabbit respectively. In the following year

Fig. 126 Group of late moulded pieces. Two pale pieces in uranium glaze, 1920's, however, match-holder/striker in royal blue, impressed mark. Cherub ash tray (several sizes)

Fig. 127 Set of Wilkinson Toby Jugs FROM DRAWINGS BY Frank Carruthers Gould, Courtesy Sotheby's

Fig. 128 Three from series Baron Toby Jugs c.1914–1918. From left to right: Marshall Foch, dark blue; Earl Kitchener, mauve/blue; Admiral Jellicoe, dark blue. all c. 9" height

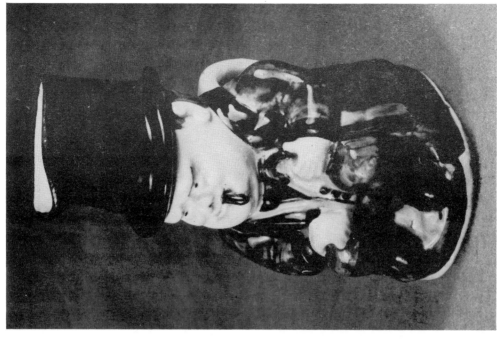

Fig. 129 Two later moulded jugs by Brannam.

a. model unknown jug   b. Mr. Churchill MND

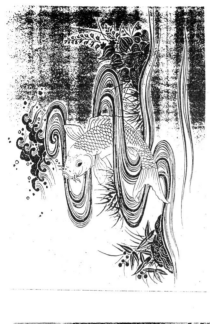

b. Designs from Cutler. NDA library

Fig. 130 a. Cover from 'Artistic Japan'

(1900) he made two more pieces — a Kruger jug, and a wall plaque showing the two adversaries engaged in a game of cards. The next to appear were in 1913 when the figures of Lloyd George (the Welsh Terrier) and Lord Halsbury (diehard) were made. There are no local records of others but there were other 'War pieces' in the 'Patriotic Series'.[3] These were small busts in unglazed biscuit-fired terra-cotta, cheaply produced and sold at $6^1/_2$ pence each. They were made from moulds and being fairly brittle probably had a short life. Pictured is Kitchener.

It is likely that other political cartoons were offered to Brannam by Carruthers Gould in the form of Toby Jugs (see original drawing from Brannam records), but the potter does not seem to have used them. They were however, accepted by the Royal Staffordshire Pottery whose Wilkinson subsidiary made a set of eleven in the World War I series.[4] However, at about this time Brannam did make Toby Jugs both plain and decorated, in various sizes. In addition, in World War II the factory made jugs — of Churchill, Stalin and Roosevelt.[5]

With regard to sizes, as many as six were produced of a pattern from the miniature up to the mammoth (three feet) and a choice was given between 'art colour' (plain) and decorated. In the latter years of the pottery each piece bore the shape number on the base, but in the earlier years they were less commonly marked in this way.

Colour and Design

It seems most likely that initially Charles Brannam had made a conscious decision to base his decorative style on the ancient local technique of sgraffito where the design was drawn on the piece and incised or cut away in the early stages before the first firing, to be later glazed and fired again. Although many pieces used other techniques, it was the sgraffito style that was most prominent in his work and first attracted the attention of the public, continuing to be used up until the first decade of the present century. It is to his credit that he never allowed the technique to dominate or to impede his progress, but was always looking for new ideas to tempt the public taste; whether it was a new shape, a fresh range of colours or a novel theme or method of decoration.

His first efforts were fairly tentative, relying on a simple fine outline for the design, using blue and yellow or red and yellow, resulting in a two-colour finished design. The first pieces, prior to 1881 presented a streaky appearance in many cases, though some achieved a good separation of colour.[6] The early jug pictured on page 60 dated 1880 and signed CHB copies the marbled style of agate ware while the jug dated 1881 copies the Fishley harvest jugs, with its faint colour tints. The pictured orange and brown vase dated 1882 (NDA collection) shows the use of red and yellow producing glazes. However, most of the popular pieces from 1881 use the blue glaze which produced pale blue and chocolate, blue/black or blue and green. According to Strong the variety of colour was largely due to the firing.[7] Most of these pieces rely on sgraffito techniques for their contrasts of design and background but there are other examples which use flat areas of colour very much in the style of Owen Davis (see page 58). It seems certain that it was this particular colour combination and design that first brought the potter's work to the attention of the public both at the local exhibitions and at the Howell and James showrooms. Such was the popularity of this particular colour combination that it was still being used as late as 1894, long after the adoption of coloured slips and pâte sur pâte had introduced a new and exciting colour range. It is certain that the jardinières made for the Queen were in two colours,[8] probably using the blue glaze and may have had some resemblance to work displayed at the Devon County Show in 1884. q.v. (see picture of jardinière with fish supports plate II).

With the introduction of pâte sur pâte and coloured slips between 1885 and early 1886, very soon after william Baron's appointment, the scene changed radically. Sgraffito worked panels were still used as a basis for designs but the emphasis shifted to applied work and the building up of coloured slips to produce a whole range of colours. By the use of six basic colours, probably yellow, red, blue, green and bronze, plus cream 'some forty tints are obtained'. It seems to be much more common to find pieces early in this period with Dewdney's signature than with Baron's. It seems likely that during the first few years at the pottery that Baron's time was occupied with modelling work to assist Bowden, but surely his experience with Doulton would have been useful in the exploitation of this new technique. However, all of the pieces so far seen are dated between 1888 and 1891. Examples of both designers' work are shown.

Because of the detailed work now involved, the new trainee designers were kept very busy finishing the designs which, because of the wide range of colours used, each of which had to be allowed time to dry, spent sometimes weeks in the drying room before being fired, then glazed and fired again. From the 1890s, with the shift of emphasis on to the decoration of the grotesque pieces, the decoration became more simple and the new youngish designers were allowed to sign their own pieces, probably much earlier than their contemporaries of five years earlier. It was clearly this new work that was responsible for the employment of so many young designers (by 1897 eight or more designers were employed in all). Then, because of the shift of emphasis from decoration to new designs and shapes, following public taste and demand from Libertys; from the turn of the century the number of designers sharply decreased until between 1901 and 1903 there was an average of four, declining until 1908 with the departure of Liverton, and the sole retention of one, Frederick Braddon who continued until 1930.

The following list shows the popular/new colours for some of the years (from N.D.J. reports and own observations):

1878 — 81 Brown, yellow, blue

1881 — 84 emphasis on blue and green in many different shades.

1885 — 87 Cinnamon, pale blue, ochres

1888   pale blue, mid blue, ochres, chestnut

1890   blue, ginger, ochre and cream. Dark brown with pale blue, ochres

1891   Brown, cream, mid blue, ochres

1892/3   green, ochre, deep cream, ginger brown, mid blue

1895 — 97 gold, terra-cotta, walnut and cream, brown, bronze and green

1898 — 99 yellowy-green, dark green , blue with brown, emerald green

1900 — 01 mid green with blue and brown, blue/green, yellow, pale blue and
                cream

1902 — 04 yellow, blue, blue with green, green with brown

1905   crushed strawberry, turquoise, mid blue

1908   blue/green

1912   matt green, du Barri rose, green/blue

1913   wedgwood blue

1914   dull gold, mauve, pink

Sources and Influences

Though Brannam's forms and designs were more often original than derivative,
Hugh Strong sees influence from many sources in his work.[9] Writing in 1888 he says:

> The owner of the Royal Barum pottery has discovered a way to make and use the thickly glazed blues
> and greens of the old Persian ware. The potter has produced ... very soft and rich combinations of
> chocolate and blue, leaf green, and pale yellow and other secondaries and tertiaries. Then there are
> Egyptian vases with designs in panels, after nature and in keeping with the beautiful shape of the vessel;
> executed in lightish blue and dark green upon a brown background. Persian designs in blue and white;
> Greek vases, appropriately distinguished for the purity of their form and Japanese pots with
> conventional decorations.

There is no doubt that the influence of Japanese art was very strong at this time.
Stemming from the 1862 International Exhibition, a growing interest had been
fostered by the pre-Raphaelite artists — Millais, Rosetti and Burne-Jones, as well as
by the artists Whistler, together with Oscar Wilde and his group of aesthetes.[10] All
were patrons of the Regent Street Oriental Bazaar managed between 1864 and 74 by
the young Arthur Lazenby Liberty. By the time that Liberty had established his own
business in Regent Street, distaste and hostility towards Wilde had had its sting
removed by the staging of the Gilbert and Sullivan production of 'Patience' at the New
Savoy theatre in 1881.[11] By this time, from being ridiculed, Japanese arts and crafts

had become 'quite the thing', as was shown four years later by the success of 'The Mikado'.

Japanese art was also featured in the new Arts and Crafts journal, 'The Studio', first published in 1893 and aimed to 'raise the standard of aesthetic sensibility'.[12] A contemporary if short-lived publication was Samuel Bing's 'Artistic Japan', a monthly journal highlighting Japanese Art and Industry. The Athenaeum library would almost certainly have purchased copies of 'The Studio' for the perusal of the young art students and the library still retains bound copies of Samuel Bing's works as well as other books on Japanese Art.

Japanese themes frequently used by designers, especially Baron include: birds in a leafy landscape, large flowerheads, a flowering branch, the stork/bamboo theme, fish in a seascape, the dragon and the peacock. Naturalistic forms were common and more especially favoured by Baron. Dewdney's designs did include natural representations but many more were formalised.

Both Thomas Liverton and Frederick Braddon had distinctive styles. Liverton's designs appear on pieces from 1890 up until 1908 so inevitably reflect strong Art Nouveau influences, using floral themes such as the lily and the fuschia. Though

being absent for some periods, Braddon's style was fluent though more noticeably stylistic. He too showed Art Nouveau trends which would have been most acceptable to Libertys'. His designs became much more simplified in the twenties when the form of the pottery became pre-eminent.

Occasionally Brannam made a direct copy of an original piece. The example shown in an exact replica of an old Italian Faience piece Plate XII.

Footnotes *(See footnote numbers in text)*

1. Fig.72 shows an exception. A purely decorative ornament by Bowden. See chapter on designers.
2. See also chapters on Carruthers Gould and the grotesques.
3. See advertisement and Figs. 136 and 146
4. See picture and note on World War figures portrayed (Fig. 127)
5. See page Fig. 129
6. The reader should study the illustrations on page 54 Fig. 44 b.
7. There are even examples of a single piece presenting two different shades (near the rim and towards the base. Plate XXX
8. These jardinieres are no longer in the Royal collection nor is there any existing record of their acquisition.
9. N.D.J.
10. The particular favourite of Whistler and Wilde was the peacock, with its marvellous eye feathers — a theme readily taken up by the Art Nouveau movement, flourishing around the turn of the century (at that time regarded by the establishment as decadent). Used by Dewdney 1884/85 Vase.
11. A satire on Wilde and the aesthetic movement.
12. The journal was published for three years or more. Bing was a collector of Japanese Art who opened his Paris shop of Art Nouveau in 1895. He is said to have invented the title.

Fig. 131 Presentation of Millenary Mug to eldest boy and girl, Pilton Bluecoat School. 1930

b. Group of Baron/Lauder commemorative mugs

Fig. 132 Group of commemorative political pieces

BRANNAM COMMEMORATIVE WARE

Brannams have made commemorative ware since at least 1897 and continued up until the wedding of Prince Charles and Princess Diana in 1981. Unfortunately there does not seem to be any record of the pieces made, so it is only possible to list those that have been noted. From 1911 up until 1937 a mug was presented to every child at school in Barnstaple, and sometimes a special run was made for a single school in the area. Swimbridge and Appledore have been noted and there may be others. A photograph shows the presentation ceremony at Pilton Bluecoat junior school in 1930 (The Millenary mug) to the oldest boy and the oldest girl in the school. Both recipients are still alive and living locally. The earlier mugs were marked in sgraffito but from 1938 most pieces were lettered with trailed slip.

COMMEMORATIVE MUGS (ROYAL)

1897	**Victoria Jubilee 1837 — 1897**	with motto and fish decoration.
1911	**George V Coronation June 22nd 1911**	mid blue not always marked
1935	**George V and Mary Silver Jubilee**	seen in yellow and royal blue
1937	**Edward VIII Coronation**	in royal blue, and pale green (angular handle)
1937	**George VI and Queen Elizabeth Coronation**	blue, and green ......
1953	**Queen Elizabeth Coronation**	seen in brown, probably other colours.
1981	**Marriage Prince of Wales and Lady Diana Spencer.**	royal blue
		also plaques. two different transfer design in several colours.

OTHER COMMEMORATIVE PIECES

1927	Penrose Almshouses	jug royal blue moulded design of building, also biscuit barrel (green)
1930	Millenary mug to mark granting of Borough	royal blue and with Borough Arms on reverse.

Single or Limited Pieces:

(These three on display in Guildhall. Photos kind permission Barnstaple Town Council).

1879 — 1979 The 'ROCK' Vase. commemorates centenary of death   royal blue
of William Frederick Rock. town's benefactor.
Presented to town by North Devon Civic Society.

1900   The 'STEEPLE' Vase. Limited number made to raise
subscriptions for repairs to the steeple of the
parish church of St. Peter. Presented to Guildhall
1981 by Miss Newcombe, formerly in possession
of her father.

1931/32   The MAYORS VASE for details see picture.

1836 — 1936 Borough Vase. commemorates centenary of granting
of Borough. Displays town seal/borough arms.

MUGS

1868 — 1968	Bluecoat School centenary	royal blue
1873 — 1973	Braunton Caen School centenary	pale green
1981	Tarka Radio Fair	royal blue

POLITICAL (Liberal)

1959	Jeremy Thorpe, M.P. North Devon, Oct 8th 1959	small blue bowl

1964   Jeremy Thorpe, M.P. 15th Oct
              1964 majority 5,136   small dish

1969   BARNSTAPLE
              PANNIER MARKET
              "THE FIRST TEN YEARS"
              PETER BESSELL — LORD FOOT
              JOHN PARDOE M.P.
              THE RT. HON JEREMY THORPE M.P.
              ALBERT COOK   EDWARD WHEELER

              jug in pale yellow, writing in dribbled slip. limited — prob. ten.

TWO LOCAL COMMEMORATIVE PIECES.
BARNSTAPLE ROTARY CLUB

1928 — 1929 Barnstaple Rotary Club. Charles William Brannam
             PRESIDENT. anagram CWB in circle (wife's MDB on reverse)

1928 — 1933 Rotary International/Barnstaple Rotary Club made to
             commemorate CH. Bradford secretary Rotary wheel on face.
             anagram CHB in circle on reverse.
             Both royal blue 'pickle jar' shape.
             Decoration in sgraffito and added slip in green/brown.

SPECIAL ORDERED PIECES

1893   Heraldic jug, bearing Talbot arms:- 'a talbot, collared and chained'
              together with motto 'Semper Fidelis'. Possibly made for John
              Reginald Francis George TALBOT, J.P. of Rhode Hill House,
              Uplyme, Lyme Regis, Dorset.

              bears verse as follows:
              "The World has battle room for all
              Go fight and conquer if ye can
              But if ye rise or if ye Fall
              Be each, Pray God a Gentleman."

              Jug is in the early colour of pale blue and chocolate and is signed
              by Thomas Liverton.

c.1937 **Furnishing of the 'King's House'.**

Erected by the Royal Warrant Holders Society as a tribute to the reign of the late King George V. 'examples of Royal Barum Ware were used'. (report in *Western Morning News*).

If this was a dolls house the pieces may have been the 'Royal Midget vase' (no. 434 in second catalogue). Examples show these to be from one to two inches in height. These may have previously been purchased for furnishing Queen Mary's dolls house. (See Fig. 111).

Fig. 133 Large Vase by Brannam dated 1886. An early example of applied slip by James Dewdney, featuring a gamecock and peaony, both with 'jewelled' applied slip in ginger, cream, ochres and pale blue. Signed J.D. 15" height

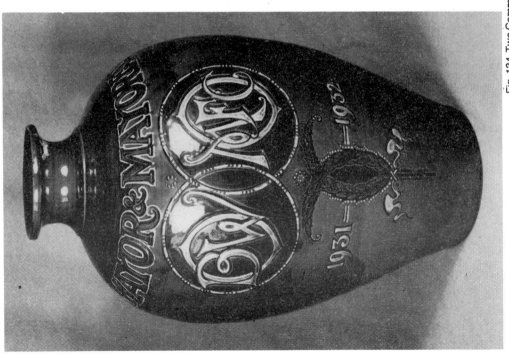

a. The Mayor's Vase

Fig. 134 Two Commemorative Vases.

b. The Borough Vase

The Guildhall collection, courtesy Barnstaple Town Council

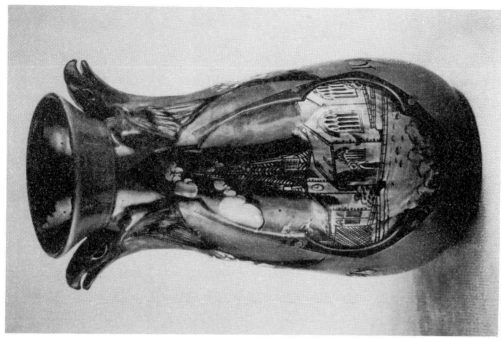

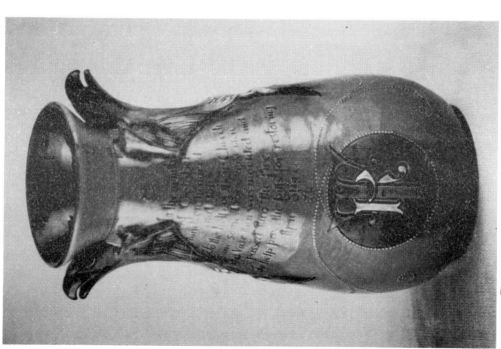

Fig. 135 The STEEPLE Vase, showing St. Peter's Church. Two views. Guildhall collection, courtesy Barnstaple Town Council

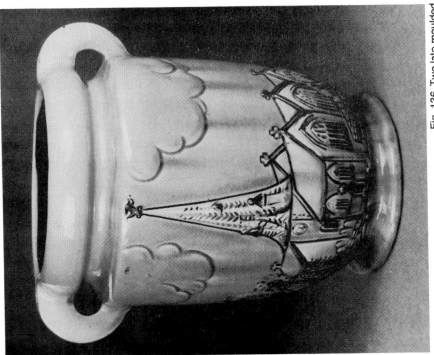

Fig. 136 Two late moulded pieces featuring buildings, c. 1924

b. Queen Anne's Walk MND

a. St. Peter's Church

ADVERTISING AND THE CATALOGUES

From the very beginning Charles Brannam was strongly aware of the value of advertising. His early contract with Howell and James, followed by his association with Libertys ensured that his name and that of his pottery were always in the public eye where it mattered — in the capital city where his reputation was first established; initially through Royal patronage, then through natural public response; widening to an increasingly cosmopolitan clientele. At the same time his participation in most of the West Country exhibitions ensured that his name became well known locally, while local coverage in the North Devon newspapers gave him wide publicity.

He placed eye-catching advertisements in the *North Devon Journal*, publicising his royal patronage, and for two or three issues just before Christmas each year made sure that possible prospective customers as well as regular clients would be reminded of the quality and ever-changing appeal of Barum Ware. He always 'thought big' and must have spent many hours and great care in the planning of each advertisement. Sometimes the layout is large, bold and simple: at others there is an emphasis on *information* — describing his latest speciality or with particular mention of his latest royal client (the appropriate coat of arms prominently displayed). At times, to show his international reputation, he would quote excerpts from the letters of satisfied overseas customers — 'December 7th, 1907 — Captain A.J. Campbell, Hart, Singapore, writes:—

"I beg to advise you that the Cask of Pottery sent to me in London has arrived here, and I have pleasure in saying there is not a single breakage nor even a chip anywhere. I am very pleased".

The potter also used these quotes on the pages of his catalogues.

His letter-heads, too showed a strong sense of publicity and the graphic art typical of the era. The order-form notepaper used in 1913 but designed soon after Princess Christian's visit is a masterpiece in itself; incorporating the potter's name with the then-recently adopted royal seal of approval, together with the impressive list of former royal clients, and including his father's early success at the Great Exhibition of 1851. The smaller, more personal notepaper, featuring a running frieze of vases appeals directly to the ladies. As may be seen, this letter, though unsigned is in Charles Brannam's own hand and addressed to Queen Alexandra's private secretary, soliciting the new Queen's patronage (though of course both she and her husband had been patrons since the first purchase by Alexandra many years earlier). Advertising photographs of the pottery were also printed — examples shown.

Without further evidence, involving wide and lengthy research it has not been possible to establish the full extent of the potter's advertising campaign, but it could well have been extensive. It is known that in later years, for example between 1916

BY

APPOINTMENT TO

H.R.H.

PRINCESS

CHRISTIAN.

C.H.Brannam's

"ROYAL BARUM WARE."

All New Goods, New Designs, New Colourings.

LITCHDON POTTERY, BARNSTAPLE. [1850]

BY ROYAL WARRANT OF
APPOINTMENT TO
H.R.H. PRINCESS CHRISTIAN.

C. H. BRANNAM'S

New Agate Ware

IS WORTH INSPECTING

AT THE ART EXHIBITION,

OR AT THE ONLY

ROYAL BARUM WARE POTTERY

LITCHDON ST. (Close to Imperial Hotel), BARNSTAPLE.

☞ NOTE CORRECT NAME AND ADDRESS.

POTTERS ALWAYS AT WORK ON THE SPOT. [7187]

Fig. 137 Two advertisements from the North Devon Journal, 1907 and 1910

and 17, he placed small ads in periodicals as well as in newspapers. Many of these, such as *The Gardeners Magazine*, and *Amateur Gardening* would have been for flower-pots and other horticultural goods; while those for the *Church Times* were probably for organisers of Church bazaars. The 'glossies', such as *Vanity Fair* and *Country Life* could have been used for Art pottery promotion.

The Catalogues:

It is not known how many catalogues were issued but according to Peter Brannam the first was in 1898 — see illustration. This was possibly the cover of the earliest catalogue, retained in the pottery records. The other, still in its original cover was probably printed in 1907, soon after the visit of Princess Christian. In the foreword the potter thanks the public for its support 'during the last 26 years'. Both catalogues feature a wide range of goods — the first illustrating 194 specimens of the pottery, with details of prices as well as the range of sizes made for each model. The specimen pages shown give some indication of the poorish quality of the originals, which of course is worsened by the photo-copying process. The other, later catalogue is even less clear, but it was nevertheless thought worthwhile to include several pages as examples. Just over 100 examples were illustrated and by this date the number of models totalled nearly 800.

Many of the illustrations in the two catalogues show identical pieces, (indicating perhaps that these had proved popular) and in some cases there were different versions of some of the grotesques. There were also many new models as well as additions to the colours and glazes. Both catalogues are extremely valuable in that they provide evidence of pieces not commonly found, for example the 'Bat' wall-pocket. However, this is not to say that they cover the whole range of goods produced, for example much of the work during the first ten or more years is not shown, and, as explained in the foreword:

... it has been found impossible to reproduce all the work, as the larger pieces are not repeated in detail.

Then there is, of course the work done for special order which probably would not be copied. There may well be other catalogues in existence. It is also likely that Libertys produced their own catalogue of the range made for them, bearing their own marks (c.1906). Certainly pages of models from that period do exist — see examples.

ROYAL BARUM WARE

—— (BY ROYAL WARRANT OF APPOINTMENT ——
REGD. NO. 44561.

Messrs. C. H. Brannam

Respectfully solicit the favour of a visit to their extensive Showrooms, where the following Goods can be seen in great variety of colour and form:—

JARDINIERES, FLOWER VASES, BULB BOWLS, TOBACCO JARS, GROTESQUE BUTTONS, HATPINS, EARLY MORNING TEA SETS, &C. PRICES FROM 6D. TO £14

No more appropriate or welcome Present from Barum can be sent than an example of ROYAL BARUM WARE in Blues, Greens, Old Gold, and Mixed Glazes .

LITCHDON ST. (AT THE BACK OF IMPERIAL HOTEL) BARNSTAPLE.

No connection with any other local Pottery.

CHRISTMAS, 1886.

C. H. BRANNAM'S

☞ ROYAL BARUM WARE.

A NEW and CHOICE SELECTION of this ART POTTERY, suitable for 'XMAS and NEW YEAR'S PRESENTS, ☞ NOW ON VIEW.

NEW COLORS, NEW DESIGNS, NEW FORMS, NEW TREATMENT.

LITCHDON STREET, BARNSTAPLE.

Fig. 138 Brannam advertisements from postcards and Mate's Guidebook. 1903

Litchdon Pottery, Barnstaple

Find these Premises when visiting Barnstaple

By Appointment to
H.R.H. Princess Christian.

C. H. BRANNAM'S
(Ltd.)
Litchdon Pottery,
BARNSTAPLE.

The Pottery noted for its wonderful colours and artistic forms. Visitors to Barnstaple must find the Pottery bearing the Royal Arms, situate at the back of the Imperial Hotel. If visitors so desire they may view the process of Manufacture.

This Pottery was visited by
H.R.H. Princess Christian.

Ask for BRANNAM'S
Royal BARUM Ware.

The Works are situated at the back of these premises.
MANUFACTURERS OF RED EARTHENWARE OF ALL KINDS.

This shows the Interior of one, of ☙☙☙

C. H. Brannam's Artistic Show Rooms.

FIND THIS WHEN VISITING THE TOWN AND BE DECEIVED BY NO OTHERS

Wonderful Blues and Greens.

Excellent and Original Forms.

Up-to-date in Design. :::

FINDS READY SALES AT BAZAARS which are literally dealt with

TAKE CARE YOU FIND IT :::

Vases, Jardinieres, Beer Jugs, Motto Goods, Pedestal and Jardiniere complete, Cream and Preserve Dishes, Quaint ::: Flower Holders.

NO MORE APPROPRIATE SOUVENIR

THE ABOVE SHOWS INTERIOR OF ONE OF

C. H. Brannam's Royal Barum Ware Showrooms,
LITCHDON STREET, BARNSTAPLE.

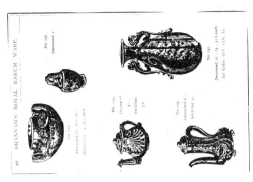

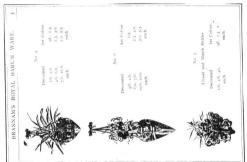

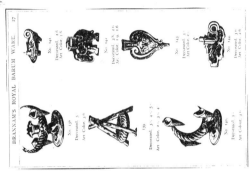

Fig. 139 Cover and four pages from the 1898 Catalogue

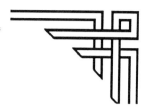

APPENDIXES

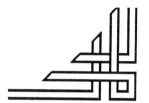

Fig. 140 a. Cover from the 1907 Catalogue   b. Two very unusual pieces for the 1907 Catalogue

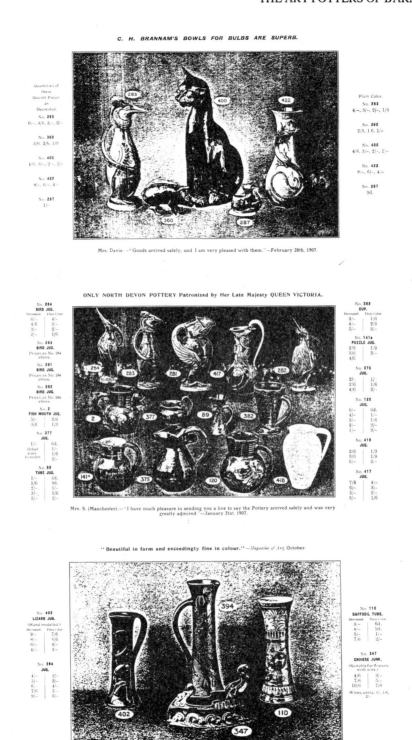

Fig. 141 The 1907 Catalogue. Some sample pages. C.H. Brannam ltd. pottery records

APPENDIX 1.A. 1891

Report on Royal Barum Ware. North Devon Journal. July 16. 1891

From time to time we have had the pleasure of chronicling fresh successes of the founder of the Royal Barum Ware Pottery in Litchdon Street which has become such an object of interest to visitors ... Mr. Brannam has accomplished many improvements since his ware first came under our notice, and in no particular of his interesting occupation has he made such a great advancement than in the perfecting of the beautiful glaze which is such a marked feature of the Barum Ware, immeasurably advancing its attractiveness. Reduced to almost transparent thinness, it adds to the pedestal, the vase and the jug that varnished brilliance which heightens the effect of the mingling tones of the scheme of colour without any perceptible addition to, or disturbance of the surface.

The effects obtained in firing have ben so closely studied by the potter that the various gradations of "smearing", "clouding" and glazing are secured with a certainty and a nicety which are obtained only by the genius which was cleverly defined as "an infinite capacity for taking pains". This much may be said without prying into the secrets of the craftsman ... the fruitfulness of design which is another characteristic of the ware. "Free Renaissance" describes the style of the original and novel productions now issuing from the pottery. Natural ornament, treated with freedom which the potter has ever claimed as his privilege is indeed the prevailing "fashion" in Barum ware. Fishes, birds and beast enter largely into the designs which are characterised by freshness and a freedom limited only by artistic restraint.

Another "new departure" that adds interest to the ware is the introduction of new colour schemes, which, for the most part, compel the admiration of the artistic mind. From deep brown to a rich orange is a very effective arrangement of tones; vases of green of four shades, with the designs in the same colour, in a triumph for the potter's art, softening down, as it does, from what is technically termed a golden green to the emerald of the verdure of Spring; and graded tones of blue.

In shape, many of the finer productions of the pottery still show an adherence to the fashioning of the classic work at the wheel of the Greek potter. Mr. Brannam's deft manipulation (the principal pieces being invariably thrown by the manufacturer) showing no falling off in the beauty of proportion. He has introduced twisted handles for some of the larger pots with very satisfactory results, and the originality of the ware is well preserved in every respect. The "Coombe jar" is in special favour with moneyed visitors to the Queen of North Devon watering places; (Ilfracombe) and toilet sets, in the scheme of shaded greens, for Liberty's, have had a great sale. Pedestals with jardinières to match, from quite a new "line", and with various designs on diversified grounds, are choice examples of decorative ware. The taste of the purchasing public has been pleased with a very novel thing in mirror and photo frames, which, in their unglazed condition in "cream" and "biscuit" colours, with Renaissance and jewelling decoration, may be counted a distinctly successful addition to the multifarious forms in which the ware now appears.

Drawing room decorative ware is much in demand, and Mr. Brannam has created a supply; the new monochrome ware, in flower-holders, fern pots and vases is of hard, unglazed pottery, the simplicity of the design and the modesty of the colour scheme together obtaining a very pretty effect. Potter, designer and kiln have conspired to produce a rich combination in the decoration of the finer Greek vases, the "slip" being of a lustrous bronze, and the design brought out in black, the retention of the lustre upon the decorations of the vase producing a rare harmony of tone.

The adaptability of the potter, which has already been alluded to is seen in some facile reproductions of the best Wedgewood designs, while the vases in shades of blue have evidently been suggested by the celebrated Chinese willow-pattern ware. Loving cups in browns to cream, and greens to cream; teapots, with snake and dragon designs freely treated; toilet sets, in which the potter has gone so far as to produce for us match-holders, here of triton shape and there of lion design; Persian flower-holders, which are also adapted for use as cigar holders; lily vases, with the new green and cream arrangement, and daffodil vases, from lustrous dark brown to rich cream; spills, flower and salt-holders in saleable grotesque designs; a butterfly match-holder, in which the marbling of the wings shows much skill; — these are some of the uses and shapes to which the ware is newly put, as result of the skill, enterprise and good taste of the manufacturer.

Not even that intensely Devon dish, of luscious strawberries and cream, has been forgotten by Mr. Brannam, who has produced a combined cup and dish in Barum ware which may be warranted to add to the tempting character of the luxury. Competition has had very gratifying results in the case of the potter: it has led to the discovery of latent beauties and new possibilities, which bid fair to yet further add to the artistic triumphs and commercial success of the Royal Barum Ware.

APPENDIX 1B

Royal Barum Ware
(from the North Devon Journal of June 18. 1903.

'Since 1880, when his exquisite Barum Ware first delighted the artistic public, Mr. C.H. Brannam has had a splendid record of success. The stages of progress have been marked by building operations. First of all the main block in Litchdon Street was built; then came a new dwelling house with handsome showroom and stores; and a few years later (in 1895-6) the small kiln block was erected. Now, in order to cope with the rapidly increasing demand for the Royal Barum ware, further developments have taken place, while magnificent additional showrooms have been provided. For the last sixteen years the portion of the ground floor abutting in Litchdon Street nearest the Square, has been used as an engine room. Accommodation for the department has been provided in the rear, while new mills have been substituted for old, the output capacity being quadrupled and superior quality of work secured.

The space abutting on the street has been converted into a splendid showroom, 30ft square and 12ft in height. The room is fitted up in a style in keeping with the artistic merit of Mr. Brannam's famous ware. The scheme of decoration is most choice. The ceiling is of Tynecastle, in Louis XV style, and there is an exquisite Anaglyptic frieze designed by Mr. Owen Davis — a distinguished Barumite. The fittings are in white enamel. The show tables are oval in shape, with fluted legs. At the back of the windows are curtains in rich old brocade, carried on handsome mahogany posts, finely fluted. There is a wood block floor. A staircase leads from this room to a showroom upstairs which has been fitted in the same dainty and artistic style. The upstairs room was previously the stockroom — a portion of premises in the rear now being used for this purpose.

In these showrooms the beautiful Ware can be seen to the best advantage. The scope offered to purchasers may be gathered from the fact that over ten thousand pieces are now on view in the showrooms. Some charming additions to the ware have recently been made, richness of colouring being combined with beauty of design and perfection of workmanship. The showrooms are brilliantly lighted by means of electricity. (Electric Co. formed earlier in 1903) Messrs. Liberty are the sole agents for the Royal Barum Ware in London, and they are heavy buyers. The alterations to Mr. Brannam's premises have been carried out under the direction of Mr. J.C. Southcombe, architect, Mr. W. Slee being the contractor. Messrs Croot & Son of High St. were responsible for the beautiful decorative work, which was carried out under the personal supervision of the head of the firm.

"Mr. Brannam has just shipped seventy sets of toilet ware to the Cape, while a

number of the choicest pieces of Barum ware — selected by Mr. Beit, the South African millionaire, who has recently been staying at Ilfracombe — have been forwarded to the Public Museum in Hamburg as specimens of British art pottery".
On the facing page of the Journal the accompanying advertisement appeared:—

C H BRANNAM
Begs to THANK the Public for the Support
so liberally extended to him during the
last 22 Years.
He has the honour to announce that NEW AND
SPACIOUS SHOW-ROOMS HAVE JUST BEEN COMPLETED
at the Works, where Customers can Select the
Ware under favourable conditions.
Amongst the present Stock will be found some remarkable
specimens of the Potter's Art.
He trusts by Close Attention to all Orders
entrusted to him to receive a continuance of
their Liberal Patronage.
PLEASE NOTE ONLY ADDRESS:
LITCHDON POTTERY
close to Ancient (1627) Penrose Homes.
BARNSTAPLE
VISITORS CAN THERE SEE POTTERS AT WORK

APPENDIX 1C.

The following account dates from 1910, the year of the Brussels exhibition and is from the Brannam records.

ALL THE PIECES SHOWN IN THE PHOTOGRAPHS ARE EXECUTED BY HAND, BEING THROWN ON THE POTTERS' WHEEL AND HAND DECORATED.

No. 1. The forms were designed and executed in blue glazes by C.H. Brannam, the large vase was decorated with fish decoration by F. Braddon, also the Plaque by the same decorator. The two other decorated vases were hand modelled by F. Braddon. The others were designed by C.H. Brannam, and are executed in plain colour in soft Blues, Greens, Reds, Old Golds, Pink and Soft Shadings.

No. 2. The two lizard vases, also the Old English Vase were designed and executed by C.H. Brannam and decorated by T. Liverton. The other forms were designed by C.H. Brannam, and are finished in the same colours as No. 1.

We are honoured by Royal Warrant of Appointment to H.R.H. Princess Christian, and have received the patronage of H.M. King of Norway this year. We exhibited at the St. Louis Exhibition, also at the Brussels Exhibition this year.

                                                              Charles William Brannam

Fig. 142 Two versions of the moulded boot. a. with cat,private collection b. with mice MND

APPENDIX 2A.

Some Original Ceramists by Cosmo Monkhouse
(From *The Magazine of Art V* 1882)

An abridged version of the article which compares and contrasts the work of Robert Wallace Martin and his brothers of Southall with that of Charles Brannam at Barnstaple.

The introduction speaks of the Revival movement, and after mentioning the firms of Messrs Doulton and the Royal Potteries at Worcester who 'have large capital which enables them to use accomplished artists', goes on to describe 'two small independent ones founded by men of especial talent in decoration whose art work deserves to be more widely known'. — viz. Mr. Robert Wallace Martin and Mr. Brannam. It describes their work as 'pure and honest' and continues: 'they do not attempt to rival nature by modelling flowers in relief, petal by petal, nor do they use the body of their jugs and vases as a canvas on which to paint Turneresque landscapes ... their jugs remain, their proper form beautified but not concealed, their use evident and unambiguous.

The brothers Martin make stoneware only, and glaze it with salt. Mr. Brannam makes ordinary porous earthenware covered with different coloured slips, and glazes it with lead. The Martins employ all kinds of decoration, from modelling in relief to flat painting; Mr. Brannam only one kind — viz. imposing a pattern in one slip on the ground of another, sometimes modelling it in extremely shallow relief, so that the flatness of the surface and consequently the shape of the article as thrown on the wheel are not perceptibly disturbed. In character 'Martin' decoration is sculpturesque, architectural, and naturalistic in turns, and is far more varied than Mr. Brannam's; but Mr. Brannam has a gift for original patterns and the conventionalization of natural objects specially suited for the decoration of pottery, and very rare in Modern European art.

Then follows a description of the bas-relief of the potters wheel, followed by a short history of Martinware.

About two years ago one of the partners of the well-known firm of Messrs Howell and James, who is a Devonshire man, brought a few of Mr. Brannam's earlier attempts to London, and showed them to Mr. Buxton Morrish, another partner in the same firm. Mr. Morrish at once divined the talent and originality latent in the rough but artistic designs, and sent down his manager to Barnstaple to make definite proposals to Mr. Brannam, to assist him in developing his new ware, and to become his sole representative in London, where he conferred with Mr. Morrish, whose taste and experience were, I believe of much value in suggesting variations as to shape and colour. Professor Church, who was then delivering his series of Cantor lectures on artistic pottery at the Society of Arts, brought some specimens of Barum-ware before his audience; and the encouragement thus received was not lost, for Mr. Brannam has not only set his inventive faculty to work in producing many excellent and novel designs, but has greatly extended the range and improved the quality of his colour.

The character of the decoration and shapes of Barum ware is shown in our cuts of bottles and vases. Some of the vases are of considerable size and executed with skill. The designs consist of panels of various forms sympathising with the shapes of the vessels, and filled with conventionalised birds, fishes and flowers which show much fertility of invention and decorative ingenuity. The panels are separated by bold scrolls and zigzags, and the corners and odd spaces filled up with globes, shells and other plain and effective forms, which give the work an individuality of a somewhat archaic character: as though an early Egyptian or Trojan potter had transmitted his simple artistic feeling to his successor in Devon. As to the colour, in addition to the contrasts of white and red and brown and yellow with which he first started, Mr. Brannam now produces very soft and rich combinations of chocolate and blue, leaf green and pale yellow, and other secondaries and tertiaries. It is impossible to say of what other beautiful developments Martinware and Barum-ware are capable, but what the founders of these potteries have already accomplished is quite sufficient to entitle them to an honourable place in the list of England's original ceramists.

"F. C. G.'S" CARTOONS.

EXHIBITION IN LONDON

[FROM AN OLD CONTRIBUTOR.]

MR. F. CARRUTHERS GOULD requests the honour of a visit to a Private View of his Original Westminster Cartoons, 1901-2, and Illustrations of Froissart's Modern Chronicles, on Friday, June 20th, 1902, 10 to 6 o'clock.

The Continental Gallery (Imperial Room), 157, New Bond St., W.

H. E. NICHOLLS, *Sec.*

Fig. 143 Entrance Card to a Gould Exhibition. 1902 from North Devon Journal

APPENDIX 2B

BARUM WARE
An article 'from a correspondent' which appeared in 'The Artist' V (1881)

Not very long ago, as a well-known connoisseur in decorative art, Mr. Owen Davis, was strolling down one of the picturesque streets of Barnstaple (of which 'Barum' is the early English name), some specimens of quaint pottery caught his eye. At once perceiving the genius and originality they displayed, he made enquiries and found the maker, Mr. C.H. Brannam was the owner of a small local pottery, and late a pupil of the Barnstaple School of Art. Besides being possessed of artistic feeling and industry, Mr. Brannam was found to be a man of sufficient modesty to accept hints; the "Barum Ware" has been developed, and some of the results may now be seen in the galleries of Messrs. Howell and James. Mr. Brannam's early specimens are quaintly shaped jars, &c of rich red body coated with creamy white slip, the incised patterns showing the red ground, the general effect old-fashioned and charming. Under the valuable suggestions of the gentleman already alluded to, the ware has grown bolder in shape, and the glaze, in ruddy browns, rich greens, and a cool celadon grey, is in itself a delight to the artistic beholder. The price of Barum ware is, so far, extremely moderate. I purchased a large jardinière, with a beautiful incised pattern of conventional orange trees, griffins, &c, for 30s.; some lovely tall jars, 'the very thing' for the top of a corner cupboard, were 18s., while smaller specimens were only 7s. or 8s. This ware has met with distinct approval from no less a judge than Professor Church of the Royal Academy, who in one of his recent lectures brought it before the notice of his audience with these words, 'The productions of this old Barnstaple pot work stand quite alone in material, decoration, and manner of their execution. This Barum ware reminds one of the rare Italian Sgraffiato ware, and some of the quaintest English work of the 17th century. Mr. Brannam designs, makes, decorates, and signs each piece with his own hand".

'SABRETASCHE'

APPENDIX 3

Frank Carruthers Gould. Political Cartoonist

Of all the ideas offered by fellow Barumites to Charles Brannam, the most unusual and productive were of a graphic nature, in the form of pen and ink drawings sent to the potter by Frank Carruthers Gould, son of Richard David Gould, the Borough Surveyor. Some years older than Brannam, he had been brought up in Barnstaple, attending the same school and; moving to London at the age of twenty to join the Stock Exchange, soon gaining a reputation for his caricatures of brokers and dealers; so much so that Mr. Labouchere, the Editor of *Truth* featured his sketches in the Xmas number of 1881,[1] this becoming an annual event. In 1887 he produced a book of Stock Exchange celebrities, 'filled with portraits of Throgmorton Street magnates, drawn with delightful ease and humour'.[2] ('Jubilee Junketings').

In this year he joined the Pall Mall Gazette, continuing later with the Westminster Gazette. His caricatures were now political. In September the 'Journal' judged that he had made 'the political hit of the season with his 'Jonah' cartoon'. 'It represents Mr. Chamberlain, the Jonah of the ship 'Unionist' being cast overboard, a whale labelled 'Fisheries' is prepared for his reception'. An added quote from a London correspondent underlines his success: 'Mr. Gould is a stockbroker by profession but he is so successful as a cartoonist and has developed such original and remarkable powers of political satire that it may be hoped that he will steadily train himself into the position of one of the first caricaturists of the day. In humour, in power of rapidly catching a likeness and in capacity for putting character as well as fun into his work, Mr. Gould I think has no more rivals than two or three famous men whom I could name. As a political satirist he improves every year, his happiest inspirations being those which are most obviously impromptu. If Punch is wise it will get hold of Mr. G. before he is much older'.[3]

Mr. Gould was not so sure. Writing some years later of his early life in London:- 'I went to the Stock Exchange when I was twenty and there I had a wide field. For many years I used to make rough sketches of personal incidents and jokes, and no doubt my experience there was a great help to me in political caricature. I am bound honestly to say that I do not look back on my early efforts with any feelings of satisfaction.

In fact he had been sketching from boyhood. Writing in*The Million* in May 1894, he described his early years. In Barnstaple where he drew

.... mostly for the amusement of my friends. I learned orthodox drawing from a drawing master (Peter Jackson); but I always had a liking for pen and ink, and I broke out naturally into caricature. I used to practise on the unfortunate borough gaolkeeper ... with youthful brutality. He was a good subject. As a borough official he had to take part in municipal processions and as the window of the Bank[4] in

Fig. 144 Two early Barnstaple cartoons by F.C. Gould. Jailer Trewin a. as Orator
b. as Prize Pig fed by the Mayor NDDA

which I was a clerk overlooked the Guildhall, he had to pass me bearing a portenteous mace. He couldn't escape but he used to scowl at me as he passed, and kick out his near hind leg viciously, to show his feelings. He went to the Mayor[5] of the town once to complain of me, and when his worship pooh poohed the matter he triumphantly exclaimed:- 'That 'baint the worst of it zur. 'E's been a caricaturin' of you too!'

Further remniscences, this time from Mr. Harper,[6] one of the town's historians, record his own memories of Mr. Gould as a young man, not long left school and working at the Old Bank. 'His chief delight seems to have been in the sketching of the customers, the manager of a rival Bank,[7] the police and the town jailer. Mr. Gould formed a music class under Mr. Belchar who had to teach Shallah's system of singing, at which however he did not seem to make much progress. He produced a very interesting caricature of the old gentleman ... and also a 'take-off' of the Blue Boys (Bluecoat Schoolboys).[8] In the picture of the first he represents him as the 'Old Cottage Clock — a composition by Mr. Belchar who tells him his sketch is very good'.

> 'But believe me dear Frank, you cannot do worse
> Than ally to your pictures such shocking bad verse,
> Be advised, go to London, enlist in the ranks
> of the artists of Punch, 'twill pay better than Banks!'

At the beginning of 1898 Mr. Gould embarked on a lecture tour, entitled *Peeps into Parliament from the Press Gallery*, the talks were illustrated with caricatures, sketches and portraits, shown by means of a 'magic lantern ' or epidiascope. After visiting many large towns he gave a lecture at Bideford on Wednesday, January 30, followed subsequently by a visit to his home town. In mid March an article in *The Rival* showed a caricature of himself 'On Tour' and in May he held his first exhibition at the Continental gallery in Bond Street, London; the first of a series of annual shows organised by Mr. H E Nicholls. On this first occasion one hundred and fifty examples of his political cartoons were displayed. (In later years he used the Doré gallery and the Brook Street gallery). The shows were usually arranged for June or July and for many years entrance cards bore an original cartoon, indicating the theme of the show. His humour appealed to all parties and the exhibitions were always well attended, the most popular cartoons having been sold prior to the opening. The 1906 exhibition featured the General Election where the favourite cartoon, bought by Lord Rosebery, portrayed 'the assimilation of Mr. Chamberlain as chief of the cannibal island, in suitable attire'. Balfour/Chamberlain relations were lampooned with a crocodile labelled 'Protection' inviting Mr. Balfour to 'Come inside and we shall be one'.

Mr. Gould was a life-long liberal and 'Whether the party was in power or in opposition his jokes were never extravagant, always good-humoured and had a gentlemanly dignity in the Tenniel tradition'.[9] He was once described as the:

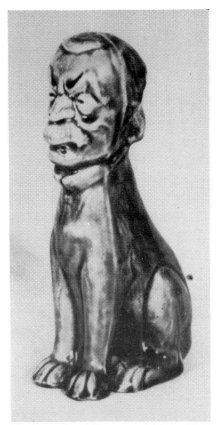

Fig. 145 a. Lloyd George model. 'The Welsh Terrier'. Courtesy C.H. Brannam ltd.

b. Lloyd George. Original drawing by Gould, pottery records

PATRONISED BY HER MAJESTY   **QUEEN MARY - - - 1913.**

ROYAL BARUM WARE

——— (BY ROYAL WARRANT OF APPOINTMENT). ———
REGD. NO. 44561.

Messrs. C. H. Brannam

LATEST ADDITIONS TO THE "BARUM" POLITICAL SERIES:

"DIE HARD" TOBY. JUG.   "THE WELSH TERRIER."

A choice of 4,000 articles, varying in price from 3d. to £4 4/-

LITCHDON ST. (AT THE BACK OF IMPERIAL HOTEL) BARNSTAPLE.

No connection with any other local Pottery.   [9406

c. Advertisement from North Devon Journal, 1913

Fig. 146 Lord Halsbury Toby Jug. Original ink and colour wash drawing, pottery records

BY ROYAL WARRANT OF APPOINTMENT

SUPPORT ONE OF YOUR OLDEST LOCAL INDUSTRIES
EMPLOYING BRITISH LABOUR BY PURCHASING THE ORIGINAL

ROYAL BARUM WARE

Reg. No. 44561.

OUR LATEST PATRIOTIC SERIES OF

H.M. King George V., Lord Kitchener, the late Lord Roberts, Admiral Jellicoe, H.M. the King of the Belgians, General French, General Smith Dorrien.

These are for sale at the Popular Price of 6½d.

A Large Variety of Goods on Show suitable for Christmas and New Year's Gifts.
EARLY MORNING TEA SETS, TABLE CENTRES FOR FLOWERS, BULB
BOWLS, GROTESQUES, &c.

NOTE CAREFULLY OUR NAME AND ADDRESS

C. H. BRANNAM, L⁵ᴰ LITCHDON POTTERY, BARNSTAPLE

NO CONNECTION WITH ANY OTHER **LOCAL** POTTERY.

Fig. 147 Advertisement from Journal, 1912, for Patriotic 'Series'

Fig. 148 Three Political Pieces. a. Kitchener, moulded figure in biscuit fired redware with detail in pale blue blue slip. 1913. One of a series of seven or more b. Baron Kruger Jug in royal blue glaze by William Baron, design of pig with head of President Kruger and comment:– 'Kruger The Old Boar' c. Chamberlain figure. 1899, C.H.B. Barum, after a drawing by Frank Carruthers Gould. 5 1/2" emerald green and black moulded design

Fig. 149 Kruger/Chamberlain Plaque by Brannam from drawing by Gould . Showing Joseph Chamberlain as Brer Rabbit engaged in a game of cards. 1990, courtesy Keith Baker, London

Fig. 150 Three Political Caricatures from Gould drawings, a. a Kruger money box in browns. greens, blue and off–white, (5 1/2"), signed 'C.H. Brannam, Barum, dated 1900 b. and c. Pair of figures – Brer Fox and Brer Rabbit after designs by Carruthers Gould, b. in blues, greens and browns, 5 1/4", signed 'C,H. Brannam, Barum' and dated 1899 c. in greens, browns, blue and off–white, 13cm, signed 'C.H. Brannam, BARUM',dated 1899. All three courtesy of Keith Baker, London

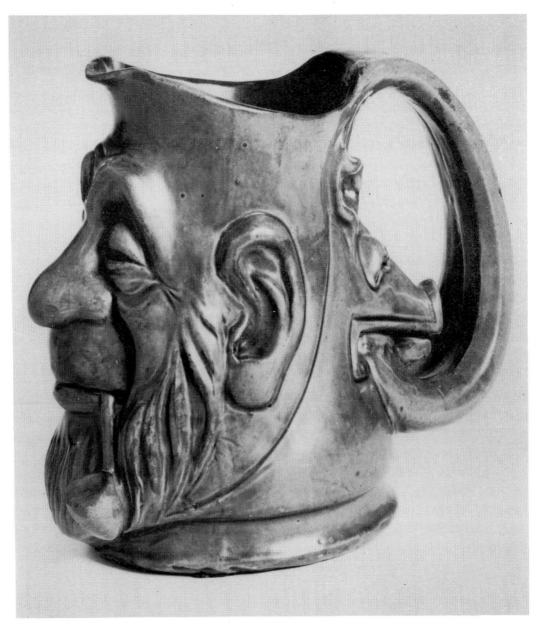

Fig. 151 Modelled jug from a cartoon of President Kruger by Gould 1900. Keith Baker, London

The trough was full, the greedy Boar
Drank quartz and quartz, yet dirtied more;
And while he quaffed the grateful flow,
He kept one eye on cruel Joe!
But Joseph when he'd cracked his whip,
Began to speak of fellowship:
He said he did but bring a letter
To ask if Mistress Boar was better.
But Boars by nature are suspicious,
He bit poor Joe—he was so vicious!

Fig. 152 From the 'Political Struwwelpeter'. 'Joe' Chamberlain and Kruger the Boar

.... biggest asset of the Liberal party. In the dark hours of Liberal dissension and of national disgrace he is always to the fore, good-humouredly holding up his accentuating mirror to men and events, compelling his adversaries to see the humorous absurdity of their position. In this way he is more than a Liberal asset. He is a John Bull, genial, facile, a natural.

During the Liberal administration of 1907/08 Mr. Gould[10] was able to 'cover every vulnerable point of the opposition to the Liberal programme' which covered the Licensing Bill, Old Age Pensions, the Irish Bill for partial self-government and the defeated Education Bill. The Irish question featured 'seven prominent Unionists in a row in a bed, Mr. Balfour a comfortable outsider, the others saying 'When Arthur says Fudge we all say Fudge': Another cartoon showed Mr. David Lloyd George defying the whole of the licensed trade and in another he is confronted by a fearsome Giant Goliath, who challenges him with "Aren't you afraid?" and the little chap replies defiantly, "Not a bit". The principal cartoon of the 1908 Exhibition, which was bought by the Earl of Crewe was the famous parody of the story of Cock Robin. Thirteen separate drawings portrayed those who were most prominently 'in at the death and obsequies' of the Education Bill, with the addition of the Prime Minister, Mr. Campbell Bannerman, and the lines:

> 'Who'll tell the people?'
> 'I', said C.B.
> 'You'll leave that to me.
> I'll tell the people'.

Mr. Gould also was the author of several books of caricatures including 'The Political Struwwelpeter' (1899) — a skit on the book of cautionary tales by Heinrich Hoffman. With verses by Harold Begbie it satirised the political figures of the day: in the opening story of Cruel Frederick (Cruel Joseph Chamberlain), the role of the faithful Dog Tray is assumed by a 'boarish' President Kruger.[11] Mr. C. makes a later appearance as the long red-legged scissor man, dealing out the 'hands off' treatment to a chastened Arthur (Balfour). Others who came under his scrutiny were Campbell Bannerman, Lord Salisbury, Ramsay Macdonald and Bishop Temple. The cartoonist also produced a Struwwelpeter Alphabet and, in a lighter vein 'in his happiest style' the illustrations for a new version of Brentanos Fairy Tales'. (1887).

   In 1903 Mr. Gould was granted the Freedom of the Borough of Barnstaple and a few years later received a knighthood. To conclude, we will let him have the last word in this chapter which is, after all, his.

'I do not profess to be a good draughtsman[12] and I am painfully conscious of hardness and crudeness but my leading motive is to get a grip on the idea I wish to convey, to give life and expression to a face. For caricature is not a mere matter of careful drawing, it is more of a faculty of appreciation.13 This

faculty enables one to store in the memory the lines which make up and give the life expression to a face, and to put subjects before the public in a form which may be crude, but bears the impress of reality. Caricaturists are not made. Like Topsy, they grow and like some larvae, they eat their way out through the husks of their surroundings'.

Footnotes *(See footnote numbers in text)*

1. The 'Journal' calls him 'The Tenniel of the Stock Exchange who keeps the brokers and dealers amused all the year'.
2. The Journal reported 'The caricature is marked by its usual pungency, Mr. Gould has outdistanced himself in his clever cartoons and henceforth takes high rank as a caricaturist.
3. In fact, Mr. Gould was never among the contributors to Punch, though his reputation seems to have been as great as any of their artists.
4. Barnstaple Old Bank was established in 1791 by partners Mounier Roch, Cutcliffe, Gribble and others. Mr. Roche had no heirs and after his death the Bank was continued at 83 High Street by the partners Drake, Gribble and Marshall. (They also occupied premises at 31 High Street for some years). However, it was through the window of 83 that the young Frank Gould watched the processions lining up in Butchers Row outside the Guildhall, as they still do today.
5. The Mayor portrayed was probably Mr Guppy.
6. Harpers notebooks. courtesy N.D.A.
7. The rival bank was the National Provincial at 86 High Street, on the corner of Cross Street, then only recently established in place of the North Devon Bank (Pyke, Scott, Law and Bencraft) The manager was at that time Mr. Guppy.
8. This school, already mentioned as the first charity boys school originally occupied premises above the North Gate but when this was demolished, new premises were built on the Strand at the end of High Street and facing the river Yeo. Continuing for a while as a boys school, it later became a mixed school when the girls from the Alice Horwood school were assimilated. Frank Gould lived directly opposite until 1898 when the area was cleared to make way for the Barnstaple/Lynton railway. Gould senior was responsible for the building of 'Monkey Island' — a small patch of land in the middle of the river Yeo. The borough surveyor had an unfortunate tic which disfigured his face and this may have been the reason for the island's title.
9. Report N.D.J. June 1910
10. 'Review of Reviews' 23.7.03
11. It seems very likely that William Baron used this cartoon as a basis for his figure of Kruger the Boar.
12. N.D.J. article. 1894.
13. The North Devon Museum have a small collection of Gould's original sketches.

APPENDIX 4

Mottoes on Brannam Pieces

Long may she live
Happy may he be
Blest with content
and from misfortune free.

Be aisy If ye can't be aisy
be as aisy as ye can.

Forbid a fool a thing
and he will do it.

Beef when you're hungry
Beer when you're dry
Bed when you're weary
Heaven when you die.

Use the means
Heaven will send
the blessing.

Good wishes to you my friend
The best of all wealth
Love, Comfort and Health
And a heart that is
thankful for all.

A Millstone and the human heart
Are driven ever round
If they have nothing else to grind
They must themselves be ground.

Do the work that's nearest
Though 'tis dull the while
Helping when you meet them
Lame dogs over stiles.

The World has battle room for all
Go! fight and conquer if ye can
But if ye rise or if ye fall
Be each — Pray God a gentleman.

From Mother Earth I took my birth
Then formed a Cup by Man
And now stand here
Filled with good cheer
Taste of me if you can.

A little house a little wealth
A little health and freedom
And at the end a little friend
And little cause to need 'em.

I slept and I dreamt
That life was beauty
I woke and I found
That life was duty.

APPENDIX 5

The Brannam Pottery in the Thirties. Two Recollections

The principals of the firm during the years I worked there were C.W. Brannam and Jack Brannam. There were nine potters (throwers) in all, including Harry Roberts who threw the large pots. The others were Charlie Guard, Thomas Parsley, Ernest Clements, Bert Gammon, William Chapple, Philip Chapple (brother), Frank Parsley and Stan Trent.[1] A Corgi deisel engine with an endless belt attached kept six potters busy every day for nine hours a day (Saturday half-day). The engineer was Jimmy Stevens. Attendants kept the potters supplied with balls of clay and took away the pots for firing. These were Bunny Clements, Eddie Pile and R. Richards. Percy Spurway and George Hill were in charge of the slips and Jimmy Cox of the glazing.

Rough clay for the flower pots, the cooking and mixing bowls and the salters etc. was processed by kneading with the feet in layers, and left for twenty four hours. The operators were Jack Dennis and Freddie Smale. The clay for the finer pottery ware was processed through presses by Dick Cann and Bill Symons. Two trips were made daily from the pits at Bickington to bring the clay by horse and cart. (Mr. McManus and one other). A four-wheeled hand cart was also used to take pottery to the market in Butchers Row on Fridays, where the pottery was sold from a showroom.

There were three firing houses or kilns: Little kiln, Big kiln and Skuttor. The last named was used for firing the plain earthenware while the Little kiln was used both for the first slip firing and also for the second. The Big Kiln held all three named. Firemen were James Hutchings, Didley Barrow, Cecil Harris and Jack Smith. The firing process took from two to three and a half days.

The packing of the terra cotta ware — mostly flower pots, was in the hands of Charlie Courtney who lived nearly opposite the pottery and kept a spare set of keys to the premises. This ware was packed in railway container vans and lorries of fifty tons or more. Sam Pinn was in charge of the glazed ware. This was always packed in large crates or barrels and mostly collected by the Great Western Railway for transit from the depot in Victoria Road.

Footnotes (*See footnote numbers in text*)

1. Also working from 1931 was the Vernon family who had come down from Staffordshire to join the firm. The father, Joe was an expert modeller and mould maker. Two sons helped in the moulding process and his wife and daughter also worked in the pottery. Joe was a weight-lifting fanatic and his strength was very useful in putting back the belt on the Jolley. Joe made the moulds for the WW2 Toby Jugs — Churchill, Stalin and Roosevelt.

APPENDIX 5

The Brannam pottery in the Thirties. Recollection from George Ovey.

George Ovey joined Brannam's pottery from school in 1929 and stayed until 1937 when he left to go to Alexanders pottery in Newport, South Wales, where the pay was better. His starting pay at Brannams was ten shillings a week and in addition he could earn 6d an hour in overtime. Most of his time at the pottery was spent as a ball maker or turning the wheel for the potter. Latterly he worked with Charlie Guard. In the evenings he was allowed to work on the wheel for half an hour when he learnt to make a puzzle jug. He worked a forty-eight hour week, from eight o'clock to six, with an hour for dinner and from eight to twelve on Saturdays. Describing his work he explained:—

> "You had to keep a potter going. One bloke used to carry the clay to the different potters and the boy would wedge it — they had the scales — say a three inch pot was a certain weight. They had a ball box by the side of the wheel — that's how it was done. It was one perpetual motion — about every hour maybe a break — sit in the toilet and smoke — you weren't allowed to smoke — only on overtime".
>
> I used to work with Charlie Guard. Old Mr. Brannam very much liked the old pieces made of white clay which he enjoyed selling in the shop; so during the summer months he asked Charlie Guard to make some for him. Mr. Brannam would say 'Charlie, will you work overtime for me for a few nights? I'll pay you — I want some white clay pots — and I'll pay the boy ...' This maybe happened twice in a season and we'd have about two or three months after six o'clock. Charlie Guard would mention it to Jack Brannam and he wouldn't be very happy about it. Looking back I don't see why not. All right, he was interrupting production but they were selling the stuff.
> "In the summer when the visitors came Mr. Brannam would be in the showroom. The place would be crowded and if anyone went for any of his old pots he loved it. I could watch — there was a glass door — it used to fascinate me — there was something about him — people would pick something up and go to *him*, not to the girls — and he'd explain — and be very disappointed if they didn't buy it. I used to like him very much — he was a nice old gentleman — not because he'd give me a tanner in and out but ..."

George continues to make and fire pots in a shed at the end of his garden, and these include his own version of the puzzle jugs he learnt to make at the Brannam pottery more than half a century ago.

PART IV

ALEXANDER LAUDER

1836 — 1921

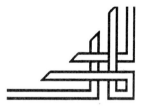

Fig.153 The Lauder Pottery at Pottington, (from an original photograph)

Fig. 154 A very large Brannam Pear–shaped Vase, decorated in blues, browns, beige and cream with fish and shells. Height 26" 1895, courtesy Phillips, Fine Art Auctioneers

Alexander Lauder. 1836 — 1921

FOREWORD

The records of the pottery at Pottington have probably long since been destroyed — at least there is very little left in local archives; while there are no remaining relatives, apart from Lauder's grandson, Brian Lauder Thomas, himself a designer in stained glass with an international reputation. Personal memories of his stay at Ravelin during the first World War recall an old man, blind for the last six years of his life; while letters to Mrs. Audrey Lloyd gave her valuable information , especially of his grandfather's early life in Edinburgh. This correspondence led to meetings with Mr. Thomas, effected by Mr. Taylor, the Town Clerk and the gift to the town of two pen and ink drawings by Mr. Lauder and cartoons of Mr. Thomas's windows.

It has been impossible to find anyone locally with a clear recollection of the pottery at Pottington, which closed in 1914:- the water colour (by Theodore Charbonnier, Headmaster at the School of Art) and the photograph are probably the sole remaining pictorial records. The greater part of the information for this account (as well as for information on the other two potters) was gleaned from the contemporary reports in the North Devon Journal, local parish records, the Census records and local Directories. Thanks are due to the patient and willing assistance of the staff of the North Devon Athenaeum over the last ten years, and also to Peter Christie for his foresight and organisation in the provision of an index of information to the Journal local news from its founding up until the 1890s:- so greatly simplifying the task of the researcher.

A complete life of Lauder has been recorded here; not only to detail his contribution to the Art pottery of Barnstaple but as a public record of this remarkable man whose whole life was devoted to the people of the town.

THE FAMILY

Alexander's father was a Scot but his mother, Mary was a local girl, daughter of John Sommerwill (Sommerville), a yeoman farmer of Landkey. Her three elder brothers do not seem to have been very interested in farming for, by their early forties John and George were working at Pottington Point, on Rolle Quay. John, the prime mover started a shipyard where, over a period of seven years he built six vessels.[1] He also managed a lime kiln adjacent to the yard where his two brothers, George and James, together with a relative, Lewis worked for between ten and fifteen years. Limestone for burning was shipped in along the Taw from Caldy. At this time lime was in great demand by farmers who relied on it as a fertiliser.[2] The chief local quarries were at Venn, Swimbridge, Filleigh, South Molton and Combe Martin. There were many lime kilns on the banks of the Taw:- at Ashford, Heanton and two at both Fremington and Vellator, near Braunton; as well as others further upstream. In the mid-century the demand for lime was so great that farmers sent their carts to Vellator for loads before dawn in order to be first and ensure a supply. Towards the close of the century, however, the industry declined owing to the importation of guano from Peru and the invention of artificial manures such as bone ash and nitrate of soda.

In the 1830s most of the wedge-shaped piece of land we now know as Rolle Quay, owned at that time by the Rolle family was very marshy, the Sommerwills being the only occupiers. By 1843 the land on the Braunton side was farmed by William Fisher who occupied a farmhouse there. Although not noted on the tithe map of that period, there must have been accommodation for the Sommerwills who, at the 1841 census occupied Pottington Cottage. This could have been the 'rather pleasant Georgian house with a walled garden' recalled by Brian Lauder Thomas[3] in a letter to a friend in the 1850s. In the mid 1840s Mary Sommerwill, her husband, John Lauder and their three children occupied the house when John took over ownership and management of the kiln.[4] It was probably at about this time that George left (though he continued as a limeburner elsewhere until his death). James followed later, leaving just Lewis, who remained with Mary after her husband's death in 1865.

After the construction of a road and bridge over the Yeo, connecting Pilton with Barnstaple, the Hon Mark Rolle developed the area, building a quay; so that by 1850 businesses were being set up there:- John How, a timber merchant, and later Rawle Gammon and Baker's on the other side of the Braunton road. At the same time houses were built to accommodate the working community, as well as an Inn.

John Lauder was a civil engineer who is credited with the discovery of the first artesian well in London. He had worked abroad for some years until ill-health forced him to return to this country. Here he met and married Mary Sommerwill, the couple living for part of the time in London where both sons, Alexander (1836) and John (1845) were born. At the baptism of Elizabeth at Landkey, in 1840, her father was described as a wheelwright. They probably visited Barnstaple a great deal when Alexander was small, especially in the summer when they could have stayed either with the grandparents or at Pottington. There was obviously a happy connection. John Sommerwill named three of his vessels after members of the family:- the 'Alexander', a 2 masted schooner in 1837, the 'Mary Lauder', a smack of 18 tons in 1841 and 'John', probably after his brother-in-law, in 1843.

All three children were educated locally, either at private schools or possibly later at the Wesleyan school, started in 1849. However, in 1851, at the age of fifteen Alexander went to Edinburgh to stay with his uncle and was educated there until the age of 24, studying both architecture and later Art. He returned to Barnstaple on the illness and subsequent death of his brother John in 1860, aged sixteen. It is touching to consider that just a year earlier, in May the family and relatives would all have attended the Bath and West Show, scarcely a stones-throw from their home.[5] Alexander did not return to Edinburgh but instead began to immerse himself in the life of the community. It was not long before he volunteered to teach the young art students at the Literary and Scientific Institution — not an easy task for a young man with no professional training in teaching, but simply a desire to share with them his favourite hobby. Many of the lads lacked even the basic skills, but for others with some training and keenness he was able to develop their early talent which laid the foundations for their future success. He also concerned himself in parochial and civic affairs and especially in the furtherance of free and full education.

Having finished his training, he set up in practice as an architect and surveyor, probably in 1864, with his first office in Barbican Terrace. Two years later he married Mary Widlake, second daughter of Pascal and Sarah Widlake, members of his church who were drapers in the town and descended from an old Huguenot family. The practice was moved to 40 High Street, then, by 1870 they were living and working at 47 High Street. Two children were born: Louis Cecil in 1868 and Evelyne in 1871 but sadly both died within a few days of each other, probably from a childish ailment such as Scarlet Fever or Measles which in those days, when assuming epidemic proportions all too often proved fatal in the very young (May 1874). However, they did have two more children: Leonard, born within a year or so and Margaret Mary in 1878. In 1865, Alexander's father who had been in failing health for some years died at his home in Pottington leaving his son in charge of the lime kiln.

Footnotes *(See footnote numbers in text)*

1. **Information from PILTON by Margaret Reed**
2. **Information from 'Some dead industries of North Devon' Devonshire Association Yearbooks, N.D.A.**
3. **Alexander Lauder's grandson.**
4. **A directory of 1850 mentions a Lauder at Pottington House.**
5. **See earlier chapter.**

Fig. 155   Marwood Chapel, from an original drawing by Ken Lloyd

Fig. 156 Two ceramic fireplaces, Ravelin. Photos by Andy Robinson

THE ARTIST AND ARCHITECT

When he was fifteen years old Alexander was sent to stay with his uncle, Alexander Lauder, at 'Goschen' near Edinburgh while he was articled to the well known Edinburgh architect, Alexander Black. During this period he was able to persuade his family to allow him to break his articles to fulfil his ambition to study art at The Trustees Academy in Edinburgh. Details of his success are contained in a letter written to him in July 1855 by a friend, John Laing, who wrote "Allow me to congratulate you by this my earliest opportunity on your great success at the Academy, the greatest success that ever any student attained there — the medal, the Academy's Prize and the Keith Prize".

All his life Alexander Lauder indulged in his love of painting and drawing whenever he could find the time, exhibiting paintings locally and nationally. In 1867 he showed a large oil painting 'Jacob and Rachel' at Mr. Ley's picture gallery in Barnstaple — described in the local newspaper as

> a work of great merit, vigorous in style and masterly in treatment ... the remarkable feature of the picture is the brilliant colouring which, however, is kept in subjection with true artistic instinct, by contrast and tone. It will be on inspection at Mr. Ley's for a few weeks and if not previously purchased will be sent to the Manchester Art Exhibition in June.[1]

Later in 1872 he exhibited further oil paintings at Mr. Ley's gallery on The Strand and these were a pair of original illustrations of old Scotch ballads. *The North Devon Journal* describes them —

> One is 'Fair Annie of Lockroyan' who is pictured reclining in the lap of her 'love Gregor'. The other, and the more attractive, is 'True Thomas parting with the Queen of Elfland' — she blooming on her beautiful palfrey and he in hunting costume with his leash of dogs by his side. The surrounding trees and their foliage are very tastefully conceived and the finished execution makes it a matter of regret that talent capable of such excellence should not have been devoted to painting instead of as a recreation merely.[2]

Further afield, in 1874, Lauder sent an oil painting 'The Sermon on the Mount' to the International Exhibition in London and later the same year he was awarded a medal at the South Kensington International Exhibition for a watercolour — 'St. Paul preaching in the Areopagus in Athens'. It is interesting that this particular painting was described as Lauder's most ambitious watercolour by his grandson, Brian Thomas, a well known artist in stained glass. Writing recently in a letter about his grandfather's influence on his own artistic career he comments:

> When I was a tiny boy I had a passion for drawing, encouraged by my old granddad who, though blind, did scribbles for me with a fluency which fascinated me and no doubt determined me to be an artist with

an architectural bias. The outcome of his rather grandiose approach to art enabled me to work in the 'Grand Manner'. Thus many years later I could design all the stained glass in the apse of St. Paul's Cathedral and six large windows in Westminster Abbey.

So for grandfather and grandson a love of drawing and painting remained with them all their lives, but when Alexander Lauder returned to Barnstaple in 1860, after his years of study in Edinburgh, it was to architecture he turned. He established a practice at Barbican Terrace moving shortly afterwards to premises in the High Street. During the early years he held an art class at the local Literary & Scientific Institution where he gave help and encouragement to many young students by giving them a start in his own office.

Among these was W.G. Davie who won the Royal Academy's Gold Medal and Scholarship in 1871 for the best architectural design for the year and who went on to the office of William Butterfield, an eminent architect of his day. G.L. Morris was also articled to Lauder and in later years exhibited at the Royal Academy. *The Builder* described his two pencil elevations with small plan as "showing a pleasing and picturesque design for a small church built on sloping ground in Gothic design".[3] Another pupil of Lauder, A. Dunn, achieved success further afield in Melbourne where he designed buildings for the Australian Temperance Life Association and a Temperance hospital.

The most notable of these talented pupils was undoubtedly William Lethaby who came to Lauder's office at the age of fourteen, a shy ambitious boy who was to benefit so much from the influence of a teacher who was not only an accomplished painter but an all round craftsman, able to impart an enthusiasm for the ideals of the Arts & Crafts movement. Many years later in 1957 Lauder's grandson, Brian Thomas, at that time Master of the Art Workers' Guild, wrote in a symposium in honour of the centenary of W.R. Lethaby:

"It's surely an example of sheer luck which attends genius that Lethaby should in his formative years have come into contact with Lauder, a man constructively interested in the materials of architecture, in the practice of various branches of craftmanship, in the training of craftsmen and in the integration of his ideas with practical politics — who furthermore was an accomplished painter, a bit of an orator, a poet and a character.[4]

During the 1860's as his architectural practice flourished Lauder served as advisory architect to a number of North Devon landowners including the Bourchier-Wreys and the Chichesters and designed various buildings for the estates. Lethaby himself said later how much he learnt about the purposes of architecture from helping to design functional buildings for the farms on these estates. But for one who devoted so much of his life to the pursuit of Methodist ideals it is not so surprising that the greater part of Lauder's work consisted of Wesleyan chapels not only locally but further afield in the west country and various other places including the London area. In the 1870's he designed five chapels in London, one of which, New Cross, was described in *The Architect* of April 1876 and illustrated by his former pupil W.R. Lethaby. The fine pen and ink drawing shows a symmetrical decorated Gothic structure. The front facade was in Suffolk and Bath stone dressings and the chapel could accommodate over a thousand people.

Locally there are at least a dozen chapels designed by Lauder, most of which are still in use. They vary in size from a style of basic simplicity as in the little chapels of Knowle and Fremington to the larger Decorated Gothic style of the chapels of Barnstaple (recently demolished) and South Molton. In his book *A History of the Methodist Revival of the Last Century* published in 1898, John Gould Hayman wrote:

> Much of the success which has attended these various chapel erections is due to the valuable co-operation of the Architect, Mr. Alexander Lauder, who in addition to generous donations, rendered his professional services in each case gratuitously.

Between the years 1866 and 1900 there are records of at least ten Lauder designed chapels in various parts of the country as far afield as West Sussex and Manchester. Several of these including Southgate Methodist Church, Chichester (1877), the South Norwood Methodist Church (1875) and South Molton Methodist Church (1882) produced historical booklets commemorating their centenaries.

All the larger chapels designed by Lauder were in the Gothic Revival style so popular in the latter half of the last century but a style which engendered some criticism, particularly among those who believed that a departure from the simpler classical form of earlier chapels was in some way a betrayal of the more ascetic ideals of Methodism.

In addition to his chapels, Lauder also designed several Wesleyan Day Schools — at South Molton, Torrington, Braunton and Newport. When the need arose for additional accommodation at the Literary & Scientific Institution he produced plans for a separate building to be erected in the grounds and this work was carried out in 1864.

There is little evidence that Lauder's work in the commercial field was at all extensive but he designed the Co-operative Stores in Joy Street in 1896 the façade of which remains, showing above the ground floor which has been converted into a modern shop-front. The first floor remains as built and is of dressed freestone, four bays wide, with roll moulded window arches. The piers between the arches are set at an angle of forty-five degrees and continued upwards to terminate in grotesque figures on the skyline. Lauder also designed the new building for Michael Squire & Sons in Tuly Street (1903) which is of particular interest in that the tympana of twin pediments contain the figures of farmworkers executed in low relief terra-cotta. This use of sculpture in architecture was evident in Lauder's earlier domestic work particularly at 'Ravelin' one of three villas he built on Shapscote ground, a gentle south facing slope about a mile from Barnstaple.

'Ravelin', Lauder's home for the last twenty or so years of his life, was built of brick and terra-cotta in the Tudor style. The house was embellished with many special brick and terra-cotta features; in chimneys, finials, moulded string courses and two fine terra-cotta figures flanking the front entrance, all manufactured by the Brick & Tile Company which Lauder founded with his brother-in-law W.O. Smith in 1876. It is interesting to note that the standard facing bricks carried the name of Lauder & Smith in a decorated scroll embossed in the frog. (See Marks).

Internally at 'Ravelin' the potter's art is seen to the greatest effect in the terra-cotta fireplaces in the main bedrooms. These fire surrounds were of highly glazed richly coloured tiles, boldly modelled in varying designs incorporating vines, frogs, lizards, owls and human figures all richly coloured and generally similar in style to the art pottery being produced in Lauder's pottery at that time. The plain cream terra-cotta fireplace in the hall was richly moulded in the form of an ogee arch supporting a gorge moulded mantelshelf with tiles of floral design to each side of the opening. The hall extended through two floors and was decorated with bas-relief sgraffito murals in pitch pine surrounds. The panels, twenty-one in all, varied in size to a maximum of five feet wide by fifteen feet high and were executed in situ by Lauder himself, there being two coats of rendering, the undercoat of a rich red brown colour, the top coat a creamy coloured sand cement mix some half inch thick. This second coat was modelled in a free interpretation of Shakespeare's *Midsummer Night's Dream* incorporating in all over one hundred and fifty figures, finely executed and with spirited movement.

Sgraffito work was also carried out by Lauder in another of the villas he built on Shapscote ground and the *North Devon Journal* published in some detail a description of the panels in the hall and round the staircase. Unlike the pitchpine panel surrounds at 'Ravelin' the borders here were of vine, passion flowers, blackberry and leaf, ivy and berries, peacocks and small birds, and these borders were described in the newspaper article as:

> remarkable for the grace which characterises the smallest detail and upon the whole of this unique series of decorative designs Mr. Lauder has lavished the fulness of his art knowledge.[5]

Lauder's enthusiasm for craftmanship led him to:

> insist that all men working on his own buildings should have understanding of one another's craft so that each might feel that he was building a house and not just practising carpentry, bricklaying or plumbing.[6]

LAUDER, THE BARUMITE

The 1880's proved perhaps the busiest years for Alexander Lauder. With his architectural practice well established and his Devon Art Pottery 'on the high-road to success', he became more involved in community activities. He was one of the original members of the Barnstaple School Board, which had held its first meeting on 16th March 1871, and acted as Chairman for many years. His concern for the welfare and education of the young led him to play a prominent part in the founding and development of the Wesleyan Day Schools and in 1880 he was instrumental in inaugurating a local branch of the Y.M.C.A. of which he was Chairman for a number of years.

In 1885/6 Lauder became the first Mayor ever to be elected outside the Town Council and this was only made possible by an Act of Parliament passed just before his election. He was very enthusiastic to establish an annual Art and Industry Exhibition and during May 1886 called a meeting at which the Mayors of Bideford, South Molton and Torrington were present as well as several local manufacturers. Lauder set out his plan in great detail, pointing out the opportunities for manufacturers in North Devon, particularly with markets so easily accessible by rail. He put forward the idea of a special exhibition for handicraft trades such as joinery, smithery, plumbing, stone and woodcarving and stressed the advantages to workers in being able to see for themselves the improvements which had taken place and the progress being made. The Mayor of Torrington promised support but the Mayors of Bideford and South Molton were more cautious in their reception of the scheme. Unfortunately the subscriptions to help finance the project, apart from an initial response from those interested in the scheme, were not forthcoming, so after a few months the project was abandoned. The timing of the scheme was perhaps unfortunate as it apparently suffered from the disturbing influence of a general election which distracted attention from the project. It is probable, however, that seeds were sown then which culminated in the Art School annual exhibitions which began in 1889.

Lauder's popularity and success as Mayor were such that in 1886 he was elected to a second term in succession covering the 1887 celebrations of Queen Victoria's Jubilee. Some of his popularity was no doubt due to his courteous manners and innate kindliness together with his undoubted gift for public speaking. He was affectionately known as 'the silver-tongued Alderman' and was in great demand as a speaker. He could be counted on to lend his support to Liberals in election campaigns and for many years was a lay preacher for the Methodist cause. Testimony to his ability as a preacher is borne out by a newspaper article which refers to:

> three Sunday Services at a local chapel, morning and afternoon conducted by the Pastor while the
> Evening Service was preached by Mr. A. Lauder — the congregations were good on each occasion, that

of the final service being so large that many could not gain admittance to the building.[7]

Mr. W.W. Hutchings writing in *Reminiscences of the Journal and of Barnstaple in the Seventies* declares "Alderman Lauder I remember even more as a gifted preacher than as a publicist". This gift he used to inspire people with the enthusiasm of his own faith which never wavered despite personal tragedy when in 1874 his two young children died within ten days of each other.

His popularity as a preacher and as a public speaker was probably due not only to his eloquence but to the fact that all his life he used his many diverse talents in the service of others. At a time when industrialisation was quickening its pace he feared, as did his contemporaries Ruskin and Morris, that mechanisation would take away men's pride in their work, so he encouraged them to use their skills for the benefit of others and felt that in this way they would gain public approval and their own self respect.

In Barnstaple a century ago Lauder's familiar figure, described by his grandson as short, thickset with bushy beard and flashing eyes, would have been easily recognised and his buildings and his pottery familiar to many.

Footnotes *(See footnote numbers in text)*

1. North Devon Journal 9th May 1867
2. North Devon Journal 21st November 1872
3. North Devon Journal 14th May 1891
4. Thomas, Brian R.I.B.A. Journal Vol. LXIV, 1957 p.218
5. North Devon Journal 1st November 1888
6. Thomas, Brian R.I.B.A. Journal Vol. LXIV, 1957 p.218
7. North Devon Journal July 1880.

Fig. 157 Three small marbled pots by Lauder

ALEXANDER LAUDER. THE POTTERY

BRICKS AND TILES. "HIGH ART"

In the following year (1876), Lauder entered into partnership with his brother-in-law, William Otter Smith who had married his wife's sister, Elizabeth. Mr. Smith worked a group of lime kilns; at Vellator, Braunton, and elsewhere along the Taw. From the Hon Mark Rolle the partners leased a marsh at Pottington, said to contain valuable clay, where Lauder proposed to start a brickworks — an undertaking they hoped would provide employment for both potters and labourers. In fact, in spite of the changing fortunes of the concern, the workforce does seem to have been kept at between thirty and forty for most of the life of the pottery and, in the more prosperous years was probably greater. Unfortunately, although the potter installed modern plant and sophisticated equipment, he encountered great initial difficulties with the clay, the 'fatness' of which demanded slow and even drying. The concern was worked at a loss for a number of years before the difficulties were overcome.[1]

There certainly was a need for good building materials. The town was expanding rapidly and new houses were needed. This fact had been foreseen by others, however — in 1880, four Bideford business men leased 90 acres on Claymoor, not far from Torrington, where there were almost limitless supplies of different kinds of clay. They built an extensive works, capable of producing a hundred thousand bricks a week. When further funds were raised two years later, the works were extended at a cost of twelve thousand pounds. In 1888, the company employed 75 hands and the patent 'continuous' kiln could fire up to 220,000 bricks at a time, while it was claimed that up to 2,500 bricks could be produced in a day. More than one kind of brick was made — all said to be non-absorbent and frostproof — a reputation that was probably justified. The bricks were popular with architects and builders alike and were used for many purposes, not the least being for houses — streets of Marlandbrick houses became a familiar sight both in Barnstaple and in neighbouring towns; while local factories and workshops still display their use — the Brannam pottery buildings and the factories of Shapland and Petters' and Rawle Gammon and Baker. In addition, the 'vitrified granite' bricks were used for waterworks as well as London subways.

This is not to suggest that there was any direct competition between the two brickworks, but Marland's cheapness and speed of production may have been a reason for Lauder to specialise in 'high art' bricks and tiles, which aimed at an entirely different market.

'High art' is a phrase coined from a Journal report in 1883 referring to the catalogue of fancy bricks and tiles that Lauder had just published:

.. an interesting work of art ... there are the sketches of various styles of plain and ornamental bricks, graduating from those required in ordinary building work to specimens which well may come under the denomination of 'high art'. Among them should be mentioned not only neat traceries for cornices, ornamental tiles and creases of attractive device; grooved, chamfered and stepbricks for windows and doors, but also elegant designs in wreath work or ornamental letters, and beautifully modelled panels.

The foregoing report gives just a brief idea of the scope and beauty of the designs. The illustrations, taken from the catalogue (courtesy of the Athenaeum Trust) may be related to the accompanying descriptions and price list:-

Designs for the Cover (See illustrations)

Wreaths	21s each
Ornamental letter tiles	3/6 doz
Corinthian Acanthus Series	15" wide 15s ft.
Acanthus Rosette	25s each
Gothic	21s each
Head & Wing	25s each
Louis Quinze	25s each

Plate 6

Patarae for panels (21 — 26)	12/6 each

Plate 8

Ridge Creases	from 4/6 per doz (plain) to 10/- per doz (fancy)

Plate 10

Ornamental tiles for string courses (1 — 18)	3/6 — 5/- a doz
Lions head (20)	4/6 a doz

But this proved to be only the beginning of the art work. In May of the following year (1884), at the Devon County Show in Exeter, Lauder had a special exhibit, made for Sir John H.T.B. Wrey, Bart; to be inserted at Tawstock Quadrangle. This consisted of 'a handsome hand-modelled escutcheon date-plate'. This was followed in September by his first figures:- 'two busts, one of Lord Beaconsfield and the other of the present

Prime Minister' (William Ewart Gladstone) 'which are modelled by hand from photographs of these statesmen'. These showed great skill as did a modelled bust of John Gay, poet and dramatist who attended the Grammar School in Barnstaple. This last piece was commissioned by William Frederick Rock and placed in the Grammar school in the summer of 1885. In January of the same year the Journal again reported — on work done for Sir John Whitaker Ellis M.P. and late Lord Mayor of London, for part of the front of an ornamental structure, (probably an orchid or a plant house) in the grounds of his house in Byfleet.

> ...The pieces consist of a central escutcheon 3ft in width, with the initials "J. W E", on each side of which is placed a handsome medallion of the mythological Pan, executed from drawings furnished to the modeller. The latter figure may be regarded as the greatest success which has been achieved in Pottington ware — the material of which it is formed gives good expression to the rubicund features usually assigned to this mythical person.

He also made a shield with central domino for the Ilfracombe Arcade — a victim of the first of the two fires which destroyed this edifice. Probably the only remaining work by Lauder in situ and made at this time by Lauder are the twin pediments above the original front to the Squires' building in Tuly Street — (1903) except of course 'Ravelin'.

Workers at the pottery

Failing records, there is little known about the staff at the pottery. However, it is known that Lauder's chief potter, (at first brickmaker) was Charles Hill. He was very talented so he was probably responsible for carrying out much of the work described in the last paragraph. (The tone of the reports suggests that the preparatory work was done, then passed on to a craftsman to carry through). Coming originally from Bideford and already in his thirties, it is likely that Charles Hill would have trained at one of the Bideford potteries. According to a relative he could neither read nor write — an omission that Lauder, no doubt would have remedied. It has been suggested, again by a relative that his employer sent him to America to gain experience in other methods and techniques — possibly even to seek for a solution to the problems of glazing that were encountered when Mr. Lauder set out to make his experimental Art pottery. His eldest son, Samuel Hill also worked at the pottery where he was a decorator, having trained for some time at the School of Art where pieces of his work were shown at two annual Exhibitions.

Relatives of the family have great pride in their connection with the Art pottery and some fine pieces are retained by them. Two other names are known for the latter years of the pottery — a Mr. Sanders, who was thrower there at the same time as a young designer named William Edward Burgess. Burgess joined Lauder straight from school, training as a designer at the same time as attending art classes at the School. He was there long enough to become skilled — a 'pair' of vases[2] which he made and decorated bear his signature but not the name of the pottery. He was allowed to keep them — until a few years ago they were still retained by the family. On his leaving the pottery — to join up, others may too have left and this was probably when the decision was made to close the pottery down (1914).

It is quite possible that Lauder followed Henry Doulton's example by employing ladies as decorators. In 1894 he was advertising for "Ladies of Artistic Talent" to apply for employment. At that time there were many young female students in training at the Art school — a far cry from thirty years earlier when classes were catering for males only (the teacher of French who had rashly accepted ladies into a mixed class, had considerable trouble with discipline and eventually gave up). Lauder himself advertised places for ladies in his Art classes in 1865, but there is no record of enrolment. In view of this gesture to the as-yet unemancipated female, it would be pleasing to confirm that in 1894 he did have applications from would-be female decorators who may have become his top designers.

Footnotes *(See footnote numbers in text)*

1. **Strong Industries**
2. **'pair' indicates two vases of the same shape but with different designs — a common feature of this potter's work.**

Lauder Commemorative Mugs

Not many have come to light, but there probably are others.

CORONATION KING GEORGE VJune 22nd 1911   pale blue jug
June 22nd 1911   A Souvenir of the Coronation   dark green mug
                       Of King George and Queen Mary.
both are written in sgraffito:

THE ART POTTER

After developing his "High Art", Lauder turned his attention to experimental Art pottery. He had already made many vases and flower pots — some 'ornamented with rich designs on a red ground' (1883) and in 1888 'handsome vases of various and beautiful designs on half pillar stands — from small tuzzas to large fruit and flower vases 5 ft in height ... orchid pots and pendants of original designs *formed of leaves and flowers* in terra cotta, with suitable openings for orchids; pretty conservatory pots and baskets *ornamented with roses, ferns* etc.

In 1886 it should have been just a short step away from coloured and glazed Art Pottery. In fact the 'brick' pottery proved to be highly unsuitable for colouring and glazing. The body was extremely brittle after firing and the colours fugitive. Examples shown of pieces ornamented with rose sprays — Lauder & Smith 1888 — have a certain charm but surely would not have satisfied the potter, though a more successful piece features an oak spray with acorns. (Plate XVIII).`

In 1888 there are also examples of vases with classical figures: — in relief (copying Wedgwood) or by using sgraffito outlines and shading — rather like a pencil drawing. The examples show use of a different clay and the use of different techniques. These pieces are either unmarked, marked Lauder & Smith or with the DEVON ART POTTERY mark. However, the progress made does not seem to fully justify Strong's claim that by 1888 the Pottery was 'now on the high-road to success as a business venture' — though his qualifying comment on the '*artistic value* of the manufactures' does not suggest complete acceptance of the Art pottery as an established fact.

It was probably at about this time or in the following year (1889) that the partnership was dissolved, this in spite of the fact that Directories of a later date still refer to 'Lauder & Smith' in their entries. One feels a certain sympathy with the departing Mr. Smith; probably already finding the profits from his own side of the business much diminished and little apparent prospect of a return for his backing of the *second* stage of the pottery venture. His departure, though probably causing some temporary financial embarassment to his partner, nevertheless gave the artist/potter a freer rein to proceed with further plans. His business sense must have counselled caution but his overriding desire to continue was obviously stronger. It was probably at this stage that Lauder decided that he would have to find a different clay or mixture of clays for his Art pottery.

The opportunity came almost immediately when Jeffery Ludlam, proprietor of the Marland Brickworks was declared bankrupt. The reason given was lack of capital rather than failing business. Lauder bought shares in the company and put in a manager — Samuel Hill. The Works was saved, the old workforce retained (though probably reduced) and Mr. Lauder had a chance to take clay from the site. An obvious choice would have been the white 'pipeclay', which the other two potters used both for slip and sometimes for the body of the ware. Lauder did, in fact make some pieces from this clay at that time, but it made very lightweight pieces. In the end he probably experimented to make a suitable clay-mix. The first mixes seem to have had a pinkish tinge, suggesting that some Pottington clay may have been used. The resulting pottery was not quite so heavy as the old but it was some time before less solid-looking shapes were developed and styling introduced: such as a baluster base, curved swirl handles and a splayed rim, sometimes scalloped. However, success followed and within a few years (1890) he had his first royal client — the Duke of Edinburgh. Renaming the pottery the Royal Devon Pottery, he moved both his architect's practice and the pottery shop to premises in The Strand (New Bridge Buildings).

In describing Lauder's pottery from 1889, there is a strong temptation to generalise, but since the early nineties was a period of experimentaton and low production; which shows itself in short runs of different styles where it is unusual to find two identical pieces; it is necessary to look at the few pieces that may be found. To add to the difficulty, many pieces believed to be of this period are undated.

The 'Lauder & Smith' soon gave way to the uncommon LAUDER & SMITH impressed mark and the various versions of Lauder's signed pieces (see Marks). The clay was now of a greyish colour, the shapes often based on the 'Indian bottle', though Grecian styles were also used. Decoration was in the form of coloured slips, often in an 'allover' design and using stylistic symbols such as the suit shapes in a pack of cards. At the same time, naturalistic decoration of flowers was used, where the outline, detail and sometimes the background were contrived by the use of sgraffito. The slips and glazes produced pastel shades, very different from the contrasts and stronger hues achieved by Brannam.

Another well-known effect that was probably developed at this time was a 'marbled' finish, used mainly on small pieces such as vases, pots, miniature jardinières, top hats etc. Many thousands of pieces must have been made and they turn up frequently, this probably being the most easily recognizable Lauder style. Almost equally well-known is the style developed next — possibly as early as 1895. This very decorative and highly successful treatment has always caught the eye of the potential collector. Basically relying on a landscape of birds in a leafy or floral landscape, or a seascape with fish and seaweed; the pattern may be free-ranging to cover the complete curving sweep of a jardinière or vase, or may be contained in panels. The detail and background are picked out with a pointed object (probably the tip of a nail). The background is less random than used by the other potters — rather than dots or dents he often used a highly stylised 'cross-hatching'. The coloration is often in the form of a spectrum, the slips being applied in stripes, like a rainbow. The colour range used is sometimes green/blue/brown, at others yellow/orange/brown and there are variations. The background was usually of a lighter colour.

Using similar techniques he also made modelled vases in the form of birds (Owls, Bittern, Kingfishers and others) as well as fish. Modelled forms of animals such as dragons and snakes were also used on vases and as handles. He also made Toby jugs, 'frog' mugs, and modelled miniature domestic animals, particularly cats. His version of the bamboo/stork candlestick compares very favourably with the Brannam 'prototype'. (Fig. 94).

By 1900 the potter was in his early sixties, still practising as an architect and deeply involved in parochial and civic work. It sems quite likely that during these last ten to fifteen years of his life in business he left the work of the pottery to a highly trained and competent staff, happy that he had brought this aspect of his work to a successful conclusion.

An appreciation

Alexander Lauder suited Barnstaple very well: or perhaps it might be more accurate to say that the town suited him. Though familiar as a home-base, initially there surely could have been no greater contrast than between his former stimulating, academic life-style in Edinburgh and this new, somewhat rugged existence in a rapidly expanding, pioneering community, seeking to establish its identity. It seems certain that his strict Scottish Methodism accorded very well with the firmly established Wesleyan congregation in the town: a community based on earlier Huguenot traditions of public service:- though a somewhat uncompromising and uncomfortable creed of teetotalism and reforming zeal may not have been altogether welcome in a town with a past record of innumerable hostelries and hard drinking!

Any regrets that he may have felt over the abandonment of an artistic career seem to have been partially compensated by his involvement with the teaching of the young art students at the 'Institute' and his subsequent career as architect; while his marriage and family, together with his immersion in civic and parochial affairs seem to have given him further joy and an even deeper commitment to the people of the town.

The business partnership with his brother-in-law, with its attendant worry concerning the 'difficult' clay could not have been without its strains and stresses. Neither partner could have foreseen the problems and no doubt all was settled in an amicable manner. It was perhaps ironic that whereas the latter twenty years of the pottery were successful, the lime/fertiliser business was, by that time scarcely viable.

However financially draining the pottery may have been, the ultimate success of both the "high art" brickworks and the Art pottery, especially in terms of artistic merit must have been a continuing source of satisfaction to its founder. Ravelin, Lauder's home during his last twenty or so years is a permanent tribute to his architectural and potting skills: a unique expression of the flamboyancy and virtuosity of the 'hidden' artist, and revealing the aesthete within the ascetic.

Fig. 158 The 'High Art' catalogue. Cover and Page 10, courtesy NDA

APPENDIX 7

THE DEVON ART POTTERY

(an abridged version of H.W. Strong's account published in book form 1889)

Twelve years ago — in October 1876, to be precise — the pottery at Pottington came into existence. Messrs. Lauder and Smith had been made aware of the existence of a valuable clay in a marsh owned by the Hon. Mark Rolle. They accordingly acquired a lease of the property and commenced a series of experiments. Their first experiences were of a most discouraging character, and in the hands of men possessing a lesser measure of that indomitable spirit which is our national heritage, the pottery would have had an experimental existence only. The concern had been worked at a loss for a few years whilst the difficulties of the material were being gradually overcome.

In the birthday of the industry the firm were content with common manufactures. But by-and-bye bricks, tiles and drain pipes gave way to ornamental ridge creases, roof finials, &c. Then Art allied itself to labour, modelling of a more ambitious character began, and the foundation of that horticultural department which is one of the staple features of the business was laid. The conservatory flower pot, various forms of "lawn buckets", tazzia vases, &c, were rapidly added to the manufactures of the firm. Ornamental orchid pots in the form of pendant baskets, through the openings in which the orchids grew and trailed their banches was a decided 'hit', and is one of the most saleable productions in this department, the rich, red ware with appropriate ornaments of oak leaves and fern fronds, being admirably adapted for this particular purpose. Encouraged by their previous successes, the firm now commenced the most ambitious and precarious development of the industry. The manufacture of art pottery was the next rung on the ladder ... (but) the fat nature of the clay, the inherent difficulty in firing colours in natural ware and the discovery of the secrets of glazes and colours and their application to the peculiar nature of the raw material in use at Pottington, may be enumerated among the barriers to success that delayed the development of the industry in this direction. But difficulties were made to be overcome. The Devon Art Pottery is now on the highroad to success as a business venture, whilst the artistic value of the manufactures is highly appraised.

The kilns are three in number, besides which there is an oven. (Then follows a description of the kilns, two of which were for firing bricks). Local talent is entirely responsible for the production of the Pottington pottery. And the watchword of the firm in all ornamental and decorative work is "Follow Nature". The modeller whom we visit at the stand supplies us with a ready illustration of the principle which guides him. By the side of the pot which he is "stippling" we notice a little bramble-bush and turning to the pot again we discover its counterpart in the dainty border of foliage he has modelled for the panel, which, in the finished piece of ware, will contain a figure.

From the modeller we pass to the designer, who, in this instance, is one of the principals of the firm. When the difficulties of the material had been overcome so far as to enable the firm to produce architectural terra cotta, in which some important work was executed for London, they sighed for fresh fields to conquer, with the result that they are now prosecuting the adaptation of the terra cotta to the manufacture of ceramic ware. The peculiar difficulties to be overcome in this direction were connected with the fixing of colours on the native red clay. By securing this object the production of an entirely new ware would be made possible. Our visit was most timely, inasmuch as it signalized the realisation of the consummation so devoutly wished. The fixity of the colour has been secured, and the development of the artistic side of the industry is simply a question of time. "The golden lustre o'er the glaze", which is a characteristic of Majorcan ware, is the latest speciality after which the firm are striving; it is a very pleasing and novel effect — the cloud of gold dust on the red clay against the rich glaze.

Naturalistic ornament — figures, with which he interweaves his birds and fruit and flowers and leaves — in various styles of Rennaissance and other phases of art, executed with the free, flowing grace of an unguided hand, is the chief type of decoration, and, it may be added, by far the best adopted by the firm. There is infinite variety in the shapes of the ware, from the dainty elicthysus and the greater Greek vase to which the rich glaze and ruddy ware give warmth of colour that together constitute the finer specimens of the ware things of beauty. The smaller vases are decked

With fadeless flowers,
That never droop in winds or showers,
And never wither on their stalks.

In the colouring of these flowers and the decoration of the ware generally the firm cherish the hope that they may create an industry in which ladies with artistic ability may be employed. So gratifying a solution of the problem "What to do with our girls", would, it is safe to conjecture, be highly popular with the "Society for the Employment of Women", and the wider, though unchartered, association of mothers and daughters.

Included among the contents of the kilns, the opening of which was contemporary with our visit, were several successful specimens of the decorative ware in the manufacture of which the firm has now, to employ an expressive Americanism "struckile". Of the larger vases one was decorated with a cock and a fox — presumably, the victim and the victimiser — with appropriate foliage, and another with a flowing Renaissance design. In these, as in the choice examples of the ware on view at the show-rooms in High Street, colours of every tint and hue mingle in one consistent decorative design, the "scale" of colour on the red clay being particularly rich in its wealth of harmonious "notes". In the Sgraffiato ware the firm have attained their highest success, the graceful freehand drawing, the bold and natural treatment of form, with the cultured sense of colour and its appropriate use, bespeaking the true artist in the designer. The latest productions in the ware are undoubted works of art.

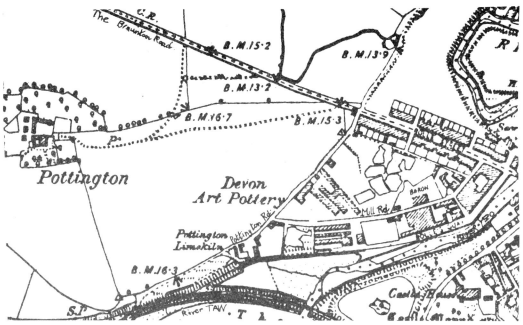

Fig. 159 a. A map showing the potteries

LAUDER'S DEVON ART POTTERIES,
POTTINGTON, BARNSTAPLE.

During December a LIBERAL DISCOUNT will be allowed on Purchases
A VISIT TO THE POTTERIES WILL REPAY.

b. Advertisement for December sale at the pottery

BARNSTAPLE
LITERARY & SCIENTIFIC INSTITUTION.

THE ART CLASS will meet, during the Winter Session, on Tuesdays and Thursdays, at 8 o'clock in the Evening, commencing on Tuesday, the 31st inst. Master:— Mr. ALEXANDER LAUDER, from the Edinburgh School of Art.
Arrangements will be made for the reception of Female Students. Intending Students are requested to communicate immediately with the Librarian.
2785]   R. W. COTTON, Hon. Secretary.

BARNSTAPLE
LITERARY & SCIENTIFIC INSTITUTION.

THE First of a Series of Public ESSAYS AND READINGS will take place on Monday Evening, November 6th, at Eight o'clock. Programmes at the Institution.
2786]   R. W. COTTON, Hon. Secretary.

Fig. 160 a. Lauder portrait, 1886 from the 'The Mayor's Book' NDA
        b. Advertisements for events at the Barnstaple Literary and Scientific Institution
        c. Two small vases with formal designs
        d. Tobacco jar in yellow, green and brown. MND

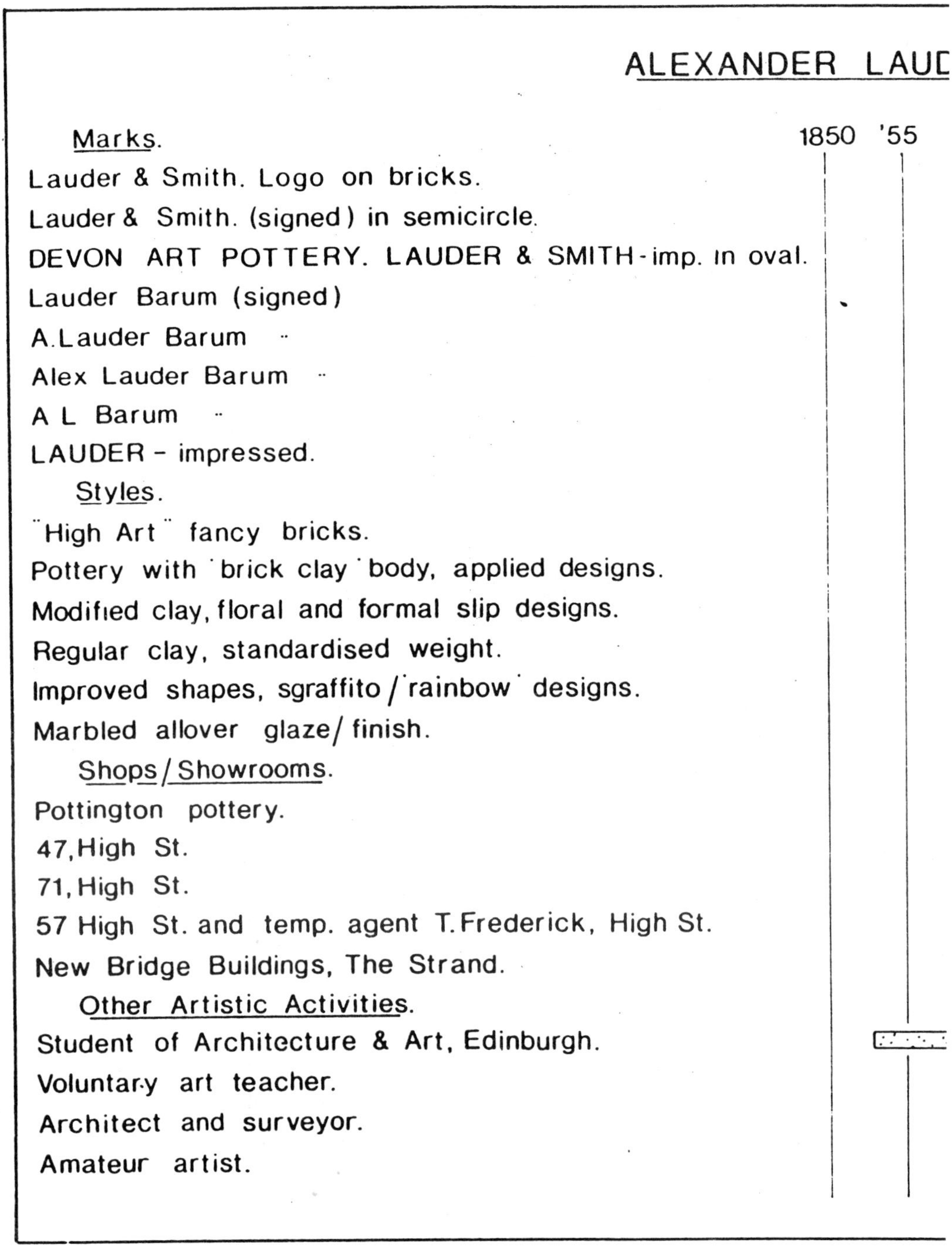

ALEXANDER LAUD

Marks.   1850   '55

Lauder & Smith. Logo on bricks.

Lauder & Smith. (signed) in semicircle.

DEVON ART POTTERY. LAUDER & SMITH - imp. in oval.

Lauder Barum (signed)

A. Lauder Barum   ··

Alex Lauder Barum   ··

A L Barum   ··

LAUDER – impressed.

Styles.

"High Art" fancy bricks.

Pottery with 'brick clay' body, applied designs.

Modified clay, floral and formal slip designs.

Regular clay, standardised weight.

Improved shapes, sgraffito / 'rainbow' designs.

Marbled allover glaze/ finish.

Shops / Showrooms.

Pottington pottery.

47, High St.

71, High St.

57 High St. and temp. agent T. Frederick, High St.

New Bridge Buildings, The Strand.

Other Artistic Activities.

Student of Architecture & Art, Edinburgh.

Voluntary art teacher.

Architect and surveyor.

Amateur artist.

Fig. 161 LAUDER Dating and Recognition Guide. Designed and printed by Jim Pinn

(Continued on page 237)

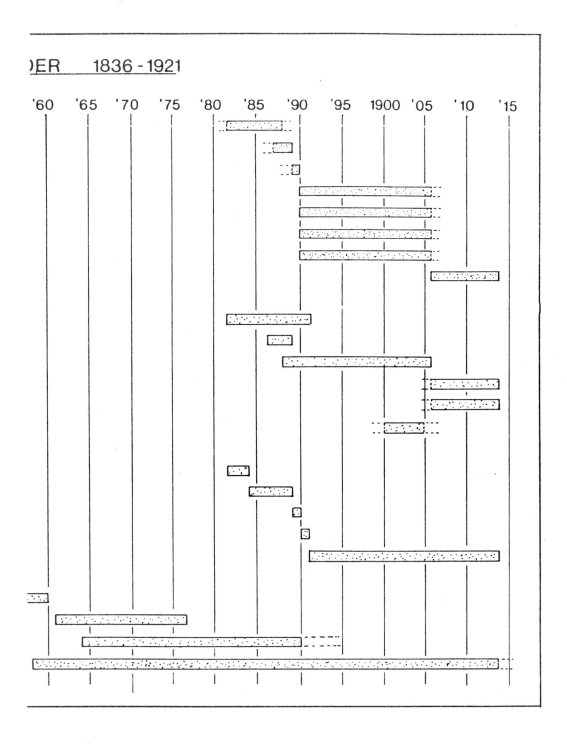

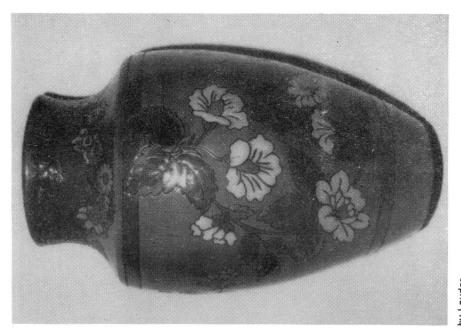

Fig. 162 Two vases by Lauder.

a. Heavy body in red clay. Central panel shows scene of
seated figures in the classical style. Ht. 10″ signed Lauder
& Smith

b. Heavy body, design of floral garlands in cream, pale
blue and ochres on leaf green slip, signed Lauder Barum

PART VI

WILLIAM BARON

1863 — 1937

HISTORY OF THE

BARNSTAPLE

ARTISTIC  POTTERY.

Made and
Decorated
by hand.

ʈe olde Borough of BARUM

No two
pots are
exactly alike

Depot
The Square
Barnstaple.

Pottery Works
Rolle Quay.

Proprietor
W.L.Baron,
late designer
Doulton's.
Certificated
Art Master.

The only North Devon Pottery invited by the Royal
Commission of which H.R.H. The Prince of Wales was President
To send at their expense, a case of Ware to the St Louis
Exhibition, as an example of British Art Pottery.

W.L.Baron has been awarded 2 Silver Medals at the
Falmouth Polytechnic. Gold Medal Bristol, Diploma of Merit
West of England, Silver Medal St Louis U.S.A. Silver
Medal Christchurch N.Z., and a National Bronze Medal.

GOLD MEDALS AWARDED AT
FRANCO BRITISH, BRUSSELS, TURIN & ROME.

Fig. 163 Cover from Baron Catalogue 1930's. Improved by Gerry Lee

a. The popular Henry Wimbush view

c. shows the other greengrocer – William Spencer

Fig. 164 Three views of Church Street, Sidmouth. From postcards 1900/10

b. shows the Baron shop at the corner of Ebdon Place

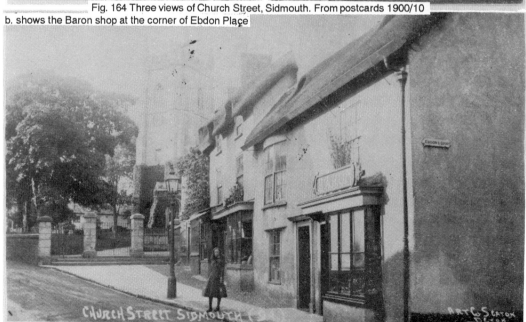

WILLIAM LEONARD BARON
Artist and Art Potter 1863 — 1937

The Early Years

William Leonard Baron was born in Sidmouth in 1863. His father William Henry Baron was a bootmaker with premises in Church Street, on the corner of Ebdon's Court and a few yards from the parish church, a quarter that was to become a much photographed corner of the town.[1] William Henry continued in his occupation as a boot and shoe dealer until at least 1870, but there is some evidence that during part of the next eight years he was in the Navy.[2] His wife, Ann was a skilled worker in Honiton lace who seems to have supplemented the family income by working and selling her lace from home. William had a younger sister, Emily born in 1867 and a brother, Percy some ten years his junior. By 1879 Baron senior had changed his occupation to that of greengrocer,[3] in which trade his son Percy later joined him.

From boyhood to old age a sketchbook and pencil were the artists's constant companions; as a lad by the seashore up to the nineteen-twenties on a 'nature walk' accompanied by his grand-daughter, Mary Cornish who well remembers his wide knowledge of flowers and birds, a reminiscence shared by his last surviving daughter, Clytie who, at the age of ninety-two years talked warmly of her father whom she survived by 45 years.[4] His parents must have encouraged his early artistic talent and it also caught the attention of 'Tommy' Dunning (RA 1906) who as a young man lived in Sidmouth and later had a studio in South Kensington Row. He struck up a lifelong friendship with the family and it may have been through his influence that William[5] became a student at the Lambeth School of Art. It seems likely that after leaving school at the age of twelve or thirteen in 1876—77, he was accepted at Lambeth where it is possible that he was a boarder. At that tender age he must have had sheltered accommodation, though he may possibly have stayed with the Dunnings. After six or seven years training he would, as was the norm for many of the Lambeth art students have moved over to join Henry Doulton at his Art Pottery.

The Lambeth School of Art had been founded in Princes Road in 1854, later on moving to new premises built on the site of the Old Vauxhall Gardens in 1860. In 1857 John Sparkes had taken sole charge of the school and within a few years trained artists who were to join Henry Doulton at his new Art pottery, established in 1866. Within the next seven years he had taken on the artist Arthur Barlow and his two talented sisters, Hannah and Florence; Frank Butler, Eliza Simmance, Emily J. Edwards and the sculptor/modeller, John Broad. The gifted George Tinworth, with his many talents had been with Doultons from the beginning and was to remain until 1913. Many of the artists that Henry Doulton took on had previously trained at the Lambeth School.

CHALONER'S ENDOWED SCHOOL, BRAUNTON

FOUNDED .... 1667.

HEADMASTER: J. L. RALPH, B.A., St John's Coll., Camb.

ASSISTANT MASTERS : F. Perry, B.A., Lond., Honours in Classics and French ; W. BARON, Art Cert. Teacher, South Kensington.

Good modern Education. Preparation for all Examinations. Boys learn Shorthand and Book-keeping. Tuition Fees, £4 and £6 per annum. Boarders are received in the house of the Headmaster. Special arrangements for Weekly and Daily Boarders.

For prospectus, &c., apply to the

HEADMASTER, The Laurels, Braunton

Next Terms begins January 21st.   [3577

EDUCATIONAL.

— W. L. BARON, —

CERTIFICATED ART MASTER,

GIVES LESSONS IN DRAWING & PAINTING.

——o——

Ladies wishing to join Class for Sketching from Nature, apply Ashleigh Road, Barnstaple.   [4610

Fig. 165 Two notices from the Journal showing Baron's teaching commitments

Ware Room, Barons Art Pottery, Barnstaple.

Fig. 166 The Ware Room, Baron's Art Pottery, Mill Road

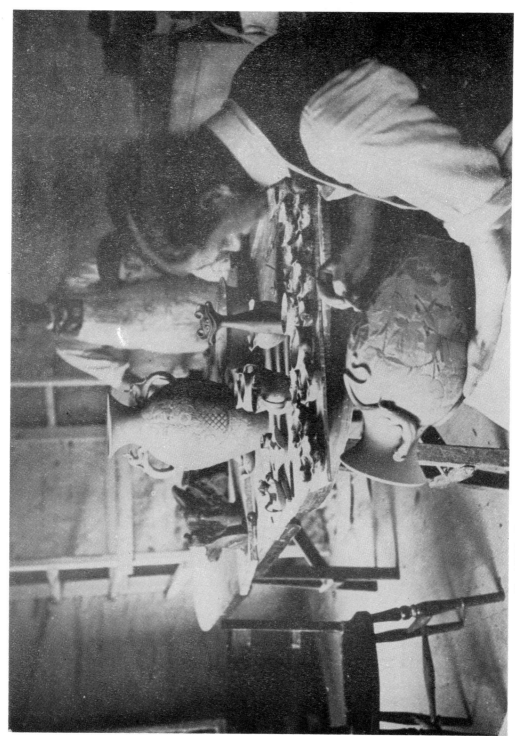

Fig. 167 The Baron Pottery. W.H. Garnish decorating. in the background .Mr. Ridd

By 1885 the firm was employing 250 artists, all but ten of whom had trained there, and by the turn of the century employed 400 artists who were Lambeth trained.

Doulton's pottery records concerning William Baron were unfortunately lost during the war so they are unable to give any precise information, but it seems likely that he joined the pottery between 1882 and 1883, remaining for a maximum of three years.[6] Evidence of his apprenticeship may be found in the two illustrations of vases, dated 1883, with decoration of fish in pâte sur pâte (plates 265 and 266 in Richard Dennis's catalogue of Doulton pottery, 1975).[7] The illustration of a small pale blue pot (unglazed, in white clay) with the Doulton mark and the initials WB establishes that Baron remained at Doultons for at least part of the following year (1884).

The expertise that he accumulated in modelling and decorating during that short time, together with the opportunities for watching major artists and modellers at work must have been an experience that enriched and moulded his future work. His contact with Henry Doulton must also have given him an insight into the ideal relationship between employer and employee working in this rarefied atmosphere. Henry Doulton was a considerate employer with a strong regard for the individuality of the artist and his or her right to express a unique talent and personality. He once said:

> To distinguish between eccentricity and genius may be difficult but it is surely better to bear with singularity than to crush individuality.

This quality of aesthetic benevolence attracted a wealth of talent to the pottery, ensuring a continuous team of artist and assistants, working in harmony to produce an astonishing range of unique art pottery that for quality and versatility has few equals.

Footnotes (See footnote numbers in text)

1. The best known view is probably by the artist Henry Wimbush whose paintings were used on many early postcards in the first decade of the present century. This view is appropriately romantic, though slightly later photographic versions show the thatched cottages becoming somewhat dilapidated. Unfortunately, the artist's view and most of the later views do not include the whole of the Baron shopfront which adjoins the greengrocers shown (William Spencer), who around the turn of the century also hired out hackney carriages — though from the view shown he may also have included bath chairs!

2. Nancy Wright (née Baron) remembers her husband, Percy recalling that when he was small, his father was away for long periods, possibly at sea, so this would be a fair assumption.

3. Percy continued the business on the same premises until the twenties when a new owner, having acquired the whole block, raised the rent. Percy moved to new premises just around the corner in Old Fore Street, soon after which fire destroyed the thatch of his original cottage together with the rest of the block, after which the whole was reroofed and tiled. His second wife, Nancy widowed in 1942 continued to run the business helped by a young assistant until 1968 when Chalmers took over, later moving to larger premises nearby. They still retain the Baron name for the business.

4. Clytie remembers holidays spent at Peter Tavy Mill, Tommy Dunning's holiday home where the artist painted her portrait, seated at the window. This was in 1908 when she was nineteen. He promised her

that if he sold the picture which was going in an exhibition, he would paint a duplicate for her, as a present. The picture was still hanging over the fireplace when she was in her ninety-third year.

5. At the 1881 census William, occupation artist, was eighteen and at home, in Sidmouth. His name appears after that of his younger sister and brother, suggesting that he was not resident but staying for a short period.

6. According to Doultons the accepted pattern was for the pottery to take on students with long training and preferably from the Lambeth School. Baron may have been able to continue in his present living quarters or possibly he may have had accommodation in one of Doultons' own cottages in Vauxhall St. or elsewhere. It is known that major artists such as Hannah Barlow had their own studio apartments but the much-read census records are so worn as to be unreadable.

7. Facts and information from Desmond Eyles and the Richard Dennis' catalogues.

Fig. 168 Small Pot from Doultons' with signature W.B dated 1884

Wheelman, Barons Art Pottery, Barnstaple.

Fig. 169 Wheelman, Baron's Pottery

Fig. 170 a. Mr and Mrs Baron in the garden of the Pottery

WILLIAM BARON. THE TEACHER

So towards the end of 1884 or in the early months of 1885, the young William Baron, aged 22, joined Brannam's pottery in Litchdon Street. At the same time he continued his studies, at Barnstaple School of Art, where Theodore Charbonnier had just been appointed Headmaster. Baron quickly worked through the range of courses and, following two summer courses at South Kensington in Design and Modelling, went on to qualify for his pupil teacher's certificate (1889) and his master's certificate in 1893. He inaugurated new courses in Design and Modelling which were both very popular and highly successful, and started a Life class on Saturday afternoons. His course of Art classes for serving Barnstaple teachers was well supported and led to a certificate for the proficient. Though some of Brannam's designers were his contemporaries at the school, others were his pupils.[1] He is known to have been an excellent teacher who was well-liked, and his expertise as an artist/potter must have greatly influenced designers such as Thomas Liverton and Stanley Williams.

More Modelling

Since the terra cotta that Baron made while he was working at Brannam's totalled only three, further work of this kind (after 1888) must have been at the School of Art. Between 1889 and 91 he modelled two more terra cotta figures, both of which were entered in exhibitions. The first depicted 'a sailor of fine physique dauntlessly fighting his way with a fainting 'middy' on his shoulder'.[2] Entitled 'The Midshipmite' it illustrated the then-popular song. It was probably sent for exhibition to the Derby Art and Craft show. The second model, made a year or so later was of 'a stalwart man of the labouring class who has a child upon his knee. 'Both figures are finely modelled, pose, expression and proportion being alike admirable'. Entitled 'The Widower' it was shown at the Royal Cornwall Polytechnic Exhibition at Falmouth in August where it was awarded first place, and again in 1891 when it gained a silver medal. Recently repaired, both figures are at the moment in my care where they are greatly admired. They belong to a great-grandson whose mother held on to them when they could have been thrown out with the rubbish.

There is also, with relatives a study from Life of a child's head in plaster of his daughter, Ethel; and an earthenware tile, bearing the bas relief of the head of a boy — probably his son, Billy was acquired by the North Devon museum from Phillips in October 1987. There was also a plaster cast of William Frederick Rock, commissioned in 1894.[3] Unfortunately this was broken some years ago and is considered irreparable. It is a pity that a suggestion by the Journal that 'a model cast in bronze be erected on a pedestal in the Square' was not followed up at the time.

Fig. 171 a. Two of the named Williams

b. Mr. Baron decorating

c. William Baron 'slipping'

WILLIAM BARON. FAMILY AND HOME

In the Spring of 1886 William Baron had married Ellen Sargent, a local North Devon girl., some nine years his senior. They lived first in Salem Street, near to the pottery. Out of a family of seven children, four girls and one boy survived infancy. Billy, the second child was born in 1888. The family soon moved to 41 Richmond Street and a few years later to a comparatively new house at 18 Ashleigh Road, By 1897 they were living above the double-fronted shop that Baron had rented at 59 Boutport Street for the sale[4] of his pottery from the kiln he had built in Mill Road, Rolle Quay. The final move was to the shop in the Square, one of a block called Bridge Buildings, owned and rented by The Bridge Trust. This premises, though designated as a dwelling house was used by Baron as a shop with living quarters above. A spiral staircase led to the upper floors.

Footnotes *(See footnote numbers in text)*

1. Many people have told me of the pleasure they or relatives had from being taught by Mr. Baron. An old gentleman who attended Challoner's School in the 1920s remembered how all the boys looked forward to Thursday afternoons when he visited the school. Others tell how he would add the 'difficult bits' like figures to their pictures. A local collector started to collect his Art pottery simply because the potter had taught Drawing to his grandfather. He now has a considerable collection. Baron was well known for his 'Squiggles' with which he entertained audiences from a platform, armed with blackboard and chalk before the start of Liberal meetings. To demonstrate:- A local lady well into her seventies remembered herself a small girl of eight, very bored and travelling on the train from Crediton with her mother. The stranger in the carriage enlivened the journey with his sketchbook. "Make a few squiggles", he suggested to my mother. "In a few moments there appeared a very smart hat — the sort my mother used to wear. He drew many more. I had no time to be bored".
2. The quotes are from Journal reports.
3. The Journal reported in full "...in the Hall of Athenaeum a cleverly executed plaster cast bust of the late William Frederick Rock, to whose thoughtful munificence the town is indebted for this grand institution. ...the artist is to be congratulated on having produced 'a speaking likeness.'"
4. Like Brannam and Fishley, Baron also had a stall in the Friday market, both before the turn of the century and also later. It was a lock-up store that looked down the market on the Joy Street side. For many years now it has been used as a store for tables.

THE BARON FAMILY

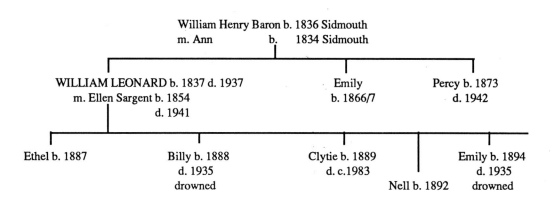

William Henry Baron b. 1836 Sidmouth
m. Ann   b.   1834 Sidmouth

WILLIAM LEONARD b. 1837 d. 1937   Emily   Percy b. 1873
m. Ellen Sargent b. 1854   b. 1866/7   d. 1942
d. 1941

Ethel b. 1887   Billy b. 1888   Clytie b. 1889   Emily b. 1894
d. 1935   d. c.1983   d. 1935
drowned   Nell b. 1892   drowned

BACK TO POTTING

Baron did not immediately set up his own pottery after leaving Brannam's but probably concentrated more on teaching; working during the day at the School of Art and also part-time at Challoners Charity-endowed school at Braunton. This last probably only entailed one afternoon a week but he was also advertising lessons from his home. All this no doubt made up for the loss of the Brannam salary: but he did not give up potting.

By the autumn of 1893 he had entered into an agreement with Edwin Beer Fishley at Fremington for the 'management' of his pottery. This would entail firing in the Fremington kiln and might even include throwing by Mr. Fishley. He called the pottery 'Barnstaple Ware' and it was marketed at Christmas of that year from William Liverton's shop at 29 High Street, adjoining the pannier market. William was elder brother to Thomas, one of Brannam's best designers with whom Baron had worked and taught at the School of Art. William had not long bought the property from his boss, Charles Crassweller, long-established china and glass merchant. The young man had recently been appointed sole agent for Doultons but gave Baron the central space in his Christmas advertisement in the Journal. The Journal reported:-

> One of the latest departures in Art pottery. This extremely attractive ware (which is sure to sell readily) ... Mr. W.L. Baron was formerly an assistant at Messrs. Doultons' and lately designer at the Barum ware potteries whilst he is assistant master at the School of Art ... Great ability characterises the various examples of the ware both in regard to design and decoration.

Just two examples are shown here, both of top quality, though these are dated 1894. The first, a two-handled vase in blue and black is remniscent of early Barum ware, though the handles suggest Fishley. The other piece is a very large heavy vase (one of a pair), using Fishley's green glaze, but in two shades. It is unique in that the decoration of fish in a seascape is achieved by the building up of the design with deep layers of white slip, then the fish being further identified with detail in sgraffito, so that distinct species may be recognised by the keen angler! The use of the white slip provides the colour contrast and is stunning in its effect. If all the pieces Baron made at the pottery were as successful as these he must have been well pleased. He also, no doubt learned something about kiln-making during his stay. It looks as if he was at the pottery for at the most a year for by 1895 he was installed at his own pottery on Rolle Quay.

THE POTTERY IN MILL ROAD, ROLLE QUAY

The Workforce

It is probably safe to assume that in the intervening two years while Baron worked elsewhere he had also acquired the site on Rolle Quay and would have built a kiln and premises to house the pottery. A relative's account[1] of the pottery gives the foundation date as 1895, so it looks as if Baron went from Fishleys' straight to the new pottery.

At the Mill Road premises he recruited his first three members of staff[2] who were Eddie Chichester Ridd, thrower and modeller; Percy Dayman, who made the mixtures for the glazes and sometimes did decorating; and Eddie Williams who was kiln layer and fireman. According to a Mr. Hill of Pilton who for many years lived on Rolle Quay, these three were recruited from the Lauder pottery.

They were later joined by Tom Williams (no relation) who was also a kiln layer. Fred Gannoway who had some training as decorator, lost a leg in WWI and after his return to the pottery worked on the finishing to the bases of the pieces. Chris Clements started with Baron straight from school (c1916) and became responsible for the glazing, while his brother Ron (who gave me most of this information) looked after the kiln, did odd jobs around the pottery and sometimes helped Mrs. Baron in the shop. Jimmy Williams was another member of staff, also probably a kiln worker, and Eddie Rice also did odd jobs. Tom Mears,[3] who like many others started by working the clay, finished up with a more responsible job, possibly decorating. Lastly there was Reg Burrington[4] who was responsible for the slips, who provided information on the final years of the pottery.

Billy junior joined the pottery straight from school, probably in 1902, remaining until his untimely death in July 1935, but serving during the war in Mesopotamia. At one time, probably betweem 1915 — 20, Baron had an apprentice thrower/decorator. This was William Henry Garnish who took over the Braunton pottery from William Fishley Holland when the latter moved to join the Elton pottery at Clevedon.

"Thrower," or "maker by hand," at BARON'S POTTERY, Barnstaple.

Fig. 172 Eddie Chichester Ridd, modeller and thrower   Fig. 173 Mr. Ridd's modelled lizard

Fig. 174 The shop in the Square

Fig. 175 Pair of Double-Dolphin Vases from the Mill Road Pottery. c. 1896 decorated in mid-green glaze shading to black signed Baron Barnstaple. Height 13"

The pottery continued until 1937 when, on the death of William Baron it was bought by Brannams'. The staff[5] remained but were later laid off for a while. When the conscription of staff into the Armed Forces reduced the numbers from eight to five, the pottery was closed down. The stock was cleared and in some cases dumped and the kilns were eventually dismantled.

In Ron Clements' time the kiln was coal-fired. It was lit on a Thursday and by Friday was white-hot (900-1200 degrees). It was then sealed with mud. Best nuts at £1 for three to four tons were used. The kiln was housed in the building next to the road.

Charles Cockram, who as a lad lived in Western Terrace, near to the pottery would often go there of an evening in the winter when the kiln was fired to keep Tom Williams company. They would cook their baked potatoes near to the kiln. He remembers two kilns, both at the back of the building which was long and narrow, running alongside the road (as it is today). At this time coke and wood were used as fuel — often long pieces of timber would be fed in at the base.

He used to get a little pocket money for the 'pictures' by going round to the backs of shops in the town, collecting 'wood wool' which had been used for packing and thrown out. Chichester Ridd, who was in charge when Mr. Baron was not there would pay $1/_2$d a pound for this commodity. 'Chich' (to his friends) was keen on sailing and kept his boat in a shed at Crow (Point). After storms the shed would get full of blown sand and the lads would help him to clear it, after which they would have a free trip in his boat. Mr. Baron's chief thrower wore a surgical boot — it was thought that he had lost several toes; so he walked with a slight limp. He was, nonetheless quite a dandy, often sporting a bow tie. Another Barumite remembers how on one occasion he launched his boat from the beach at Crow to rescue a very large and heavy lady who had 'capsized' into the shallow water from a boat returning passengers from Crow to the Sand Barge, which used to run Sunday trips between Castle (or Rolle) Quay and Crow in the summer months (when the tides were favourable). The large lady was very uncomfortable and muddy: so presumably was Mr. Ridd. As a modeller he was extremely adept — his well-known lizard was complete and grafted to the pot or vase in just a few minutes.

Visitors were always welcome at the Baron pottery. Small girls (now elderly ladies) tell how they would wander in and stay to watch Mr. Baron at work. "Mum always knew where I was", one confided to me. In the summer season of the thirties when the tourists would arrive by the charabanc-load from Ilfracombe, Baron the entertainer would come into his own. Surrounded by a large crowd he would do the finishing work to a puzzle jug and then challenge his listeners to try to drink. "The fun he had with those visitors and the puzzle-jugs they couldn't master"! remembers Mary Cornish. There was a garden behind the pottery — where the picture of the potter and his wife was taken. For a number of years he had a pet owl who used to travel around on his shoulder and was very useful for keeping down the rats. He also had a succession of dogs, often bulldogs or bull terriers both of whom were favourite models for his small animal pieces. One of his bulldog pieces bears the motto — "The more I see of some men, the better I like my dog"! His cats, however were less straightforward, with long necks and aristocratic faces. He also modelled pigs and rabbits, and even an elephant!

His life-style was busy but money was never his primary concern. Mary Cornish describes him ruefully as 'most unbusinesslike' and 'often short of money'. However, he may have also been a trifle absent-minded as when the shop was dismantled after Brannam wound up the business, a bundle of notes and several guineas were found tucked away somewhere.

Outside business he had many interests as well as sketching and painting. He was a staunch Liberal and sometime Chairman of the local group, a keen Rugby fan (his brother Percy was at one time an international player), and an amateur bee-keeper. To travel, he owned first a motor cycle and sidecar and then a little Morris. Reputed to be the world's worst driver, he was somewhat accident-prone. On one occasion, following an accident with his motor cycle at Saunton he was admitted to hospital where he had a skingraft on his eye and cheek. His daughter Clytie still recalled the drive down the 'zig-zag' at Arlington and on another occasion Mrs. Baron broke her arm when she jumped from a moving car. He had parked the car at the top of a hill 'to answer the calls of nature' but returned to find it no longer there. He had left the brake off and it had sailed down the hill to finish in a hedge.

The death by drowning[6] of his son Billy in July 1935 was a bitter blow. Billy's son, young Billy showed little interest in the pottery and the old man lost heart. He was, in any case over seventy. I think he would have been glad that the pottery did not drag on, under alternative management. He certainly would have been pleased that his family would continue to cherish his work and that there would be a rekindling of public interest in his Art pottery almost half a century after his death.

Footnotes *(See footnote numbers in text)*

1. The account, in the Athenaeum records is from Mrs. Baron of Landkey.
2. Percy Dayman's sister said that when the pottery closed Percy moved to join Brannams but caught T.B. from a workmate and spent some time in a sanatorium. Her daughter had a pair of plaques that he made and decorated for his apprentice piece (in 1910).
3. A nephew of Tom Mears, visiting the town after an absence of several years remembers watching him at work, doing decorating. " and all he had to work with was an old shaving brush and a six-inch nail"! he told me.
4. Reg Burrington joined the pottery straight from school, aged fourteen in 1929. He too says that his boss had little business sense. They were on friendly terms — he used to take Reg to Cardiff to watch the Rugby. He remembers that they used a lot of white clay for the body of the ware in his time. In summer they worked longer hours because of the tourists and when the money ran out they worked shorter

hours. When Brannam closed the pottery — he says in 1938, he continued with Brannam but was later called up. After the war he returned to the pottery where he remained until 1977 when a threatened stroke caused him to leave.

5. Brannam's Wages list for Baron's pottery. 1937. (from Brannams records)

	Rate	Hrs	Gross Wage
E. Ridd	1.9	39	3.9.0
T. Mears	1.3	39	2.5.0
C. Clements	1.3	39	2.2.5
P. Dayman	1.4	39	2.10.0
R. Clements	1.0	39	1.16.7
J. Williams	1.0	41	1.18.7
F. Gannoway	9	39	1.7.10
R. Burrington	9	39	1.9.0

6. Towards the end of July the family party was on a picnic on Stanbury Beach, Morwenstow. The day was fine and sunny, a notice described the beach as 'safe for bathing'. The party included Mr. and Mrs. Baron senior, Billy and his wife and their two small children, Mary (Cornish) and her fiancé together with her sister and their parents; Baron's daughter, Nell and her husband, George Barker; and another daughter, Emily (Jo) and others. Several of the party were strong swimmers and Billy held life-saving certificates. Quite suddenly the wind picked up and the sea became very choppy so that the three or four of the party who were bathing found themselves in difficulties. Billy plunged in and managed to bring his sister Nell to the shore, but when he went back to rescue his other sister, Jo, he was himself swept out to sea. The bodies of Jo and Nell's husband George were recovered but it was too late to revive them. Billy's body was not recovered until more than a fortnight had passed when it was found floating off Tintagel Head.

Fig. 176 Two Baron Plaques a. with grapes (mid blue) and wreath of vines (yellow) on bright blue b. has favourite floral branch with perching BlueTit, mid blue/pink and pale green, both 9 1/2" diameter

THE POTTERY IN MILL ROAD, ROLLE QUAY

THE WARE

It does not seem to have taken long for the pottery to start producing saleable ware. The new kiln would have been a challenge to both Mr. Baron, and his staff; some with workers at the pottery, there was a happy, informal atmosphere — which is often conducive to successful results. By the evidence of early dated pieces:- 1895 W.L. Baron Barnstaple and 1896 Baron Ware Barnstaple; the potter seems initially to have used Fremington clay (red body) and Marland clay (white, lightweight) with of course the white clay for slip. The blue and green colours produced suggest the use of metal oxides while other colours were provided by the use of coloured slips, usually applied very thinly (perhaps with a brush).

One of the pieces made in the first year is an Owl wall-pocket in white clay. This is a version of the model made by Brannam in 1893, and likely to have been modelled by Baron at that time., so the potter may have felt himself entitled to use it (though it is unlikely that Mr. Brannam would have agreed)! Baron also later used other models — the serpentine teapot and the 'double dolphin' bowl. The staff complement at the pottery at this time would probably have been ten at the most. A later family history gives it as about twenty — but this would have been in the busy years of from 1905 — 1910 and the twenties. In the latter years it was probably never more than fifteen.

After 1896 the pottery was never dated on the base — the mark was a signed Baron Barnstaple (from various hands).[1] The only dating evidence that can be supplied is in the case of either commemorative ware or where pieces were made especially for customers (a service offered over a number of years). In the case of the series of Toby jugs featuring War Leaders a date would be irrelevant as they were only made from 1914.

For the purposes of description of the ware it therefore seems apposite to use Baron's own classification, mentioned in a letter in the Royal Albert Memorial Museum, Exeter in 1911, when he sent a consignment of goods to a customer seeking orders.

"We make in four styles viz. Decorated, Motto, Plain and Grotesque".[2] If modelled animals were added to the list, this classification would probably apply throughout the lifetime of the pottery. Further notes on the use of the white clay for the body, the various glazes and the differing styles add further information.

Fig. 177 A group of tourist ware. From left to right: Ilfracombe mug, Puffin (The Lundy Parrot), Joke potty, Shrew–bill and early puzzle jug 1904, 8"

b. Two pieces by Baron

a. Vase with design of roses

b. another, more sophisticated version of the Bell

Keith Baker, London

PLAIN WARE

This indicates any piece with a single colour used (Brannam's term was 'art colour'). It covers a wide variety of plain pieces as the following list indicates.

vases	pitchers	ash trays	beads
jugs	egg cups	plaques	buttons
bowls	teapots	toilet sets	cuff-links
pots	coffee pots	candlesticks	hat pins
beakers	tea sets	jardinières	

favourite colours were mid blue, matt blue, pale green, pink and mauve.

MOTTO WARE

This was a popular 'line' with Baron and made primarily for the tourist trade. The mottoes were usually written around the mug, jug, vase or bowl — in two, or more often in one continuous line. The recipient would need to turn the piece round to read it and since the wit of the saying was usually in the last few words, this made it most effective. The potter had a fund of very witty mottoes — a selection of which are given. Some of the lines were used for specific pieces, such as the shrew/suffragette bell or the 'naughty' miniature potty with an eye inside on the base, supplemented by a verse around the perimeter which read:-
'Wipe me dry and keep me clean and
I won't say what I have seen'

GROTESQUE WARE

To the extent that Baron used a few of the Brannam grotesque models, he followed the tradition of the caricature but most of his original pieces, especially his face jugs were much more in the tradition of 'Folk art'. These are reminiscent of the Cornish 'piskie', with their primitive features, hands often being added to the decoration. The effect was obtained almost completely by modelling, not so much emphasised (as with Brannam) by the addition of decorative slips, as *heightened* with one colour slips or the use of a marbled, thinly applied all-over slip, of which the long-nosed/spouted teapot is a good example. His modelled candlesticks, wall pockets and other pieces also rely on modelling rather than on polychromatic decoration for their effect.

In general, his own designs are more effective, being more finely modelled on the whole than those of Brannam — compare the two fish wall-pockets or Baron's

b. Advertisement 1913 from 'Devon Past and Present'

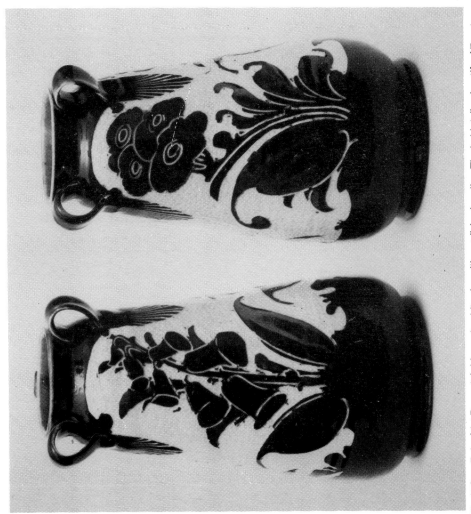

Fig. 178 a. Pair of Art Deco style Vases in white clay with small ring handles. The bold stylised motifs of Foxgloves and Alkanet are in mid blue, turquoise, browns and fawn. height 9" b. Advertisement 1913 from 'Devon Past and Present' Courtesy NDA

candleholder with the other's 'chubby dragon'. In most cases the former's sparing use of slip is not allowed to dominate the design. There are just two examples to hand of political 'skits' (rather than cartoons); both featuring President Kruger — the first a jug with a design in flat blue/black relief of the Boer leader as a boar — the pig body having an excellent likeness of the well-known features in the added head. The other is a modelled pig on a flat base where the familiar piskie face is used — with the addition of an unmistakable beard (fairly crude, this one). There may be others.

The potter also made models as features for his jugs, vases etc, the lizard probably being the best known. There was also the ubiquitous dragon (griffin) used by all three potters for handles. There is also an example of a jug modelled in an owl shape, with pointed feet, owl features and glass eyes. There was also a selection of small modelled animals, most of them in naturalistic poses. These include a rabbit, a pig (with a seraphic expression); an elephant (rare); and at least three dogs. He made several versions of the bulldog — sometimes inscribed on the body with the motto: 'the more I see of some men the better I like my dog'. He also made at least four different models of cats — one the familiar fat-cat-on-the-mat image, the rest of a more slender and aristocratic bearing. There is also an unidentifiable creature with a froggy face, made in sizes from the very small to the very tall, usually with glass eyes. He also made figures of puffins — the 'Lundy Parrot' — a tourist piece.

Probably the rarest and most prized specialist pieces were those modelled for the series of Toby jugs featured in the 'War Leader' series, made from 1915, for which he took out patents. There were probably only a limited number of each model and they are not easily found. From information supplied by a collector of Toby Jugs, there seem to have been at least seven, each bearing a registered number, name and apposite motto. The following list gives details, where available, though not necessarily in the correct order. Three are pictured. They are of similar height — app. $9^1/_2$ inches.

King George V		651723 ?
Marshal Joffre	'Vive la France'.	651724
Admiral Jellicoe	'England expects every man will do his duty'.	651725
Earl Haig	(field marshall 1917)	651726 ?
Lloyd George	(Minister of munitions, later Prime Minister)	651727 ?
Earl Kitchener	'Your King and country need you'..	651728
Admiral Beatty	(who succeeded Jellicoe)	651729 ?

DECORATED WARE

To a certain extent Baron employed the styles and techniques he had used while with Brannam, continuing the use of sgraffito for background and to delineate/add detail to designs. However, slips were seldom applied very thickly, often being brushed on thinly, sometimes being allowed to mingle, so that after glazing a harmonious effect was achieved. He kept his palette within a colour-mingling range rather than relying on contrasts of colour. Raised effects were achieved either by cutting deeply into the slip or, in the case of modelled pieces by the fineness of the modelling. His favourite themes were still fish in a seascape; flowering branches, sometimes with birds; and, in particular bunches of grapes.

He achieved different effects/styles through the use of particular glazes as well as by the use of white Marland pipeclay for the body. The most effective and popular glaze he used was probably the mauve/pink/blue glaze, said to have been 'bought in from Staffordshire'. This produced a variety of colours, presumably through firing — a particularly charming example is a bowl, featuring a vine branch around the perimeter, just below the rim, the curve of the bowl exploiting the hanging bunches of grapes and the vine leaves which are coloured in shades of blue, purple, yellow and green; which the glaze complements perfectly. Floral designs work equally well in these colours. The white clay pieces are, of course, very light in weight. They are usually only partly glazed, with a narrow band around the outside of the rim and sometimes another next to the base. The colour of the clay and the slips used produced very pastel shades of blue and green. The design was very finely drawn and was usually outlined with a graving instrument in white, the shapes being filled with a layer of flat, painted-on slip. Sometimes the background was picked out, exposing the white body. Altogether the effect was delicate and very art nouveau in feeling. The two vases shown are splendid examples of this genre.

Occasionally, as must occur with most potteries, a single piece with unusual features almost escapes recognition — in this particular case, a vase decorated with a blackberry branch, the body covered in cream slip. It is the *mode* of decoration that is unique — the colours being painted on in the same way as an artist would work on a water colour or oil painting, the piece being finished with a matt glaze.

Footnotes (*See footnote numbers in text*)

1. There is also a mark in 1896 which is in variance with the rest of the pottery being produced in that year, most examples of which are of a lower quality, some being over-fired and others with patchy glazes. The mark is Baron & Hill (or B & H) Barnstaple (signed). Most of the pieces are vases, though one fish-mouth jug has been noted. The identity of the Hill is not known, though it seems likely that he could have been related to Charles Hill, Lauder's foreman. One theory that seems tenable is that he was a younger son of the above, who, in 1896 would have been sixteen. This young man, Charles Henry died three years later from consumption. A 'Journal' report of December 1899 describes the funeral...

    'In the presence of nearly a thousand persons the mortal remains of Mr. Charles Hill of Rolles Quay were on Sunday afternoon interred in Barnstaple cemetery. The deceased who was only nineteen years of age succumbed on Wednesday to Consumption'.

    Perhaps not a potter but most certainly a well-known and popular young man.

2. The letter-head gives details of his awards.

WILLIAM BARON — ADVERTISING AND THE CATALOGUE

There is little evidence that William Baron advertised widely. There are very few examples of advertisements in the local press, but latterly he paid more attention to this aspect of the business. A number of photographs were taken and printed in the form of postcards, so providing pictures of some of the staff at the pottery. In addition, in the mid nineteen-twenties he produced a catalogue, with a brief history of pottery in the area, photos of the inside of the pottery and three plates showing the ware. There is an attractive cover, with details of the potter's prizes. The many photos and an advertisement from Mate's Barnstaple are shown among the illustrations.

An example of his headed notepaper[2], printed for use after 1906, is fairly modest in comparison with that of his former employer. He does, however list his successes at exhibitions up until 1910 (facsimile shown). He also erected a sign board at the entrance to the town pointing 'To the Pottery'. Not to be outdone Brannam erected a hoarding in a field by the side of the Braunton Road directing visitors to the *Brannam* pottery. Peter Brannam's account of the 'Tourist war' in the thirties makes amusing reading.

BARON COMMEMORATIVE WARE

Commemorative Mugs Royal

The first mug recorded seems to be 1935 and there were two others in 1937

1935	George V and Mary. Jubilee	pale blue, orange
1937	Edward VIII. Coronation	pink, pale blue
1937	George VI and Elizabeth. Coronation	mauve/blue, green/blue

Other Commemorative pieces

Commemorative Victory Ball   6th Battalion Devonshire Regiment c.1928-30
                                            Lincoln green and scarlet

B & N.D.   Aerodrome   1935   pale blue
Barnstaple and North Devon Aerodrome

Other

BWLA (Barnstaple Whist League Association) 1937-38 prize   mauve vase

Mottoes on Baron pieces

May the hinges of friendship never grow rusty.
A hair on the head is worth two on the chin.
A thorn on the bush is worth two in the hand.
All things come to those who wait on themselves.
Don't take a load you can't carry.
Hasten slowly.
If you chop your own wood you won't burn so much.
May your children have rich parents.
More waist less speed.
The largest part of a fish is usually the tale (on a fish-mouth jug)
The more I see of some people the better I like my dog.
Water is alright if taken in the right spirit.
Where there's a will there are relatives.

(On bells with a shrewish face under a bonnet:-)
The perfect woman speaks only when told (tolled)
The perfect woman tongue tied.

I am a bell   There are many good reasons for drinking
As you may tell   One has just entered my head
If you hold my head   If a man can't drink when he's living
And shake me well.   How the H —l can he drink when he's dead.

"From rocks and sands and barren lands
Kind fortune set me free
And from great guns and women's tongues
Good Lord deliver me".

The manners which are neglected
as small things
are often those which decide
men for or against.

On puzzle jugs:-

This jug was made your skill to try
Drink if you can when you are dry.

Within this jug there is good liquor
'Tis fit for parson and for vicar
But how to drink and not to spill
Will try the utmost of your skill.

This jug was made to try your skill
Drink if you can but do not spill.

Here gentlemen come try your skill
I'll lay a wager if you will,
That you don't drink this liquor all
Without you spill or let some fall.

Fig. 179 Two family photographs of the two Barons at work c. 1930
of Baron senior and son Billy at work in the pottery. Courtesy Mary Cornish

Fig. 180 a. Three Face Jugs by Baron 3 1/2"– 6" (a.) relies on modelling and colour mix of yellow and green glazes
(b.) blue and white 'piskie' (c.) another piskie face with hands, and slips in mixed blues

d. A brightly decorated vase with fishy panels and
modelled lizard. NDA and MND

e. A very dainty piece in white clay, with lively and
colourful design. MND

EPILOGUE — THE FADING YEARS

It is probably better for an historian to record without bias. A collector may be partisan but a writer needs to guard against such temptations. One anticipates a spirit of healthy opposition between firms competing in the same market, but in Brannam's case this became, one might say, a more personal rivalry. It is a pity that the senior potter's displeasure over his former employee's 'desertion' was allowed to colour the scene in the early years of the century when the 'Queen's potter' saw his own pottery as unique and competition to be resisted at every turn. His contemporary Journal advertisements clearly demonstrate this attitude, while a continuing family feeling of criticism show how strong these sentiments must have been.

Initially, while the pottery on Rolle Quay was being put on a secure footing, there was probably no real threat, but when Baron moved to his new shop in the Square (c.1904/05) and at the same time began to enter his work in large exhibitions, the picture changed. Traffic entering the town no longer passed along Litchdon Street, past the pottery; whereas the position of the Baron shop was ideal — being visible to all visitors by road from that end of the town as well as travellers coming from the Junction station; and alerting potential customers even before they found their holiday accommodation. Baron's exhibition successes from 1907 to 1910, both at home and abroad, (which included two silvers and a gold medal) showed that his fingers were, at that time, closer to the pulse of public taste.

This was a time of changing fashions. Brannam's highly decorated ware which had been so popular up until the turn of the century was no longer in favour and the potter was not finding it easy to find a new formula. The change-over was accomplished only very gradually, first by simplifying the design, then by creating new art nouveau (and later deco) styles, particularly acceptable to Libertys. The shop in the Square seems to have kept pace to a certain extent with public taste, or perhaps the styles were never excessively Victorian and a wider range of modes and styles were continuously explored. The rivalry continued through the thirties and the tourist 'boom', (amusingly if wryly described in Peter Brannam's book). By then the Art Pottery era was long past and interest in contemporary ceramics would never quite match that shown during the last quarter of the nineteenth century and the first quarter of the next.

WILLIAM BARON

	1875	'80	'85

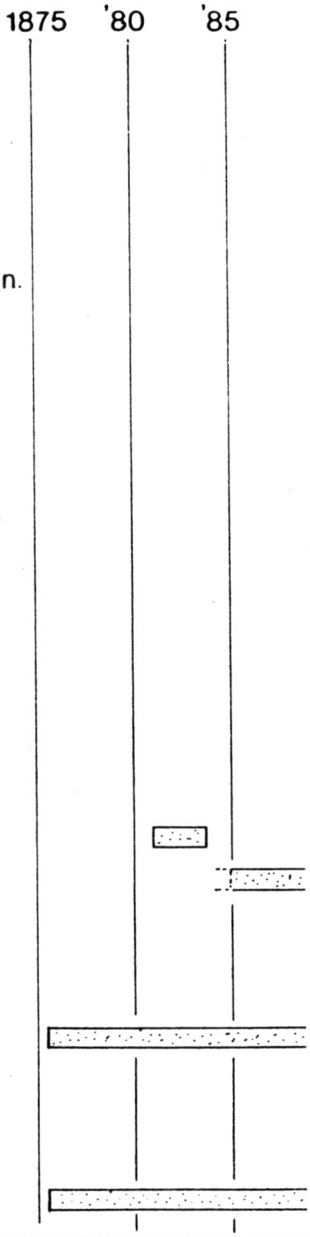

Marks.
W L Baron Barnstaple Fremington. (signed)
Baron Ware (signed) & W L Baron. Barnstaple.
Baron & Hill (B & H) Barnstaple. (signed)
Baron Barnstaple (signed) many hands.

Styles.
Experimental, possibly decorating only, often green.
Usually small pieces, low quality, overfired, etc.
Often larger pieces, good quality, fishy designs.
Series of face jugs.
Puzzle jugs, motto ware, tourist ware.
Use of pinky/mauve glaze.
Pieces in white clay in biscuit ware, (fired once.)
Series of jugs. War leaders.
Deco styles in design.

Showrooms & Shops.
William Liverton, 29 High St. - Agent.
59 Boutport St. First shop/home.
Bridge Buildings, The Square.

Potteries
Working at Doultons, Lambeth.
Modeller and decorator for C.H.Brannam.
Working at Fremington with E.B.Fishley.
Mill Rd. Rolle Quay. Own pottery.

Other Artistic Activities.
Art student.
Teacher at Barnstaple School of Art.
Part time teacher at Challoners School.
Teaching from home.
Artist in pencil, water colours & oils.

Fig. 181 BARON Dating and Recognition Guide. Designed and printed by Jim Pinn
(Continued on page 269)

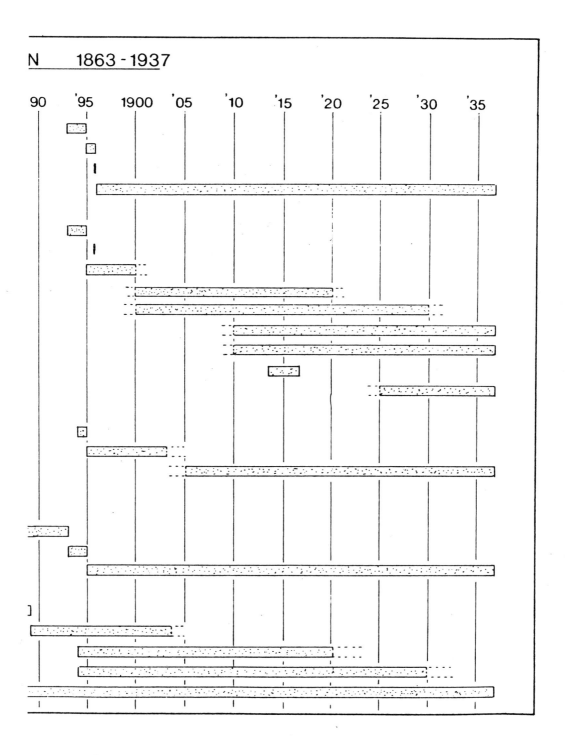

N   1863 - 1937

Fig. 182 Three pieces by Baron, in blue with detail in black

a. Moulded Owl Jug, 4 1/2"   b. Cylindrical Vase with Deco design painted in black on blue/mauve slip dated 1894, 8"   c. Vase from Fremington

PART VII

THE BRAUNTON POTTERIES

WILLIAM FISHLEY HOLLAND
WILLIAM HENRY GARNISH

Fig. 183 Work by Fishley Holland at Clevedon. a. Puzzle jug, and two–handled mug in Somerset dialect. Centre Fishley beaker

Fig. 184 Two late commemorative mugs and face jug all with signature W.F. Holland

HOLLAND FAMILY TREE

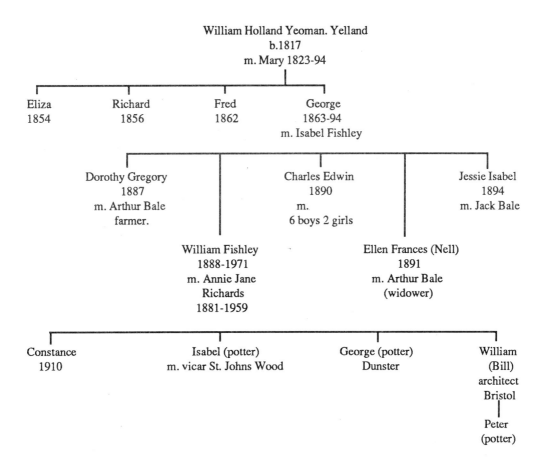

WILLIAM FISHLEY HOLLAND. THE BACKGROUND

When William Fishley Holland joined his grandfather, Edwin Beer Fishley at Fremington just after the turn of the present century, he became fifth in line and both observer and participator in the final ten years of this remarkable and unique peasant pottery: active and thriving for more than a century. Always catering basically for the utilitarian market, each member of the family had indulged his pleasure and flair for decoration by accepting commissions for items such as harvest jugs for yeoman farmers or pieces for special occasions — very much in the tradition of the Barnstaple and Bideford potters of the seventeenth century.

Edwin Beer Fishley was no exception; but whereas his forbears had used their gifts perhaps as much for their own pleasure as for financial gain; his own decision to make decorative ware *on an experimental basis* was both a response to changing tastes and an attempt to find an alternative market to the rapidly dwindling demand for common earthenware. During the late 1870s he began to experiment with new designs on pottery and with raw lead glazes as an alternative to the old galena glaze formerly used. Encouraged by J. Phillips, local gentry and other friendly craft and pottery enthusiasts; who made regular visits to the pottery to see his latest work; he decided, in 1881, to send examples of his wares to the Exhibition at Plymouth. Among these were three vases, inspired by a visit to London museums[1] where he saw the Schliemann collection and the work of Trojan potters. These remarkable pieces won awards, and were kept by the potter, remaining at the pottery until after his death, when they were acquired by members of the family.

It is not clear how many pieces of decorated ware were made, but they are seldom found and one must regretfully conclude that only a limited number were produced — perhaps mostly for special order. It is, however, sure that Mary Fishley did decorations on Fremington ware (1890 Exhibition, School of Art) and since she did not marry and move away from the pottery until the close of the century, it may perhaps be significant that the complement of staff (at the 1881 Census) had risen to *eighteen*, seven of whom were women.[2] These last would not have been expected to do the heavy work and were probably well suited to the tasks of slipping and glazing. (In the four Census records of 1841 to 1871, the maximum number of staff employed was twelve (of whom four could have been women). (When William Fishley joined the pottery in 1902, the staff numbered eight).

What had happened in the intervening years? Obviously the market for the traditional functional earthenware had continued to shrink — though Brannam's reduction in output following the success of the Art Pottery may have given the Fishley pottery a temporary advantage; but this would not account for the substantial increase in the number of staff (shown in 1881). It seems fair to assume, therefore that the 'Art pottery' venture was continued at least for a few years, with some success; though it does look as if some years before William's arrival the staff[3] quota had been gradually cut down and the production confined[4] to simply glazed pieces in green, blue and yellow (old gold), in the production of which the young man was later to be concerned.

Writing of the raw lead glazes, Mr. Fishley Holland describes how some were achieved:

> Red lead was used instead of galena for the glazing, and it was not fired in saggars. This was the secret of the variety and beauty obtained, as the pots got alternate oxidization and reduction and often came from the kiln with most interesting lustre and bloom. In those days there was not the variety of colours and glazes... available and we relied on coarse-ground copper, cobalt and iron oxides which we ground with pestle and mortar. This gave us varied textures... Grandfather used red lead, flint and stone, the most successful trial having two parts red lead to one each of flint and Cornish stone. I have since found that a little china clay improves the glaze. This makes a good transparent glaze, but if black oxide of copper is added in various proportions, some brilliant greens, running through to a blackish lustre are obtained. This was on a red body, fired up to 1000°C. If we wanted a matt effect we increased the china

clay and flint. If a green slip of copper was used we got a sparkling silver effect, which, under glaze gave a mottled finish peculiar to grandfather's pots. Previous to the copper slip he used a very thin wash of manganese. He also made a very clear darkish blue, often running into Royal by using cobalt in various quantities. His yellows, made with red oxide of iron, sometimes nearly an ounce to the pound, were beautifully full and varied. There are now numbers of books on glazes and pottery in general, but I have always found that trial and error are the best teachers.[5]

Footnotes *(See footnote numbers in text)*

1. See Page 16.
2. Staff at the time included Herman, Edwin Beer's eldest son, aged 22/3 who presumably had worked at the pottery for nine or ten years. It is not known when he left, but his presence as one of the executors of his father's estate did not act in William's favour. Mr. Holland sensed a feeling of jealousy that he had been so successful at the pottery and was coping well with the management.
3. From W. Fishley Holland. 'Fifty Years a Potter'.
4. Though dated examples of ordered pieces exist up until 1911, and a Coronation George V commemorative beaker was made, also in that year.
5. From W. Fishley Holland. 'Fifty Years a Potter'.

Fig. 185 Double advertisement from NDJ, 1890. Lauder in competition with Brannam after Lauder received the Royal Warrant from the Duke of Edinburgh

THE MOVE TO BRAUNTON

On the death of his grandfather in 1912 (February), the future was uncertain. William was the obvious candidate to continue with the pottery, but his two uncles were called in to administer the estate. William agreed to continue with the work of the pottery, but after a few months interference with the running of the business led him to hand in his notice. The pottery was advertised for sale and it was not long before a potter from Staffordshire — Ed Sadler showed interest in buying it. He had been led to suppose that William would continue to work there as before, but there was some difference of opinion about a fair wage. Having heard about the possibility of a pottery being set up in Braunton, where deposits of blue clay had been recently discovered, William made enquiries from a[1] solicitor who was concerned with the enterprise. After a short interview he was accepted as manager and offered a higher wage than he had expected to get from Sadler. The latter, meanwhile, having decided to buy the Fremington pottery, contacted William, agreeing to his terms; but for the new manager of the Braunton Pottery there was no turning back.

After the discovery of the clay, a company had been formed to carry through a scheme for a brickyard and pottery. An orchard in South Street and another near the station were purchased as sites and the building began in August. Mr. Holland was on the site to supervise the building of the pottery and the work at the pits at Knowle where, after a fortnight's work a certain amount of suitable clay had been obtained. There was some public speculation as to why the pottery was not being built adjacent to the claypits until it was pointed out that it would be less costly and more convenient for all concerned to have the pottery near to the station, where it should prove a great attraction to visitors. By the first week in September the building was already completed. There were two spacious rooms on the ground floor; one for preparing and for throwing the clay and the other for drying and glazing. The large upstairs room with shelving for stock was also the showroom and in addition there was a small, private room for mixing the glazes and an office with a telephone. Plans for a square kiln had been considered but on the advice of Mr. Holland a modern round kiln was built close to the other buildings. The machinery, which included two potters wheels had already arrived.

Interviewed, the new manager said that the rings and saggars would be made at the pottery which would be producing 'ware of the Fremington and Barum type, using the famous Fishley blues, greens, yellows (or old golds) and lustres'.

Work at the claypits was held up because of heavy rain and subsequent flooding; nevertheless nearly fifty tons of clay had been dug up. However, it soon became clear to both Mr. Holland and the owner that the prohibitive cost of extracting the clay could be avoided by buying in clay from Fremington. It is also possible that trial tests in firing the local clay had not been altogether satisfactory. In any case, the decision to use the clay which he knew so well must have been most acceptable to Mr. Holland if not to the founders of the Braunton Pottery Company who from the beginning had planned to use the clay for brickmaking.

THE POTTERY

By all accounts the first pottery was a redware, similar to that produced at Fremington, together with domestic ware decorated with combed patterns in white slip.[2] Mr. Fishley's blue glaze was also used with great success. It was not easy to work up connections and to anticipate public taste. Mr. Holland found several London shops who were interested in 'peasant ware' but at the outbreak of war in 1914 business became very slow. In addition he lost two of his trainee staff. For a while he developed the peasant ware with the assistance of two agents who had previously brought in pottery from Europe. He was able to copy these styles which became quite saleable.

At about this time he employed a designer. From the evidence[3] gathered his initials were 'A J' and he also worked for a while with Ed Sadler at Fremington. The Braunton pieces both bear the signed mark Braunton and the date 1914, though only one is signed. This is a boat-shaped bowl in a royal blue glaze, while the unsigned piece is a modelled cat in the typical Fishley green lustred glaze. The two Fremington/Sadler pieces are more distinctive, each bearing the mark 'Devonia Art' together with the artist's signature but no date. The vase is plain but stylish, with a classical design in applied slip. The other piece is a charming modelled head and shoulder of 'Sunny Jim', (a well-known character from the advertisement for FORCE corn flakes) but in the Brannam style of a match holder/striker, the features being picked out in brown and cream.[7] The mark is clear and explicit:- 'Ed Sadler. 107. Devonia Art. Fremington. Barum, together with the artist's signature, but no date. What a pity that he stayed so short a time at either pottery and that Mr. Sadler sold the pottery (in 1915) to Brannam's.[4]

At the outbreak of the first World War, two of Mr. Holland's trainees joined up, while he himself later joined the Royal Flying Corps. In the interim he engaged more apprentices but for the rest of the duration his wife managed the business side of the pottery, with one thrower to do most of the work. After the war business seems to have picked up quite quickly. People were looking for colour and there was some interest in hand-made pottery. At this time the potter developed a turquoise glaze of which the two shown examples (small pot with painted black line and jug with an attractive streaky glaze could well be examples. However, most of the piece of this potter bear the signature W F Holland (or WFH) and it is not easy to tell whether the piece was made at Braunton or Clevedon. Unfortunately at this time (1921) the solicitor/owner Mr. Hooper ran into difficulties and was declared bankrupt. Mr. Holland expected to have the opportunity to buy the pottery at a reasonable price but the business had already been registered in the name of the owner's wife. He could have stayed on to work there but preferred to take the opportunity to move elsewhere. At the Clevedon pottery both Sir Edmund and his chief potter, George Masters had died, and there was no one at the pottery with sufficient knowledge to continue the work. Ambrose Elton employed Mr. Holland to do a day's throwing at the pottery and he was given his own premises to carry on his own work.[5]

Before he left Braunton, however he was visited by Michael Cardew who had traced him from Fremington. Mr. Cardew's parents had a house at Saunton which they occupied in the holidays and were great patrons of Edwin Beer's peasant pottery, visiting the pottery by boat across the estuary. In 1921 Mr. Holland taught the young Mr. Cardew the elements of throwing and bowing — (making handles). After the move, the new owner allowed the young man to come in after five o'clock to practice after the others had left.[6]

Footnotes (*See footnote numbers in text*)

1. **A Mr. Hooper**
2. **From 'Fifty years a Potter' page 45.**
3. **As above.**
4. **Brannams used the pottery mainly for making coarseware, especially ovens, work previously done at North Walk which had closed at the turn of the century. (This information also from 'Michael Cardew. A Pioneer Potter'.**
5. **Work at the pottery is not mentioned in this account, though examples of the potter's work at Clevedon are shown.**
6. **This information from 'Michael Cardew. A Pioneer Potter'.**
7. **See also ashtray with head of Ramsay MacDonald.**

THE BRAUNTON POTTERY. 1921 — 71

After Mr. Holland's departure, together with his assistant, George Manley, the pottery came into the ownership of William Henry Garnish. Mr. Garnish had trained at the School of Art and also with William Baron at the Rolle Quay pottery. Frederick Luscombe remained and Tom Haydon was brought in as thrower from Brannams. Much of the output of the pottery was domestic ware such as cups, saucer, plates, jugs, bowls, vases and the like. The shapes were pleasant, functional and unfussy; while glazes were in clear colours. A black glaze, similar to the one adopted by Prinknash was very popular for a time. In 1928 Henry Chichester joined the pottery and worked as a glazer. When Mr. Garnish retired the pottery was carried on for the last twelve years by Mr. Luscombe and Mr. Chichester in partnership.

I am indebted to a niece of Mr. Garnish for the photographs of the pottery and the exhibition pieces, and to Mr. Chichester for much of the information.

Fig. 186 Tyg or Loving-cup and small jug by E.B. Fishley, green glaze 1890's

Fig. 187 Two pieces, Sadler group Fremington 1912–18   a. Two moulded vases in blue and green. 'Devonia Barum'
b. Centre: blue/green vase signed Devonia Art, Fremington, Barum A.J.

c. Small 'Sunny Jim' match–holder

d. Ramsey Macdonald ash tray

Fig. 188 Group of pieces by E.B. Fishley, including 'Pair' of dogs possibly by George Fishley.Two pieces from the Fishley family . RAMM, Exeter

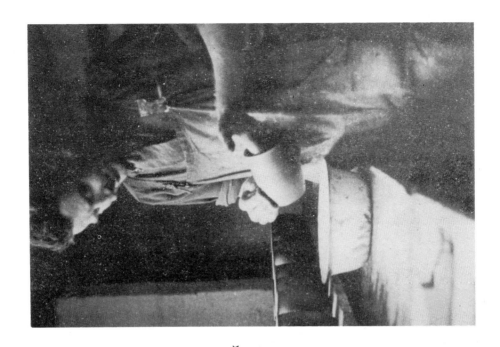

Fig. 189 a. The Ware Room at Braunton b. Tom Haydon, W.H. Garnish and Fred Luscombe at work
photographs courtesy Mrs. Aggett

Fig. 190 Two later Lauder pieces.

a. Three handled vase with floral and bird decoration in blue, green and brown. 8".

b. modelled fish. Length 9 1/2", turquoise/cream/browns

Fig. 191 Two vases by Lauder a. cylindrical waisted piece
height 10" floral/bird design in sea green and brown   b. in the Grecian style c.1910

Fig. 192 Jardiniere with design of birds. In green with cream sgraffito background

a. Birds in a floral setting   Fig. 193 Two later Lauder vases   b. birds in flight

b. Lauder & Smith piece with parrot courtesy Keith Baker, London

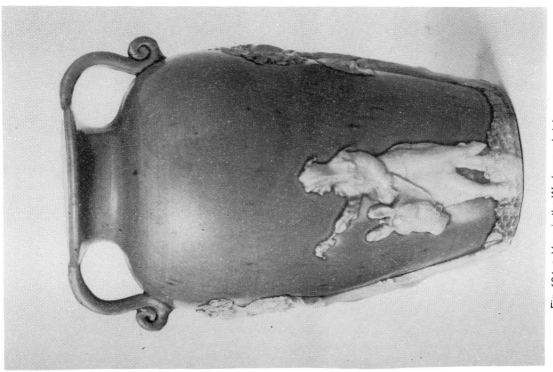

Fig. 194 a. Vase in the Wedgewood style

Fig. 195 Third fireplace, Ravelin photographs by Andy Robinson

Fig. 196 Details of exterior of Ravelin a. gothic chimney b. terracotta figure

C H Brannam
Barum
1880

C. H Brannam
Barum 1886 F. 73

C H Brannam
Barum Ware
1886

Registered mark 1886

RP
447561

Barum Ware
Jas Dewdney 1888
Del

C H Brannam
Barum
J.D 1888

Impressed mark 1930
19/4 —
C H BRANNAM
LTD
BARNSTAPLE
MADE IN ENGLAND

Impressed mark 1911
c 1900 – 1914
C H BRANNAM
BARUM
N. DEVON

c H Brannam Ltd
Barnstaple B

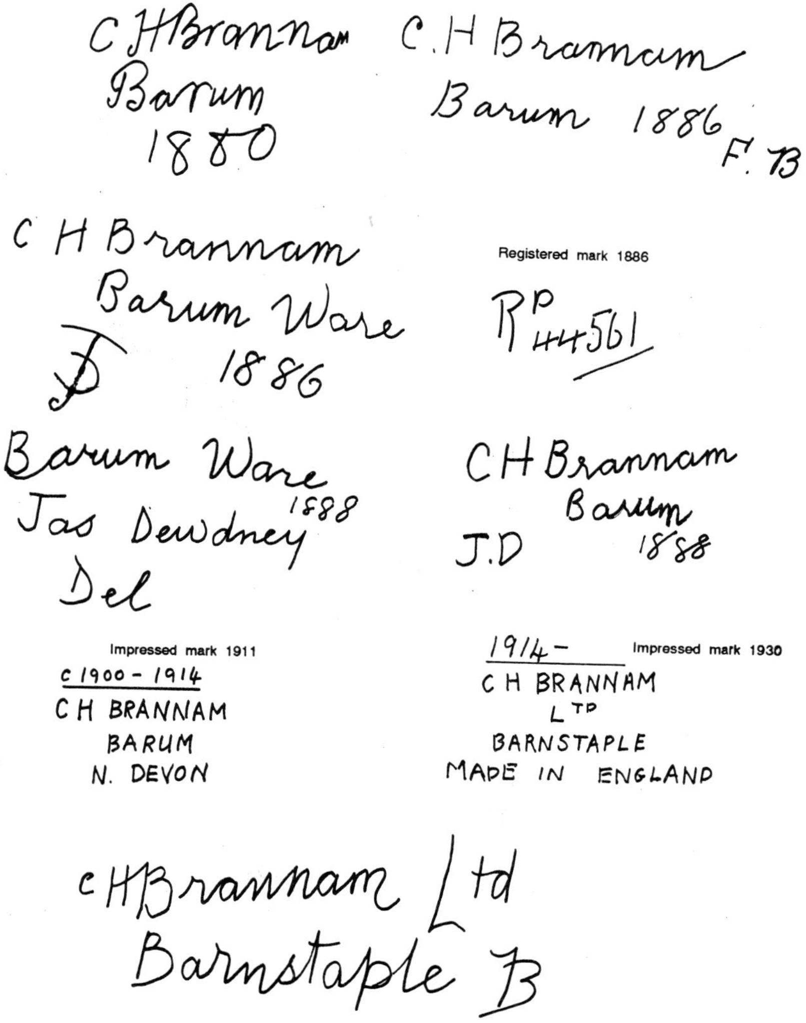

Fig. 199 Page of Brannam signatures

Fig. 197 Pedestal plate 1888, with J.D. signature

Fig. 198 Small early pot 1885 with Baron signature

Fig. 200 Bases from three large Brannam pieces and signatures of decorators

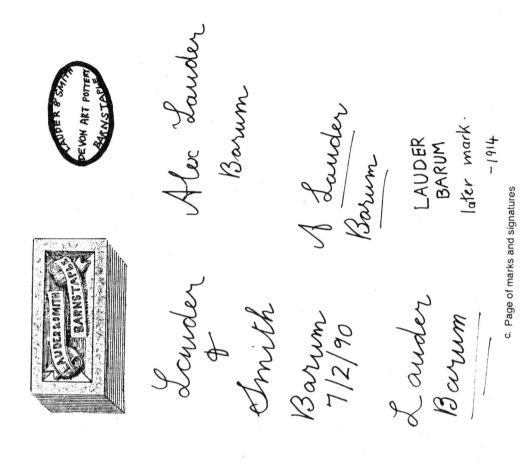

c. Page of marks and signatures

Fig. 201 LAUDER marks. Two bases

a. Lauder & Smith Barum 17/8/89

b. Alex Lauder Barum 13/12/90

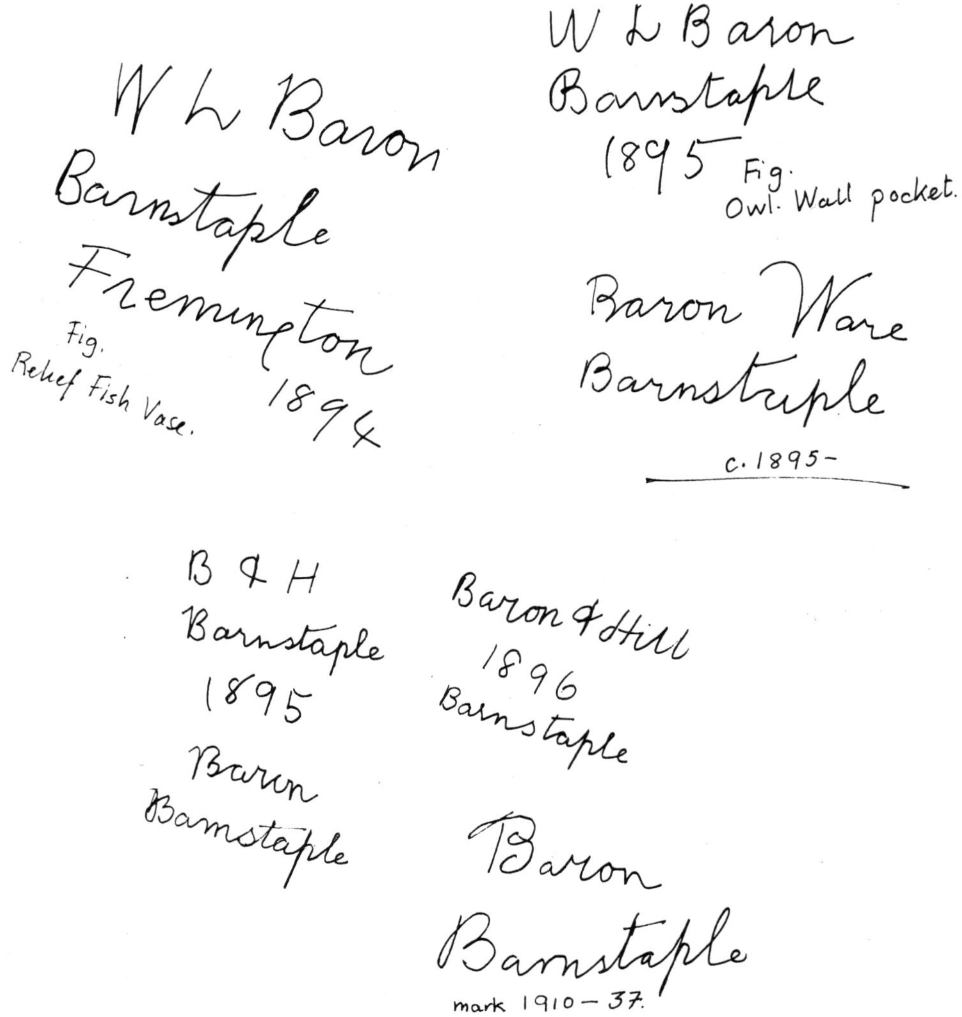

a. Baron Barnstaple
b. W.L. Baron Barnstaple, Fremington

W L Baron
Barnstaple
1895 Fig. Owl. Wall pocket.

Baron Ware
Barnstaple

c. 1895 —

W L Baron
Barnstaple
Fremington 1894
Fig. Relief Fish Vase.

Baron & Hill
1896
Barnstaple

B & H
Barnstaple
1895

Baron
Barnstaple

Baron
Barnstaple
mark 1910 – 37.

Fig. 202 BARON Marks. Page of marks and signatures and marks from two bases

Fig. 204 Signature on base. Sadler Devonia Art Pottery

Fig. 205 E.B. Fishley

Braunton Potteries.

Braunton
AF 1914
Blue Boat.

WILLIAM FISHLEY HOLLAND. 1912 - 1921.

Sadler. Fremington.

E? Sadler
Devonia Art
Fremington
Barum
AF
'husky Jim'
Fig.

Devonia Art
Fremington
Barum
Vase. Fig
Ash Tray Fig.

Devonia
Barum
moulded
Vase. Fig

1912-1915. SADLER FREMINGTON. (A.J. connection)

1921-71   Braunton Pottery.   W.H Barnish and
others.

BRAUNTON
impressed.
Blue jug. Fig.

BRAUNTON
POTTERY
DEVON
stamped.
in black.

Fig. 203 Page of marks. Braunton Fishley Holland. Braunton later marks
Sadler Devonia Art Pottery

REFERENCES/BIBLIOGRAPHY

BRANNAM Peter   *A Family Business*. 1982.
BREARS Peter C.D.   *The Collectors Book of English Country Pottery*.
CARDEW   *Michael Cardew. A Pioneer Potter*.
                             An Autobiography. Collins. 1988.
DENNIS Richard.   *Lambeth Art Pottery*. Catalogue of an exhibition
                              at the Fine Art Society. 1975.
EYLES Desmond.   *The Doulton Lambeth Wares*. Hutchinson. 1975.
FISHLEY HOLLAND William.   *Fifty Years a Potter*. Pottery Quarterly. 1985.
GRANT Alison.   *North Devon Pottery. The Seventeenth Century*.
                             University of Exeter. 1983.
LEARY E. and PEARSON J.   *By Potter's Art and Skill*. Pottery by the Fishleys at
                             Fremington. Handbook for exhibition Royal Albert
                             Museum and Art Gallery. May/June. 1984.
LIBERTY.   *Centenary Exhibition Catalogue*.
                             (Courtesy Mr. D. Coachworth) Curator 19/20th
                             Century Ceramics. Victoria and Albert Museum.
REED Margaret A.   *Pilton — Its Past and Its People*. 1977. and
reprint.
STRONG Hugh.   *Industries of North Devon. 1889*, North Devon
                             Journal 1888/1889 and David & Charles Reprints.
                             1971.

and the following resources, courtesy of *North Devon Athenaeum*.

        Census Records. 1841—81.
        North Devon Journal
        North Devon Directories.
        Parish Records.
        Devonshire Association Yearbooks: 1890. Fremington Clay and Others.
                                            1881. J. Phillips. The Potter's Art in
Devonshire.

GARDINER W.F.   Barnstaple. 1837—1897.
HARPER'S Notebooks.
R.H. Phillips.   The Bideford Pottery Industry. The Devon
                             Historian 1971. 2 parts.

Y